Critical race theory and inequality
in the labour market

MANCHESTER
1824

Manchester University Press

Critical race theory and inequality in the labour market

Racial stratification in Ireland

Ebun Joseph

Manchester University Press

Published by Manchester University Press
Oxford Road, Manchester M13 9PL
www.manchesteruniversitypress.co.uk

British Library Cataloguing-in-Publication Data
A catalogue record for this book is available from the British Library

ISBN   978 1 5261 3439 4   hardback
ISBN   978 1 5261 6030 0   paperback

First published 2020

The publisher has no responsibility for the persistence or accuracy of URLs for any external or third-party internet websites referred to in this book, and does not guarantee that any content on such websites is, or will remain, accurate or appropriate.

Typeset by
Servis Filmsetting Ltd, Stockport, Cheshire

Contents

Figures

All figures are the property of the author.

Tables

Acknowledgements

This book would not have been possible to complete without the help and expertise of many people. First, I would like to thank the community of academic friends and allies who have supported me, received my work and shared their spaces with me. It provided me with opportunities to develop further. I would like to thank Dr Alice Feldman for her long-standing friendship and transition from research supervisor to colleague and friend. I really appreciate you for always being available to discuss critical race theory with me and encouraging my continuous growth. I would also like to thank Professor Kathleen Lynch for her constant support, and Dr Barbara O'Toole, someone I met only a couple of years ago who has become a good friend and ally. Thank you for the prompt feedback on chapters in this book.

Special thanks to my family and community of friends for the encouraging words and prayers that effuse me with love. Thanks for your patience, encouragement and support of my every ambition and success. Special thanks to Alex and Patrick, my amazing sons who continue to be so understanding in sharing their mum with this writing and my many pursuits! Their constant care and selfless love free me to pursue my dreams. Thanks sons, love you in every way possible. My biggest gratitude always goes to God for the grace to surpass my own strength. Lastly, I would like to thank in particular the people of migrant descent whom I interviewed in the primary study, who not only shared their stories with me but also trusted me with their feelings and innermost thoughts. Without their willingness to share their personal stories on such deep levels, the depth and richness attained in this book would never have been possible.

Introduction

Human societies are racially stratified; why is this and what are the implications? If migration is the reason for racial inequality in the labour market, then all persons of migrant background should have the same experience and economic outcome when comparing like with like. This is not, however, the case in Ireland nor in any other part of the Western world today. Neither has it been so for a very long time. Europe is a migratory hub; a milieu of intra- and inter-continental movement of people where every immigrant has to adjust to their new environment and access its socio-economic resources and status. Some groups, however, routinely appear at the bottom and some at the top of both the economic and racial ladder. This is despite the consensus that race or biology does not influence IQ or work performance. Out of 4.4 million immigrants in Europe in 2017, an estimated 2.4 million to the EU-28 were from non-EU countries, with 1.9 million people previously residing in one EU member state migrating to another (Eurostat, 2019). Despite their commonality as immigrants, there is evidence of an extant differential in socio-economic outcomes among migrant groups. The tacit agreement that society is hierarchical is met with a dearth of scholarship on the racial order not just in Ireland but across Europe. Labour market researchers routinely blame the differences in outcomes on individual motivation, route of entry into the state, foreign qualifications, the migration process itself and culture shock – which all suggests a migrant deficit. While these indeed influence outcomes, little focus is given to how a similar racial order is maintained across different societies, with the same groups appearing at the bottom of the ladder. Critical race theory (CRT) scholars have on the other hand taken the view that racial stratification assigns immigrants to different strata, thus influencing their outcomes. The theory of immigration and racial stratification (Zuberi and Bashi, 1997) is pivotal in this regard as it presents insights into how on arrival in the US, immigrants are assigned a racial identity. Having been developed in the US, this work is valuable to the European context, particularly at this time where old and new arrivals are categorised and given a racial tag which determines how they are treated – including status and access to resources. Zuberi and Bashi argue that rather than the human difference and behavioural patterns that are often blamed for the inassimilability of newcomers; racial stratification and how difference is treated is the problem. These arguments on racial stratification, which indeed helped shift the focus of social critics from the individual to the collective, are often built on secondary data analysis.

Three key notions inform the data collected for this book. First is the theory of immigration and racial stratification (Zuberi and Bashi, 1997), which insists migrants know and have a way of knowing the racial order in their host country. Second is in accordance with the CRT tradition which centralises race as a macro-level variable in comparing how human differences are managed among groups who routinely fare better on the labour market with those at the bottom. Third is the positioning that all modern states are racially stratified based on the perspective of social critics like Crenshaw (1989), Mills (1997), Zuberi and Bashi (1997), Bonilla-Silva (1997, 2013) and Delgado and Stefancic (2012).

Two questions intrigue me concerning differentials in outcomes among migrants, particularly when I am faced with race scepticists who insist race does not influence a person's labour market outcome. The first question I ask is, do you think society is equal or unequal? Although most people answer that society is unequal, they erroneously focus on the outcome, which is the stratum on which individuals and groups end up. In our quest for a more equal society, however, it is clear that the starting point of all human subjects in society is different. It can differ based on race, gender, class or any number of grounds. Many people today are, however, reluctant to attribute the differential in labour market outcomes to race on a substantial level because it paints a picture about us and our society we thought we had outgrown and left behind. For racial scepticists, I ask this second question. Since migration is often named as the reason for the labour market differential in outcomes, all people of migrant descent should have the same labour market outcome when comparing like with like in terms of achievement attributes. Why then is it that in all of the Western world with predominantly White populations, some groups consistently appear at the bottom of the labour market ladder? More specifically, why are Blacks at the bottom of the economic ladder in the Western world? Unless we return to racist arguments that there is something wrong with this group that predisposes them to the bottom of the economic ladder, such patterns suggest a systemic problem that operates across various countries which makes it inevitable for this group to appear at the bottom. Don't get me wrong. There are exceptions that have made it to the top, and we can list Barack Obama, the forty-fourth president of the United States who made it to that country's highest elected office. It does not nullify the fact that Blacks are at the bottom of the economic ladder.

In this book, rather than focus on where groups end up on the strata, I argue that all groups have a default starting position which influences where groups and their members end up irrespective of their country of migration in the Western world. By shedding light on the role of racial stratification in the disparity in outcomes among migrant groups, the central task of this book is to examine the socio-political and economic structures which maintain the system of racial stratification in European labour markets. This book is built on data generated by bringing together two scholarly traditions for social change: egalitarian theory and critical race theory. It is foregrounded on the egalitarian notion that all human persons are equal in fundamental worth. Theoretical assumptions from CRT are employed to examine and outline the mechanism through which racial stratification is (re)produced and maintained; how it is recognised by citizens; the dialectical interaction/s of actors negotiating its inherently hierarchical arrangement, and the ways it limits and benefits human agency and mobility based on racial category. It draws on secondary statistical data, together with interviews with first-generation immigrants of Spanish, Polish and Nigerian descent negotiating the Irish labour market, to reveal how people are positioned on a racial stratum. Considering the messiness of racial stratification occurring contemporaneously with a heterogeneous labour force, this book particularly emphasises how race, gender and class, along with age, act as intersecting stratifiers which not only influence inter-group outcomes but also intra-group hierarchies. The combination of theory and praxis in this book in addition provides a method for researching racial stratification and the racial order to decipher and outline how states assign a place (racial positioning) to their migrant groups. The ways migrants know, negotiate and change their place on the racial strata in the process of migration to labour participation are explored through meso-level analysis of counterstories from migrant groups. The key dynamics and experiences among groups and their hosts in Ireland, and what these teach us about how racial stratification operates in the labour market and migrants' working lives, are also made explicit in this book.

The importance of context

To have a radical critical understanding about race and its effects in the labour market, the centrality of race and race consciousness is crucial. These two themes run through this book and I discuss them further in the concluding chapter. Although, unlike in the United States, the notion of racial stratification has not been prominent in European scholarship, particularly in relation to labour market disparities, many CRT theorists insist the world social order has effected the racial structure as we have it today (Mills, 1997; Gillborn, 2006; Verdugo, 2008). The title of this book alludes to its focus on investigating inequality in the labour market and explicitly centring race as a key factor in determining migrant chances, and addresses this through the adaptation of CRT.

While the immigrant types and populations in Ireland might be some-what different from those in older immigration countries such as Britain, Germany, France, Sweden and other European countries where people of immigrant descent are up to the second, third and fourth generations, Ireland's relative newness to mass immigration means we are able to access raw data on the experiences of immigrants in a new environment before assimilation and acculturation fully set in. Racial stratification has been chosen in this book as the angle to speak to the differential in labour market outcomes among groups in Ireland. The Irish case in this book provides a model for studying racial stratification with applicability to other settings as its research population is representative of three broad groups (Eastern Europe, Western Europe and Africa) in addition to data from an employment programmes' database of people of migrant descent from seventy-seven different nationalities. This book focuses on Ireland for a number of reasons. My role as a career development specialist in Ireland brought me in contact with migrants of over eighty nationalities, who were making immense efforts to increase their employment chances. I observed that despite the number of years they have lived in Ireland, being European and/or naturalised Irish citizens, they were all still encumbered with minority status. This was not helped by the higher risk of poverty and underemployment associated with Black Africans in general and Black men in particular in the Irish labour market, who, based on the 2011 and 2016 Census record, are five to eight times more likely to be unemployed than a White person. This piqued my interest to understand what influences migrants' economic success in order to better serve the target group.

I was also personally invested in the search for answers. As a parent of two teenage boys who are Irish citizens by birth, I wanted to understand if investing in developing their achievement attributes will suffice in reducing this risk and grant them access to the privileges enjoyed by citizens categorised as White in Ireland and the acclaimed intergenerational mobility in spite of their darker physiognomy.

Background to the study on which this book is based

The ideal in an equal and meritocratic society is that qualified and hardworking individuals will gain entrance and mobility on the labour market. However, empirical research demonstrates that multiple factors aside from personal effort and competence affect people's chances of gaining employment (see McGinnity et al., 2009; EU MIDIS 11, 2016; Arnold et al., 2019; Joseph, 2019). The European model of managing cultural and racial diversity through integration and multiculturalism has operated on the premise that access to the language of the host community, citizenship or citizenship rights, housing, access to medical services, basic education and employment skills are required for migrants' successful employment, which it suggests in turn facilitate integration. This model has resulted in social scientists, employment activation projects and migrant support groups routinely recommending that new migrants should be equipped with these skills, particularly the language of the host community, to enable newcomers to gain entrance onto the labour market.

As a career development specialist, the natural expectation is that there would be some difficulty for migrants seeking to gain employment in Ireland, which turned out to be the case. I, however, also observed a remarkable difference in outcomes between job-seeking migrants from different nationalities despite similarities in their educational attainment, age, gender and right to work in Ireland. My position, based on my experience as a migrant who has been through the employment-seeking process and prior research, is that race undoubtedly influences migrants' outcome in the job-seeking process. There were, however, in addition to this some worrying patterns which suggested a systemic interference in the differential in outcomes. I observed that when race was centred in analysing the outcomes of participants in an employability programme (EP 2009–2011 database), the Nigerians of Black African descent who appeared to have the highest labour market activity had the lowest progression rate on to paid employment. While their progression was mainly on to unpaid, voluntary roles, the participants from Spain gained access to paid employment. The database statistics showed that Nigerians who are Black Africans were over-represented at the bottom of the employment ladder in low-skilled, low-paying roles, a view which was confirmed by the Irish 2011 and 2016 Census data.

By taking the parameters of the 2011 integration monitor known as the Zaragoza Indicators (McGinnity et al., 2011) as the starting point, a preliminary investigation through a focus group with migrants who possessed the stipulated requirements which, according to the Zaragoza report, foster the integration of migrants, was carried out.[1] The main research findings suggest that: 'Though the ability to function effectively within the society provided a spring board for the participants to make some advancement in their individual process of integrating in Ireland, it, however, proved insufficient by itself to bring the participants to feel fully integrated' (Akpoveta, 2011: 70). Secondary findings of the research indicated that the participants presented as oscillating between Ireland and their home countries, and they did not feel at home in either country. This was not a new finding, as the ground-breaking book of 2001, *The Psychology of Culture Shock*, suggests such phase of oscillation is one of the stages experienced by migrants in their integration process (Ward, Bochner and Furnham, 2001). What was remarkable, however, was that rather than name the cause of the feeling of oscillation as racism per se, the research participants attributed this experience to 'not feeling accepted by the host community' (Akpoveta, 2011: 72). This was more pronounced in the reports of the participants whose country of origin was outside the EU, while those of EU member state descent expressed a higher level of feeling accepted.

From these findings, three dynamics required further exploration. First, an understanding of 'acceptance' and how it influences migrants' experience, and their cultural and socio-economic outcome in the labour market. Secondly, what ascriptive or achievement attributes contribute to how migrants are positioned in Ireland? The third dynamic is how migrants are racially positioned in Ireland, which morphed into a need to understand racial stratification, and how it is produced, reproduced and maintained.

Why a critical race theory methodology?

Adopting a CRT methodology springs from the search for a theoretic framework which includes empirical methods and methodology to investigate the disparity in labour market outcomes within the context of racial stratification. While Silverman (2001: 3) succinctly states that 'without theory there is nothing to research', theories can be described as 'travels' (Tweed, 2006: 20). In Ireland, race and nationality of descent are nuanced in ways that certain groups are more likely to appear at the bottom of the socio-economic ladder than others. Although 'racial stratification is real' (Zuberi and Bonilla-Silva, 2008: 10), biology or genes are not the root causes. In instances where there is an obvious distribution of power and resources which disproportionately marginalise racialised people's position in society, CRT insists that race remains central to research investigations. Indeed, frameworks such as critical race feminism and critical whiteness studies, which are offshoots of CRT, have been known to centre particular problematics which accounts for their progress. Contrary to many labour market practices today, race should not be piggybacked on other well-established theories (Mills, 2009). Many of the traditional approaches to inequality and inequity in the labour market or the outcome of Blacks the world over, particularly when juxtaposed with that of migrants with phenotypic whiteness, do not adequately speak to my lived experience as a person of Black African descent.

In terms of race, a CRT methodology offers a theoretical frame that can sharpen the critical lens and draw from other scholars who have challenged the racialised order in society. It provides avenues to challenge narrow ideologies and traditional ways of knowing (Hylton, 2012). Similarly, Zuberi and Bonilla-Silva (cited in Zuberi, 2011) maintain that white logic has proved to be more ideological and less transformative.[2] Extant knowledge epistemicide in the social sciences sees a university knowledge system still heavily reliant on 'the Western canon, the knowledge system created some 500 to 550 years ago in Europe by White male scientists' (Hall and Tandon, 2017: 7). Collins (1990), however, specifically urges researchers to search for ways to reflect the experiences of Black people without borrowing passively from White social science.

CRT, like any other theoretical framework, is recognisable by certain characteristics, including its centring of race in the problematising of social relations and its social justice agenda. It also resists colour-blind, race-neutral, ahistorical and apolitical perspectives (Crenshaw, 1995; Delgado and Stefancic, 2012). Taking cognisance of the increasing debate on intersectionality in the development of CRT as a methodological framework, for example the intersection of race and gender (Crenshaw, 1995) and the intersection of race and class (Cole, 2009; Gillborn, 2008), means ensuring that twenty-first-century research on race incorporates avenues to explore how class and gender (including gendered roles and responsibilities) might account for labour market outcomes.

What is critical race theory?

CRT is a theoretical and methodological framework which attributes racial inequalities, particularly in the US, to structural as opposed to individualised causes (Delgado and Stefancic, 2012). As a methodological framework, CRT provides analytical tools for critically investigating the concept of racial stratification, hierarchy in modern states and the othering of those categorised as Blacks or non-Whites. CRT started by focusing directly on the effects of race and racism while at the same time addressing the hegemonic system of white supremacy on the meritocratic system of the United States (Cook, 1995; Crenshaw, 1995; Matsuda, 1995), and it developed initially from the work of legal scholars Derrick Bell, Alan Freeman and Richard Delgado. It started in the mid-1970s, as a number of lawyers, activists and legal scholars interested in studying and transforming the relationship among race, racism and power realised that the seeming advances of the civil rights era had stalled and, in many respects, were being rolled back in what Omi and Winant in their 1994 theorising described as racial formation projects. CRT takes as its starting point the conception that race and races are socially constructed thoughts and relations that have no bearing on either objective reality or biological traits. In other words, one's race should not determine one's ability, contrary to Herrnstein and Murray's (1994) writings in *The Bell Curve*. It sees race as a product of the human imagination that manifests and reinvents itself through articulations of distinctions, as opposed to the hegemonic thinking that defines racial cleavages as natural, permanent and essential (Bonilla-Silva, 2003).

One of the defining features of CRT is that it insists on analysing race and racism by placing them in both historical and contemporary contexts, and its scholars view racial distinctions as having a historical ring which is open to change (Delgado, 1984; Harris, 1995). CRT theorists, however, argue that there are difficulties encountered in the process because of the ways in which hegemonic thoughts that are maintained by supremacist structures control the nature of relationships between majority and minority groups. This provides interesting scope in research, particularly in investigating the nature of the relationship between minority workers, their work colleagues and the systems within those structures. The activist dimension in CRT brings to the fore the fundamental role that the law plays in the maintenance of racial hierarchy (Zuberi, 2011). It 'sets out not only to ascertain how society organises itself along racial lines and hierarchies but to transform it for the better' (Delgado and Stefancic, 2012: 7) with the possibility of implementing social justice. CRT is more than a theoretical framework. It is a call to action. You cannot really do CRT and not act.

In recent years, social scientists and Western societies have routinely used 'ethnicity' and 'diversity' interchangeably with 'race'. However, the twenty-four people who started CRT defined a kind of racial consciousness as a necessary element in fostering and understanding the contested position of those in power with racialised minorities in a position of subjugation. Thus, in this general context, critical race research should be based on the epistemology of racial emancipation and examining the practices of racial power while working towards the elimination of the effects of white supremacy. Although research can be informed by various informants, in a racial stratification research the critical race perspective should be informed by the experiences of racialised groups suffering from the various forms of white supremacy. Studies that have employed CRT, particularly in Education, analyse the role of race and racism in perpetuating social disparities between dominant and marginalised racial groups (see Ladson-Billings and Tate, 1995; Ladson-Billings, 1998; DeCuir and Dixson, 2004); they do not simply describe the story, they also examine how race influenced the outcome. CRT initially borrowed from the insights of radical feminism, some European philosophers, American radical traditions and critical legal studies (CLS) which challenged the meritocracy of the United States. However, unlike traditional civil rights, which embraces incrementalism and step-by-step progress, CRT scholars are critical of three basic notions that have been embraced by liberal legal ideology: the notion of colour blindness, the neutrality of the law and incremental change. In organisations describing themselves as equal opportunity, the colour-blind perspective holds that 'one's qualifications, not one's colour or ethnicity should be the mechanism by which upward mobility is achieved' (Gallagher, 2003: 3).

The promotion of colour-blindness and neutrality is a perplexing one seeing that it should ordinarily promote equal opportunity. Colour-blindness has, however, been adopted as a way to justify ignoring and dismantling race-based policies such as affirmative actions that were designed to address societal inequity (Gotanda, 1991). Moreover, as has been proved in the French nation state, adopting a colour-blind position does not eliminate racism and racist acts; rather, in the law, the notion of colour-blindness fails to take into consideration the persistence and common-place experience of racism and the construction of people of African descent as other – a process which automatically disadvantages them. Colour-blindness and its purported neutrality cannot adequately address the harmful effects of being othered. In fact, its supposed disregarding of race is clearly false as colour-blindness serves a social and political function for Whites while disregarding racial hierarchy. Through acts of shared consumptions, the notion of colour-blindness turns race into nothing more than an innocuous cultural symboliser by taking racially coded styles and products and recoding these symbols to commodities or experiences that Whites and racial minorities can purchase and share (Gallagher, 2003). This chimera of sameness is portrayed by multinationals like McDonalds and at shopping malls, which have made not just American culture but Western culture more homogeneous and also created the illusion that everyone is the same through consumption (Gallagher, 2003). The notion of colour-blindness has made the interrogation of both the ways that white privilege is deployed and the normalising effects of whiteness nearly impossible. Since 'difference' in the colour-blind discourse almost always refers to People of Colour because being White is considered 'normal' (DeCuir and Dixson, 2004: 29), it follows that practising colour-blindness will affect the people with the most need.

As part of a general movement against racial powers, CRT makes its contributions by its articulation of the contours of racial power, 'undermining the logic of the postracial reality' (Zuberi, 2011: 1587). It is a forerunner in the critical analysis of historical racial projects. It has over the years developed perspectives which challenge the dominant narrative. CRT is open to further development and it encourages researchers to develop methods for their research. This, however, proves challenging particularly for those new to CRT as a methodological framework. Its labour market research has mainly employed the analysis of secondary or administrative data, while education research has employed the various tenets of CRT, particularly counterstorytelling (Delgado, 1995; Solórzano and Yosso, 2002; DeCuir and Dixson, 2004; Martinez, 2014). With the continuing worldwide crisis and increasing racial inequality, the development of a CRT methodology in the labour market is paramount, now more than ever. This chapter makes such contribution through the development of a reproducible framework to carry out scientific labour market research on racial stratification.

The relevance of the tenets of CRT

CRT, like other critical theoretical frameworks, is evidenced by an ontological position which is best defined by its main tenets. These tenets provide both an analytical and conceptual framework to help uncover the ingrained societal disparities that support a system of privilege and oppression. Since CRT originated in the United States, the tenets are mainly explained through the original arguments employed in its development. The four main tenets of CRT discussed in this chapter will give an insight into how it can travel to Europe and be employed beyond American shores.[3]

Voice-of-colour thesis and counterstorytelling

A tenet of CRT is the voice-of-colour thesis which holds that because of their different histories and experiences with oppression, Black, Indian, Asian and Latino writers and thinkers may be able to communicate to their White counterparts matters that Whites are unlikely to know (Delgado and Stefancic, 2001: 9). In other words, 'minority status … brings with it a presumed competence to speak about race and racism' (Delgado and Stefancic, 2001: 9). Thus, the legal storytelling movement urges Black and Brown writers to recount their experiences with racism and the legal system, and to apply their own unique perspectives to assess law's master narratives. A monovocal account engenders not only stereotyping but also curricular choices that result in representations in which fellow members of a group represented cannot recognise themselves (Montecinos, 1995: 293–294). Counterstorytelling forms an essential part of CRT because of its numerous advantages. It has been used by many CRT theorists, particularly in education research (Solórzano and Yosso, 2002; DeCuir and Dixson, 2004; Gillborn, 2006) and law education in the United States (Bell, 1992 in *Faces at the Bottom of the Well*). Counterstorytelling is 'a method of telling the stories of those people whose experiences are not often told' (Solórzano and Yosso, 2002: 26) and 'a means of exposing and critiquing normalised dialogues that perpetuate racial stereotypes hence giving voice to marginalised groups' (DeCuir and Dixson, 2004: 27). Counterstorytelling is premised on the idea that the views of the dominant, 'privileged,' powerful (those who decide who the other is) and the marginalised or 'other' are different; that the storyteller determines the view(s) expressed in each story; that there are hidden or untold stories of the 'other' (DeCuir and Dixson, 2004: 27). While it encourages the marginalised to tell their stories, its strength lies not just in the stories it tells but the depth it uncovers. This epistemological standpoint serves to expose, analyse and even challenge master narratives which 'essentialises and wipes out the complexities and richness of a group's cultural life' while putting human faces to the experiences of often marginalised and silenced groups (Montecinos, 1995). It also aids the telling of stories that aims to cast doubt on the validity of accepted premises or myths, especially ones held by the majority (Delgado and Stefancic, 2012).

There are various methods of generating data through the telling of stories by interviewees, imaginations or unreal creations. While counter-stories are a form of storytelling, it is 'different from fictional storytelling' (Solórzano and Yosso, 2002: 36). A story becomes a counterstory when it begins to incorporate the five elements of CRT (Solórzano and

Yosso, 2002: 36). Critical race scholars have practised counterstory-telling in at least three general forms, including personal stories or narratives, other people's stories or narratives, and composite stories or narratives (Solórzano and Yosso, 2002). When gathering individual stories to form a counterstory, CRT scholars suggest the importance of maintaining theoretical and cultural sensitivity. Theoretical sensitivity, which is a personal quality of the researcher that can be further developed during the research process, refers to the special insight and capacity of the researcher to interpret and give meaning to data (Strauss and Corbin, 1990). More succinctly put, 'theoretical sensitivity refers to the attribute of having insight, the ability to give meaning to data, the capacity to understand, and capability to separate the pertinent from that which isn't' (Strauss and Corbin, 1990: 41–42). Cultural sensitivity refers to the capacity of individuals as members of socio-historical communities to accurately read and interpret the meaning of informants (Bernal, 1998, cited in Strauss and Corbin, 1990). In order to create counterstories, Solórzano and Yosso (2002: 34) relied on four sources of data: the data gathered from the research process itself, the existing literature, and their own professional and personal experiences.

Despite its ability to present views rarely evidenced in social research, the inherent weaknesses in storytelling arise from the fact that stories are socially constructed. They can represent limited versions of reality for subjugated people and their everyday experiences, especially where oppressive social arrangements remain unchallenged (Hylton, 2012). Nonetheless, the advantages of counterstorytelling far outweigh its weaknesses not just for CRT theorists but for victims, as 'hearing their own stories and the stories of others, listening to how the arguments against them are framed, and learning to make the arguments to defend themselves can be empowering for participants' (Solórzano and Yosso, 2002: 27). Counterstories also enable victims of racism to find their voice, and those injured by racism and other forms of oppression discover they are not alone in their marginality (Solórzano and Yosso, 2002: 27). Note that counterstorytelling is not about 'developing imaginary characters that engage in fictional scenarios', instead, the 'composite' characters that are developed 'are grounded in real-life experiences and actual empirical data and are contextualized in social situations that are also grounded in real life, not fiction' (Solórzano and Yosso, 2002: 36).

Permanence of racism

The notion of the permanence of racism in society is a tenet of CRT. It is the belief that racism is the usual way society does business and is the common, everyday experience of most People of Colour in the United States (Delgado and Stefancic, 2001). With its history steeped in immigration, Bell (1992: 13) contends that 'racism is a permanent component of American life' that plays and continues to play a dominant role in American society. This epistemological stance within a CRT framework would involve adopting a realist view which would suggest that 'racist hierarchical structures control all political, economic, and social domains and allocates the privileging of whites and the subsequent othering of People of Colour in all arenas' (DeCuir and Dixson, 2004: 27). In a racial stratification framework, 'white-over-colour ascendancy serves both psychic and material purposes of working class people and White elites respectively' (Delgado and Stefancic, 2004: 3). And 'the ordinariness of racism means that racism is difficult to cure or address and that colour-blind, or "formal," conceptions of equality, expressed in rules that insist only on treatment that is the same across the board, can only effectively address the most blatant forms of discrimination' (Delgado and Stefancic, 2001: 3).

This pessimistic view of society which seems to offer no way out of racism is one of the main reasons CRT is critiqued. However, using CRT as a methodological framework can be quite a useful tool, particularly in light of DeCuir and Dixson's (2004) CRT analysis in Education which utilised five of its prominent tenets.[4] One of the main reasons for the underreporting of racism is the lack of action when people actually report. Some victims of racism are made to feel they are being oversensitive to a little joke. They are offered meaningless platitudes and a handshake. DeCuir and Dixson (2004) illustrate some key considerations for analysing events to comprise: examining the disparity and dismissal of both the import and impact of racist acts on the victims and victimiser; exploring the ways in which states and their practices serve to support the notion of the permanence of racism; and then examining the disciplinary process employed when racist crimes are committed or reported. The uniqueness of using CRT as an analytical tool means exploring not just the event but also the nature of the particular threat or event, its meaning and intent. It should also explore the culture of the establishment that allowed the victimiser to feel comfortable in producing the threat. Taking a CRT stance in investigating an event will in addition consider the manner in which the threat may have encouraged racist and violent behaviour or supported a hostile and alienating environment for the victim (DeCuir and Dixson, 2004). If schools, organisations and businesses cover these elements in reported racist incidents, victims will feel heard, perpetrators will be in no doubt of their crime and organisations will be indicted for the ways they collude with perpetrators of racist acts or create environments that are conducive to racism.

Interest convergence

Interest convergence is a tenet of CRT that was advanced by Derrick Bell (1980). The notion originated in the US and it suggests that civil rights gains within communities of colour, particularly those for African-Americans, should be interpreted with cautious enthusiasm. The argument is based on the idea that White people will support racial justice only insofar as there is a 'convergence' between the interests of the White people and racial justice. This means Whites pursue racial justice and equality for others when they have vested interests or something to gain (Bell, 1980). The dominant narrative of the 1954 decision in Brown v. Board of Education – that Brown was a watershed moment in US history, marking what is popularly seen as a collective moral, political, and cultural shift in attitudes towards race and inequality – has been argued to be a 'convergence' of interests by Derrick Bell. He insists the decision was because the White elites were willing to concede on the segregation battle, albeit on the legal front only, because they were concerned about international condemnation of the US on racial segregation. In other words, the desegregation may have resulted more from the self-interest of elite Whites than a desire to help Blacks (Delgado and Stefancic, 2001). In developing this notion, Bell (1980) also indicts the US Supreme Court that they supported Brown because it served the United States' cold war agenda of supporting human rights. He concludes that the self-interest of the elite White coincided with the interests of civil rights leaders, which brought about school desegregation. The interests of those who were making the decision converged with the interests of the Black plaintiffs. This notion of interest convergence adds a further dimension to the permanence of racism (Delgado and Stefancic, 2001): because racism advances the interests of both White elites materially and working-class people psychically, large segments of society have little incentive to eradicate it.

This close interaction of the outcome of individuals and groups in society with the law, in accomplishing such feats as Brown v. Board, is problematic and has strong implications in managing equality and social justice, not only in American society as it applies specifically to those cases but to other parts of the Western world. First, it implies a close connection between judges and the interests of the White dominant community; secondly, it suggests that there is relatively little room for judges to have autonomy to make their own decisions; thirdly, it denies the marginalised community a role in shaping the law; and lastly, because the will of the majority tends in the direction of self-interest, it can be problematic for meeting the equal needs of all citizens (Bell, 1980; Delgado and Stefancic, 2012). Indeed, the early civil rights legislation seemed to have provided only basic rights to African-Americans without addressing the racial and social injustices they had experienced – rights which many argued had been enjoyed by Whites for centuries. Those acclaimed initial gains are seen by critical race scholars as superficial opportunities because they were basic tenets of US democracy (Bell, 1980), and as concessions which were offered to the extent that they were not seen as (or exacted) a major disruption to a 'normal' way of life for the majority of Whites (DeCuir and Dixson, 2004: 28). Interest convergence provides analytical tools which I have adopted to problematise specific projects within an Irish context. The dearth of such critical analysis in state projects in Ireland and social justice curricula shows a need to adopt such a framework. I return to this in a later chapter in my plea for the adoption of critical race theory in the social sciences in Europe and in Ireland more specifically.

Intersectionality: when race, class and gender intersect

Though CRT insists on the centrality of race in its application as a theoretical and methodological framework, one of its tenets is intersectionality which addresses the interaction between interlocking identities. The notion of intersectionality challenges the traditional tendency to treat race and gender as mutually exclusive categories of experience and analysis. It suggests that we cannot talk about the lives of people when we examine only one dimension of their lives, and at the same time it debunks the idea that there is a monolithic identity detached from other forms of identity. Many (Crenshaw, 1989; Collins, 2000) insist that when we talk of racial domination, we must examine how it interacts with other forms of domination including gender, sexuality, class, religion and all forms of disadvantaging identities. The concept was advanced by feminist writers including Hook, Davis, Crenshaw and Smith – it was Crenshaw (1989) who put the term into the public domain, since when it has become a buzz word in social science research. Crenshaw (1989) illustrates intersectionality as a 'crossroad', Nancy Fraser (1995) called it 'bivalent collectivities' and Patricia Hill Collins (2000) termed it 'matrix of domination', while Yuval-Davis (2006) termed it 'axes of difference'. This includes many other variants of intersecting identities. While the central purpose of the concept is to advance the telling of the relegated identities of women (Crenshaw, 1989, 1991), it is presently being used to address various interlocking oppressions. Intersectionality is an integral aspect of CRT with applicability as a 'methodology for studying the relationships among multiple dimensions and modalities of social relationships and subject formations' (McCall, 2005: 1771). Kimberle Crenshaw argues that:

> Feminist efforts to politicize experiences of women and antiracist efforts to politicize experiences of 'people of colour' have frequently proceeded as though the issues and experiences they each detail occur on mutually exclusive terrains. Although racism and sexism readily intersect in the lives of real people, they seldom do in feminist and antiracist practices. And so, when the practices expound identity as 'woman' or 'person of colour' as an either/or proposition, they relegate the identity of women of colour to a location that resists telling. (Crenshaw, 1991: 1242)

Intersectionality holds that the various oppressions within society, such as racism, sexism, homophobia and religion-based bigotry, do not act independently of one another; instead, these forms of oppression inter-relate, and are connected to each other to create a system of oppression that reflects the intersection of multiple forms of discrimination. The idea is based on the need to think of identities and experiences as being shaped by the intersecting vectors of race, class and gender (which are the most often named) in order to address the hierarchies which marginalise them.

While Black women are indeed the quintessential case for inter-sectionality, Kimberle Crenshaw's (1989: 139) potent analogy of an accident at a crossroads depicts how employing a single-axis analy-sis distorts the experiences of Black women such that they are also 'theoretically erased'.[5] The 'dominant conceptions of discrimination condition us to think about subordination occurring along a single categorical axis' (Crenshaw, 1989: 139) because it limits inquiry to the experiences of otherwise-privileged members of the group. Both feminist theory and antiracist politics marginalise and exclude Black women when their experiences are viewed under those single categories. This is not to say that Black women do not experience discrimination in the same ways as men or White women. Rather, due to their intersec-tionality, Black women often experience 'double discrimination' – the combined effects of practices which discriminate on the basis of both race and sex (Crenshaw, 1989: 149). Discrimination can sometimes be experienced as Black women, which is not the sum of race and sex discrimination (Crenshaw, 1989: 149). Such combined identities can include 'Muslim women' and how their experience of the hijab is unique to them. It is fair to say that 'no person has a single, easily stated, unitary identity' (Delgado and Stefancic, 2001: 9). For example, a White feminist may also be Jewish and/or gay because 'everyone has potentially conflicting, overlapping identities, loyalties, and allegiances' (Delgado and Stefancic, 2001: 9). It also, however, means that people are members of many groups, such that we have complex identities which can shape our experiences. An Irish person may also be Black, or Muslim. An Asian Irish may be gay, female and a single parent. A Black Irish person may have a parent who is German or a grandparent who is British. All of these occupy different positions on the social stratification in different societies. These multiple differences interact and can be experienced in various ways. Gender influences the experience of racism by men and women differently sometimes, just as women of different races can experience sexism differently. Feminist theory has, however, remained *white*, and 'its potential to broaden and deepen its analysis by addressing non-privileged women remains unrealised' (Crenshaw, 1989: 154). Considering that (white) feminism evolved from a white racial context that is seldom acknowledged, its value for Black women is diminished. According to Crenshaw (1989: 154), 'not only are Women of Colour in fact overlooked, but their exclusion is reinforced when White women speak for and as women. The authoritative universal voice – usually White male subjectivity masquerading as non-racial, non-gendered objectivity – is merely transferred to those who, but for gender, share many of the same cultural, social and economic characteristics.'

Black women, it would appear, can only be protected insofar as their experiences coincide with the two groups – White women or Black men. 'This is because anti-discrimination doctrine ... generally forces[6] them [Black women] to choose between specifically articulating the intersectional aspects of their subordination, thereby risking their ability to represent Black men or ignoring intersectionality in order to stake a claim that would not lead to the exclusion of Black men' (Crenshaw, 1989: 148). Viewing Black women this way can be problematic because they can be seen as either too female or too black, thus positioning them on the margin of both feminist and black liberation agendas. We see Women of Colour situated within at least two subordinated groups that frequently pursue conflicting political agendas. However, the dimension of 'intersectional disempowerment' that Men of Colour and White women seldom confront is manifest in this need to split their political energies into two (Crenshaw, 1991: 1252). Intersectional subordination need not be intentionally produced. Rather, it is frequently the imposition of one burden that interacts with pre-existing vulnerabilities to create yet another dimension of disempowerment (Crenshaw,

1991: 1249). It doesn't matter which of our social categories caused the harm, the focus should be that women are being harmed.

CRT has been critiqued because of the belief that the focus on race obscures other aspects of difference that serve to marginalise and oppress People of Colour. However, CRT theorists in their analysis routinely adopt a stance which includes class, gender and race and how they interact. 'Intersectionality addresses the most central theoretical and normative concern within feminist scholarship: namely, the acknowledgement of differences among women' (Davis, 2008: 70). It 'promises an almost universal applicability, useful for understanding and analysing any social practice, any individual or group experience, any structural arrangement, and any cultural configuration' (Davis, 2008: 70). Moreover, it allows researchers to see race, gender and class as interlocking systems of oppression rather than monolithic categories. This makes it possible to extend the understanding to other oppressions, such as age, sexual orientation, religion and ethnicity.

Mind-map for studying race and racial stratification in the labour market

When we talk about the multifaceted nature of race, what does this mean, and what is involved? What is a comprehensive view of race and its impact like? With the growing significance of race in Europe today, the dearth of a comprehensive theory on the labour market which centralises race is egregious. Rather, the ubiquity of implicit bias, group favouritism, inferiorisation of difference and harsh workplace environments consigns people of migrant descent, particularly people of Black African descent to the bottom of the racial ladder. Even with increasing diversity in society, the labour market in Ireland is still a white space of white privilege that invisibilises difference. We need a critical race theory of the labour market similar to CRT in Education and legal scholarship where the focus of researchers, policy makers and educators is not on difference but on how we respond to difference for racial equality, equity and justice in our social world.

When I began my travels in studying race and how it influences the disparity in outcomes among groups, I developed a race consciousness which grounded my understanding of racial stratification and whiteness. I have pulled these together in a comprehensive mind-map (Figure I.1). It captures the complexity of race and the myriad ways race is nuanced in the labour market as a roadmap for thinking through and making meaning of racial stratification. This guide for structuring an anti-racist examination of society comes from insights gained through researching

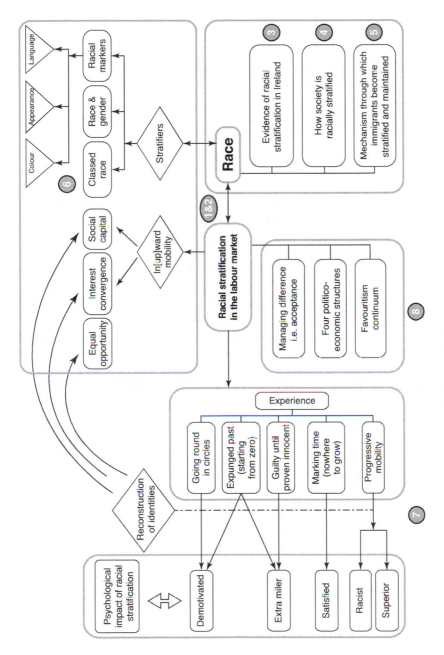

Figure I.1 Mind-map of analysing race and racial stratification in the labour market

labour market differentials among migrants in Ireland. It represents my understanding of racial stratification as a critical race theorist of Black African descent. The key question this map addresses is 'what accounts for the differential in outcomes among different groups in the labour market?'

This comprehensive examination of the labour market is structured in accordance with the CRT tradition for the following reasons. It commences by rejecting a colour-blind approach to racial difference in the labour market because it silences people who are categorised as Blacks or non-Whites while they are impacted by the racial order within the racial stratification systems in Europe. The centrality of race and the voice of colour – the marginalised; it provides and encourages new anti-racist lenses and structures to examine the outcomes of groups by under-standing how racial stratification influences human outcome; it gives voice to marginalised group/s and sees the world from their perspectives; and it does not assume a black deficit approach to understanding race and its impact.

In the mind-map, race is centred as the main construct/variable in the analysis. A CRT assumption embedded in the study is that the construc-tion of race creates racial stratification and racial stratification only exists because race is seen as real. Thus both elements (race and racial stratification) are central to any study on society. When race is centred in a CRT study, some key understandings about race become imperative – refer to the sections mapped as 1 and 2. This means a study of race should start with and include a contemporary and historical understand-ing of the meaning of race in the country/setting of the study. The next section, marked out 3 to 5 on the map, is where you gather any evidence of racial stratification and the racial order. Next, your study needs to identify the racial stratifiers as depicted in the mind-map section 6. This concerns our intersectionalities, a main tenet of CRT – because people do not live monolithic lives. In my study, there were three broad areas of intersectionality in the lives of the people in the study (see discussion in chapter 6): the classed race – where a person's race is classed; the intersection of race and gender; and racial markers (physical appear-ance, language and skin colour). These racial stratifiers in turn influence labour market mobility – which is how migrants and minorities change their place on the labour supply chain. Mapped at number 7 is the form of reconstruction of immigrants which occurs in Europe where their experiences influence their actions which consequently becomes solidi-fied through identity reconstruction as discussed in chapter 7. Next, we have the political system that powers racial stratification. This is the favouritism continuum discussed in chapter 8. Note that to use this map, the sections can be reproduced as separate units or as a whole. While the complexity and multifaceted nature of race, race relations and racial stratification are evident from the mind-map, it also means there are still further depths to be explored.

Structure of the book

This book begins with the ontological view that all societies are stratified (Ultee, 2007) and that racial stratification is instrumental in maintaining economic injustices. This introduction sets up the Irish case as an empirical roadmap for race scholars across Europe to research and uncover the often unspoken and obfuscated aspects of race. It provides insight about the genealogy of the study on which the data in this book are based, with a detailed section on how the chapters are set and connected. Critical race theory and four of its tenets are discussed to ground readers in the theoretical understanding and race consciousness underpinning this book. A bonus mind-map is also provided which captures the complexity of racial inequality and the myriad ways race is nuanced in labour market differentials as a roadmap for thinking through and making meaning of racial stratification. It provides a useful guide for structuring an anti-racist examination of society.

Chapter 1 highlights the pernicious use of race as a means of categorisation to determine access to scarce and desired resources. The way whiteness selectively privileges groups is discussed. The chapter introduces readers to the everyday performance of white supremacy as the underlying structure of white privilege. In this regard, whiteness is counterposed as privilege against whiteness as dominance as the locus of understanding the effect of whiteness and the resulting marginalisation and subjugation of Blacks and non-Whites. The chapter ends by defining some key terms for understanding racial stratification.

In order to introduce a CRT perspective to how we look at and talk about racism in Ireland, chapter 2 examines the symbolic use of colour in emphasising the perceived difference of racialised Irish people in their diaspora settings. It also discusses how whiteness has historically been mobilised to centralise Irish interests both at home and abroad, altering their positioning from colonised to colonisers. The cartography of the top tiers of the Irish labour market presents us with a false picture of a monocultural Ireland. This is in contradiction to Census data which demonstrates the presence of newcomers within its borders, including Ireland's ethnic minorities – the Irish Travellers. A key argument in the chapter is that rather than racism between White bodies invalidating skin colour as a locus of understanding racism, deviation from

Eurocentric norms was employed to darken actors and influence the symbolic colour of the perceived difference ascribed to racialised Irish people on both sides of the Atlantic. While Ireland has been a welcoming state, this chapter discusses inconsistencies through its relationship with the Irish Travellers – the Irish racial other, and Ireland's relationship with its migrant population from the early 1900s to the present.

The comparative chapter 3 is a deviation from traditional ways of presenting data on discrimination and labour market differentials and converts statistical data to show the ways groups are racially stratified in the labour market. It provides evidence of racial stratification in Ireland by analysing the disparity in outcomes among migrant groups and how it is divided along racial lines. It utilises three main sources of data: a selected employability programme (EP) with a database of 639 unique individuals; the Irish 2011 and 2016 national Census statistics and various OECD reports of migrants' outcome in the EU; and data from 32 semi-structured interviews with first-generation migrants of Spanish, Polish and Nigerian descent. The conflating of nationality of descent and race in the society, coupled with the separation of White workers to paid labour and Black workers to unpaid labour, is also discussed.

There is a growing interest in Europe among early researchers and race theorists in CRT as a methodological and analytical framework. While we all know on some level that society is unequal and hierarchical, what is unclear – which is the focus of chapter 4 – is who is at the top and who is at the bottom of the economic and racial ladder and how they are connected. More importantly, how do we determine what group/s are at the top and what group/s are at the bottom? This chapter answers those questions through a step-by-step guide for researching racial stratification and the racial order. It also outlines some key considerations for researching the racial order drawing on insight from a racial stratification study of immigrants' experiences in the Irish labour market. This chapter should be read with chapter 5, where a racial dichotomy of White over Black is unveiled in the Irish case.

Based on extensive empirical evidence from labour market outcomes of migrants in Ireland and analysis of semi-structured interviews, chapter 5 presents racial stratification as a 'default' starting position assigned to newcomers on arrival. It shows how the interaction of class and race produces a classed race to influence this default positioning of group members. The key features of racial stratification discussed within this chapter include its homogenising attributes, inter- and intra-group layering of group members, and the available hierarchies and how migrants fit into them as members of racial groups. The chapter provides insight on how immigrants know and occupy their place on the racial strata. It concludes with a discussion of the implications of racial stratification on the socio-economic outcomes of Black and White workers and how it differs along colour lines.

Migrants and people of migrant descent experience different forms of labour market mobility. Micro-level analyses of their everyday experiences reveal how migrants change their place on the labour supply chain. Chapter 6 presents interest convergence, social capital and equal opportunity as three vehicles with which migrants negotiate their way through racially stratified societies. The way the labour market experiences of migrants align to any of these concepts has long-term implications for everyone, including the creation of racialised ghettos and tripartite segmentation in the labour market. Intersecting vulnerabilities including gender and age that foster inter- or intra-group layering also form part of the chapter.

Although racial stratification influences the outcomes of groups and their members, chapter 7 shows that it is not deterministic because individual migrants can and do express minority agency which influences labour mobility and intra-group hierarchy. This dialectical interaction between minorities and racially stratifying systems in their new country of settlement is the focus of this chapter. It presents a framework for interrogating the migration to labour market participation process within four strands which every migrating person goes through: expectation, experience, negotiation and identity reconstruction. It also presents the typologies identified from migrants' trajectories that reveal five characteristic labour market experiences which in turn become solidified into reconstructed identities. The presence of racial stratification in the labour market participation process selectively metes out an endemic colour-coded migrant penalty which proliferates racial inequality.

Chapter 8 presents the favouritism–disfavour continuum as the system through which racial inequalities, injustices and economic exploitations are proliferated in modern states. It introduces the following four processes: implicit bias, social acceptance, group favouritism and human contact, and discusses how they operate interdependently to maintain the positioning of actors on the continuum. The chapter makes three key arguments. First, it illustrates how the favouritism continuum determines the outcome of actors by the position they occupy on the continuum. Secondly, it illustrates the restrictive yet fluid and changeable nature of this positioning through minority agency and individual mobility. Thirdly, it illustrates how this continuum operates the machinery employed to maintain homogeneity in a heterogeneous labour market, thus producing racial inequality. The chapter also addresses how groups on lower racial strata attempt to avoid triggering implicit bias in others in order to circumvent its negative consequences. The chapter concludes with a theoretical contribution on how to manage difference through the recognition–tolerance continuum and posits that acceptance is the missing link between both concepts.

The concluding chapter argues for a critical race theory in labour market inequality. Racial stratification is a default position ascribed to all citizens, old and new. The way it operates today means that racism will continue to be a permanent fixture in our society unless we deliberately reveal whiteness and white supremacy for what they are – invisible markers and silent affirmative action for Whites. This chapter discusses the limitations of current methods of addressing disparity in outcomes in labour markets across Europe and outlines the benefits, strengths and weaknesses of a CRT approach. It considers the ways in which racial stratification and CRT approaches are thus relevant and necessary for understanding/application in wider societal and global contexts – outside the issue of labour. It contends that for a deracialised, anti-racist analysis and understanding of the labour market, three core elements of CRT become vital: the centrality of race, race consciousness and the voice of colour through counterstorytelling. This chapter reminds readers that racial inequality is not about where people end up but about where they start.

Notes

1 The data-rich informants were a cohort of migrants who were in a position to successfully access the Irish system in that they had either Irish or EU citizenship; they could speak the language of the host community; they either owned their own homes or were in good rented accommodation; they had access to medical services, and they were either in middle-management roles or employed in well-paying jobs.

2 'White logic' refers to a context in which white supremacy has defined the techniques and processes of reasoning about social facts. It assumes a historical posture that grants eternal objectivity to the views of elite Whites and operates to foster a 'debilitating alienation' among the racially oppressed, as they are thrown 'into a world of preexisting meanings as people incapable of meaning making' (Zuberi and Bonilla-Silva, 2003, cited in Zuberi 2011: 1583).

3 Other tenets of CRT include the Social Construction thesis and Differential Racialisation.

4 DeCuir and Dixson used the counterstories of African-American students at Wells Academy, an elite predominately White independent school, to interrogate the relationship between the students of colour, their peers and how conflictual issues were resolved.

5 'Consider an analogy to traffic in an intersection, coming and going in four directions. Discrimination, like traffic through an intersection, may flow in one direction, and it may flow in another. If an accident happens in an intersection, it can be
caused by cars traveling from any number of directions and, sometimes, from all
of them. Similarly, if a Black woman is harmed because she is in the intersection,
her injury could result from sex discrimination or race discrimination' (Crenshaw,
1989: 149).

6 It is important to note that intersectionality as conceptualised by Kimberle
Crenshaw was very specific to how looking at the situation of Black women in
the US through the lens of either gender discrimination or racism alone led to
an incomplete and distorted picture. She grounds her argument using the meta-
phor of a road intersection in the experience of Black female workers in General
Motors in the US and other cases where anti-discrimination policies based on
racism and patriarchy failed to address the needs of Black women who experienced various levels of difficulty in legally establishing their particular problem
of discrimination on the grounds of either race or gender, unlike Black men and
White women. She also argued that the emphasis should be on addressing the
'injury' experienced by Black women rather than the focus of the US judiciary
system on the origin – if sexual or racial discrimination.

1

Race: the unmarked marker in racialised hierarchical social systems

> Race is constructed for the purpose of maintaining a racial hierarchy. Race does not exist as a neutral attribute of each individual. Race exists as a signifier of group and individual social status. Race is real in its social consequences. If race existed only on its condition of being believed, its life would have ceased long ago. (Zuberi and Bonilla-Silva, 2008: 335–336)

Race is a social construct that has been utilised in separating people into groups for positive or negative treatment. The way it impacts on a group will depend on where group members are located on the strata. The effect can include limiting or granting group members access to esteem, status, power and resources. We might, then, erroneously think that race is the problem; to this I say no. The real problem is what race is used for: the creation and maintaining of a racial hierarchy where some – more specifically, Blacks – are at the bottom and some – Whites – are at the top. This arrangement of people on strata based on their race in very simple terms is racial stratification and it affects all groups differently. For Blacks and non-White groups at the bottom of the racial strata, racial stratification is a site of oppression, while for non-Blacks or White groups, it is a site of domination. Racial stratification is only possible because race is possible, because race is constructed as real.

Let me start my travels with race by giving you a glimpse through a personal story of my first realisation living as a person of migrant descent in the white world – an experience I have titled, '... For a black person'. Before I arrived in Ireland, my country of naturalisation, I was just a person – a female person. I experienced the world as a human being, as a woman. So among those who looked like me, neither race nor *my* 'race' was ever an issue. From the day I arrived in Ireland, I became a social construct. I became my race and my intersectionality. I became my skin colour, the gross domestic product (GDP) of my nationality of descent. I became a *Black* woman. No one sought my consent. As I arrived at the state's borders, these categories were already existent and I was expected to fit into them. They would go on to mark my experiences, rights and access to resources. My education became embodied in my Black[ness], such that when I performed well, I would hear, 'that's quite good' as if I just surprised them. I often wondered about the silent comparison and the source; *good for who or what?* ..., I would think, as I waited, silently urging them to say more. ... Would they say it? ... *for a Black person?* You speak really well, for ... *a Black person.* You've achieved a whole lot ... *for a Black person.* I quickly came to the realisation that I was simply my race.

Not everyone understands the angst Black people have about the way race is defined and employed both historically and in contemporary times – and the impact it has on their being, in their everyday lives. This is because of the ambivalence of Whites who though they know that race is an issue; their race is not an issue. The little piece from my lived world is the experience of every person of migrant descent in one shape or form of the other who crosses the borders into the Western world.

The central themes in this chapter include the way race is employed as a means of categorisation to determine access to resources; and whiteness and how it selectively privileges groups. The chapter introduces readers to the everyday performance of white supremacy as the underlying system of white privilege. In this regard, whiteness is counterposed as privilege against whiteness as dominance as the locus of understanding the effect of whiteness and the resulting marginalisation and subjugation of Blacks and non-Whites. The chapter ends by defining some key terms for understanding racial stratification.

The contentious nature of race

The concept of race is not static but has been employed in various ways, making it open to contestation. Its use, particularly in human categorisation at individual and group levels, raises significant questions about race relations and race dynamics. While statisticians may employ race as a category in the collection of data and in providing services to the public, it becomes problematic when we consider who categorises people, the power dynamics involved, and the meaning(s) associated with the categories in terms of where, how and with whom individuals are categorised. All of these have implications, for example if a person is categorised as EU or non-EU; from the Third World, developing or developed world. More recently, development studies have used the term 'global North' and 'South'. Other pertinent concerns include the arrangement of the categories, if flat – signalling racial equality, or top-down – signifying a hierarchical ranking; the status, privileges or negative judgements attached to each category, and the challenges they present to the categorised person when exercising their agency, all of which make the concept of race an ongoing concern. In social identity theory (Tajfel and Turner, 1979), mobility within and between groups plays a vital role in group conflict, and attempts to answer such questions have been the basis of different schools of thought. Race has also been problematic in relation to whether it should be acknowledged or not. Some scholars argue that researching and referring to race reifies it. Those who ignore the concept have been accused of being colour-blind.

The complexity of race is evident from the myriad ways in which it has been conceptualised, though the various positions seem plausible. A major line of contestation, however, has been on how races are formed. Some claim race is an illusion, some see it as an ideology, others take an essentialist view and see it as biological, and yet more see it as socially constructed. The concept of race emerged in the European languages in the fifteenth century, where it was used to emphasise nobility and supe-riority of some groups, while at the same time depicting the inferiority of the other (Omi and Winant, 1994; Cornell and Hartmann, 1998). Race has been applied as a category imposed by others who use it as a foundation for oppression and discrimination, including the promo-tion of slavery in America and apartheid in South Africa. Across Europe today, race is one of the main determinants of socio-economic outcomes and the mobility of people across geographical borders particularly as we consider the 2016 refugee crisis. Race has also been conceptualised and applied by craniologists like Samuel Morton, who claimed to be able to determine the inferiority of others by their skull size, and eugeni-cists who believed in good genes and sustained discriminatory acts like racial segregation, forced sterilisations and genocides. A little over twenty years ago, the authors of the controversial book, *The Bell Curve* claimed that genes and the environment accounted for racial differences in intelligence in the human population (Herrnstein and Murray, 1994). However, it has since been argued (King, 1981) that the biological exist-ence of race is an ideological concept loaded with questionable scientific value. Race operates as a social construct that has material impacts and outcomes. It functions as a category that implicitly and explicitly assigns values, status and positioning on the social, racial and economic hierarchy. Race is not simply about an individual outcome but a group/ collective outcome. It is not personal but structural.

Race creates a hierarchy – a racial hierarchy; one that was established as natural within the social fabric of Western powers and now global systems. One of the most contentious uses of the concept of race is that it orders racial groupings, whereby Africans are inserted at the bottom and Europeans at the top (Zuberi and Bashi, 1997). The incongruence in such hierarchical systems that insists on categorising the human race on the basis of difference is made obvious by Todorov (2000), who cautions that such a belief in the superiority of one group over another may imply the possession of unique and integrated value structures, or serve as an evaluative framework for making generic judgements. Todorov's concerns are worthy of note, as to reasonably compare and decide if one race is better or superior to the other, there is a need for racial groups to exhibit a certain level of sameness to be comparable. Extant evidence also shows that race is commonly applied to distinguish, classify, tag and pigeonhole groups through the application of a scale of values that is markedly ethnocentric, with the racialist's own race usually positioned at the top of the hierarchy (Todorov, 2000).

Individuals take various perspectives on race, and scholars have attempted to categorise such positions. Moschel (2011), for example, uses the label 'racial scepticists' to describe those who maintain that races do not exist at all. Such people or organisations will simply eliminate race from political and normal everyday usage and life. For Crenshaw (2000), the appellation 'racial constructionists' can be used to describe those who believe that races do not naturally exist but are in some ways socially defined. While some of these believe that talking about race should be eliminated, CRT theorists see race as part of the real world and the use of the term should be continued as an effective strategy to combat racism. Todorov (2000: 66) noted a third category, the 'racialists' – individuals who, while not satisfied that races differ, recognise racial superiority. Racialists exhibit ambivalence, and simultaneously believe that people are different while judging them based on a set of rules that indicate sameness.

Traditionally, race is a comparatively simple idea that is applied to certain outward signs of 'social visibility' such as physiognomy (Myrdal, 2000: 96). The literature suggests that race also derives from racial systems, or ways of classifying people, usually by judging how closely their phenotype fits with the somatic norm imagery of what the different races 'look' like (Zuberi and Bashi, 1997: 669). This ability to categorise the other implies a power dynamic where 'Whites categorise Negros' Myrdal (2000: 96). This point is illuminated by Fanon (2000: 257), who contends that 'as long as the Black man is among his own, he will have no occasion, except in minor internal conflicts to experience his being through others'. He thus insists that in the discourse of race, being black is usually viewed in relation to being white, and because of the racial positioning of Black people in the global hierarchy they become the racial 'other'. Goldberg (2000: 156) makes a similar claim that hegemony wielded through race does not take effect in isolation but through contact with others. Consequently, he adds, people adjudged as the racial 'other' are sacrificed at the altar of an idealised and superior category, stripped of personhood and disregarded in matters of social benefits and political (self-) representation. The Negro, in essence, is given two frames of reference within which to place himself (Fanon, 2000: 257–258).

Undeniably, race is a social fact that shapes the concept of identity and collective representation organising social experience (Winant, 2004). It is for this reason that race is widely employed to socially define and categorise individuals based on their physical characteristics that are not predetermined by biological facts (Cornell and Hartmann, 1998). But the concept of race has morphed and become even more pejorative in its use to separate people into groups, such as Europeans and others (Spickard, 1992). The taxonomy of race operates in a way whereby the dominant groups exercise the power to stipulate the status and place of the less powerful, thus maintaining their own power, status and authority (Cornell and Hartmann, 1998). Such classifications usually involve a power relation with racial designations that imply some kind of inferiority. The positioning of White Europeans at the top of the pinnacle, where they were seen as naturally superior to all other 'races' in virtually every aspect, was vital for the imperialist expansion in all parts of the world, including the inception and practice of slavery. Without it, Song (2007: 3768) argues, 'it would not have been possible to subordinate and dehumanise conquered peoples'. Therefore, how race is employed for the inferiorisation and superiorisation of groups makes it continuously problematic and contentious.

While there is consensus among race theorists today that race is a socially constructed category, its influence does not seem to have lessened. One's race is thus an objective reality, a sort of agent that dictates the position of the individual on the hierarchy; determines and influences the individual's life chances and outcomes, and even affects the individual's relationships with others. It is not only in the contemporary United States that the way race is practised is an objective fact where 'one simply is one's race' (Winant, 2000: 185) but also in contemporary Europe. Race is a very real social classification that has cultural ramifications as well as enforcing a definite social order (Omi and Winant, 1994). In this sense, race operates as a matter of both social structure and cultural representation that indicates difference and constructs inequality. The negative implications of race still prevail by its ability to disadvantage some groups while privileging others. What is evident from this trend is the continuous devising of new justifications to institute racial difference to promote the superiority of one group over the other, more specifically, Whites over Blacks to enact white supremacy. It would indeed appear, as Zuberi (2011) argues, that the move from eugenic to cultural arguments on race seems only to be a move from one type of essentialist perspective to another – the biological evolutionary to the cultural perspective of European superiority which came to replace the biological justifications of race. Thus, despite anti-discrimination laws and equal opportunity policies, racial inequality in the labour market persists.

The 'post-racial' discourse, particularly after the election of the first Black president of the United States of America, is that researching and centring race is discouraged by some who claim it reifies it. Contrary to Crouch's (1996) predictions in his essay 'Race is over', there is a continued preoccupation with physical characteristics as the central indicator of race which societies have used to create racial stratification – an ascribed ranking in society which can affect a person's opportunities, status and access to resources. Empirical data show that race still matters in modern states, particularly in view of the festering dissatisfaction with migrants within the EU. In a 2007 survey of forty-seven nations, nearly half (46 per cent) of the UK respondents named race relations and immigration among the most important issues facing Britain, ranking it ahead of education and placing it almost at par with crime (Transatlantic Trends, 2010). A similar poll in Ireland in 2009 found that 72 per cent of people wanted to see a reduction in the number of non-Irish immigrants living in Ireland (O'Brien, 2009). Race, as has been argued, is always an issue (Dyer, 2000). Through immigration debates, race has been central in all political spheres in the Western world, from the 2016 election of President Donald Trump, his fight to build a steel wall costing billions of American dollars, to the 2016 Brexit vote in the UK, or the near election of Marie Le Pen in France. Indeed, race still matters. It is insidious, highly contentious and is often used pejoratively the lower down the racial strata a person is assigned. We cannot forget that race was originally created to separate groups and promote white superiority which is the same as white supremacy. The origin of race was for racial hegemony; and its consequence domination.

Whiteness the invisible norm

Critical Scholarship on whiteness is not an assault on White people per se: it is an assault on the socially constructed and constantly reinforced power of White identification and interests. (Gillborn, 2015: 278; see also Ladson-Billings and Tate, 1995)

While there is a growing acknowledgement among Whites that whiteness privileges Whites, it is still used matter-of-factly; while many people do not necessarily really see how whiteness operates materially, in their embodied lives. They rather see it simply as a debate, ideological position and opinion while some Whites see it as an attack on Whites.

Although there is widespread acknowledgement that race is an illusion that is socially constructed, skin colour and nationality of descent still influence socio-economic outcomes (Joseph, 2018). Race doesn't just exist because of anecdotal beliefs. It is a protected phenomenon maintained by both legal and political powers. Otherwise, its reign as a signifier of difference would have been terminated long before now. Within the CRT scholarship, whiteness is central to addressing race and its consequences for three reasons. First, because CRT focuses on white supremacy and centralises race as the determinant of groups' positioning on the racial strata. Secondly, race is relational (Fanon, 2000; Goldberg, 2000), therefore understanding whiteness, which is presented as the norm against which all other races are compared and measured, is vital. Thirdly, whiteness operates on the right to exclude others (Harris, 1993). While whiteness is not often explicitly named in Ireland as a major factor that structures the lives of its inhabitants, extant evidence shows the possession of whiteness affects both the possessors and non-possessors of whiteness. It is therefore important to understand what whiteness does to both its possessors and non-possessors, and the ways it structures lives.

Although skin colour has been described as the universal calling card of difference (Jacques, 2003), and race is a form of differentiation that operates to separate, classify, hierarchise and (de)value, Whites rarely openly acknowledge that the possession of white skin colour advantages and oftentimes protects them in society. One of the earliest White scholars to endorse the view of whiteness as protected and unacknowledged privilege was Peggy McIntosh (1988).[1] She argued that whiteness, just like what being male did for men, privileged White people and put them at an advantage while it disadvantaged non-Whites. She went on to identify some of the daily effects of white privilege which she saw as attached more to skin-colour privilege than to class, religion, ethnic status or geographic location. She described whiteness as 'an invisible package of unearned assets that I can count on cashing in each day, but about which I was "meant" to remain oblivious. White privilege is like an invisible weightless knapsack of special provisions, assurances, tools, maps, guides, codebooks, passports, visas, clothes, compass, emergency gear, and blank checks' (McIntosh, 1988: 291).

The study of whiteness has undergone a shift in the last two decades from the perception of whites as having a symbolic and optional ethnicity to the conceptualisation of whiteness studies, in which whiteness is an ideology tied to group social status. Ruth Frankenberg also researched this concept from her positioning as a White woman and her interviews with other White women. She viewed whiteness as having three linked dimensions. First, as a location of structural advantage of race privilege; secondly, as a 'standpoint' from which White people look at themselves, others and society; and thirdly, as a set of unmarked and unnamed cultural practices (Frankenberg, 1993: 1; 2000: 447). Whiteness has since then been framed not as a cultural identity but as a racial social category characterised by a privileged position in society typically at the top of the economic and racial hierarchy. Unlike other racial categories, however, whiteness is not racialised. This is because White people in white culture are given the illusion of their own infinite variety, while in the representation of non-Whites stereotypes are used to present them as fixed (Dyer, 2000). Although stereotyping can be complex and contradictory, 'it does characterise the representation of subordinated social groups and is one of the means by which they are categorised and kept in their place' (Dyer, 2000: 543–544).

Early research focused on the unique status of whiteness in a number of ways. Whiteness has been described as the 'unmarked marker' – unmarked insofar as it is identified with a 'neutral' universalism while serving as a criterion against which all other groups are marked and racialised (Dyer, 1997). This is evident in the everyday speech and imaging of People of Colour, while at the same time there is a marked absence of reference to whiteness, as is prevalent in media and movie representation where Whites are just people and non-Whites are referred to, for example, as 'Black man' or 'Chinese neighbour' (Dyer, 2000). Whiteness in this way is presented as the norm that might be classed, gendered but not raced. The 'invisibility of whiteness as a racial position in white/dominant discourse is of a piece with its ubiquity', assuming that White people are just people, which is not far off saying that other colours are something else. At the level of racial representation, 'there is no other more powerful position than that of being just human', where 'whites are not of a certain race, they are just the human race' (Dyer, 2000: 541). Such power positions of not being raced mean that 'the claim to power is the claim to speak for the commonality of humanity. Raced people can't do that – they can only speak for their race. But non-raced people can, for they do not represent the interests of a race' (Dyer, 2000: 539).

This purported invisibility of whiteness has been recognised among other scholars. Frankenberg (1993) at first established the understanding of whiteness as a transparent, invisible category and later went on to write that 'White people are raced just as men are gendered' (Frankenberg, 2000: 447). She modified her own position, arguing instead that whiteness is invisible mostly to White people, while it is quite visible to the 'other' or non-White groups. Non-Whites from their inferior position on the social hierarchy are keenly aware of the colour and privileges of whiteness and to claim that 'whiteness is invisible' is to 'repeat the gestures of hegemony' (Frankenberg, 2001: 73). Another scholar to take this view is critical race theorist David Gillborn, who writes that 'Most White people would probably be surprised by the idea of a "white-world" as they see only the "world", its whiteness is invisible to them because the racialised nature of politics, policing, education and every other sphere of public life is so deeply ingrained that it has become normalised – unremarked, and taken for granted' (Gillborn, 2006: 319). The invisibility of whiteness is no longer a tenable notion, particularly with increasing diversity, where living alongside difference is commonplace. In order to see their particularity, 'White people need to see themselves as White' by whiteness being made strange – not in terms of ethnicity which is linked to national identities such as Irish or British, but in terms of being White (Dyer, 2000: 541). Scholarship on the hegemony in the way whiteness operates and is positioned is, however, rare in Ireland. Critical legal scholar Cheryl Harris, who examined how whiteness, initially constructed as a form of racial identity, evolved into a form of property, exposes its hegemonic operation. She contends that:

> Whiteness is simultaneously an aspect of self-identity and of personhood, and its relation to the law of property is complex. Whiteness has functioned as self-identity in the domain of the intrinsic, personal and psychological; as reputation in the interstices between internal and external identity and as property in the extrinsic, public and legal realm. ... Whiteness at various times signifies and is deployed as identity, status and property, sometimes singularly, sometimes in tandem. (Harris, 1993: 172)

Building the concept on a number of ideas, including expectation, privilege, property as a right rather than as a thing, and property as metaphysical rather than physical, she posits that 'racial identity and property are closely related'.[2] In her argument, white identity and whiteness are sources of privilege and protection while their absence means being the object of property which included being subject to enslavement and its associated disadvantages. She argues that 'slavery as a system of property facilitated the merger of white identity and property' (Harris, 1995:

1720–1721), thus making whiteness 'something that can both be experienced and deployed as a resource' (Harris, 1995: 1734). The elevation of whiteness enabled it to be deployed to fulfil the will and to exercise power: 'The law made it possible for whiteness to be elevated through race from a passive attribute to an object of law and a resource deployable at social, political and institutional level to maintain control. ... Whiteness as the embodiment of white privilege transcended mere belief or preference; it became usable property, the subject of the law's regard and protection' (Harris, 1995: 1734).

While the focus has typically been on difference and how it disadvantages non-Whites, Harris (1993) put forward an interesting argument concerning the actual possession of whiteness itself, as the act necessary to lay the basis of rights in property. By taking a historical look into the time of Black enslavement in the United States, she suggests that because the system of slavery was contingent on and conflated with racial identity, it became crucial to be 'White' to be identified as White and to have the property of being White (Harris, 1995: 1721). Through this, Harris introduced actual possession as a relevant aspect of whiteness. It is important to say here that possession of whiteness was not simply in having white skin colour, it included the cultural practices of Whites and, in the times of slavery and segregation in the US, it involved not having tainted blood. The rule of first possession became qualified by race and backed by the law in a process which 'infused whiteness with significance and value and because it was solely through being White that property could be acquired and secured under law. Only Whites possess whiteness, a highly valued and exclusive form of property' (Harris, 1995: 1724).

Whiteness (including cultural whiteness) quickly came to represent a very desirable resource for those who possessed it while the law busied itself in deciding and separating those who were White and those who were not. For example, America employed the one-drop rule to decide who was Black and determined the race of a child by the mother's race or nationality by depriving babies born to Black women of white status irrespective of the race of the father. In other words, as long as one of your parents is Black, you cannot be White. White identity is not just about skin colour, but it confers tangible and economically valuable benefits which have historically been jealously guarded as a valued possession allowed only to those who met a strict standard of proof. This strictness increased its value by reinforcing its exclusivity. Thus, white privilege became an expectation and whiteness became the quintessential property of personhood (Harris, 1995; Dyer, 2000).

People with one Black parent, who have lived in Ireland all their lives and speak both English and Gaeilge with a strong Irish accent, are still being asked the annoying question – where are you originally from? While it is rarely openly stated that you have to be White to be Irish, Irishness in the everyday experience is often equated with whiteness. In the UK, Member of Parliament, Diane Abbott was referred to as 'coloured' and many people did not understand why that was wrong or offensive. She was not referred to by her British identity or role as an MP, but rather she was reduced to her skin colour. Any system of differentiation affects everyone, including those it privileges and those it oppresses. Although Blacks and non-Blacks live racially structured lives, 'white discourse implacably reduces the non-White subject to being a function of the white subject, not allowing her/him space or autonomy, permitting neither the recognition of similarities nor the acceptance of differences except as a means of knowing the white self' (Dyer, 2000: 544). To fully address this invisibility of whiteness, the colonial construction of whiteness as an empty cultural space has to be displaced and decentred as socially constructed rather than as the norm.

Whiteness as supremacy or whiteness as privilege

White supremacy is seen as 'the unnamed political system that has made the modern world what it is today' (Mills, 1997: 1)

The trio of class, race and gender have conflicting central themes and views of how the social world operates. The belief of CRT theorists that white supremacy is at the base of racial categorisation and stratification has been one of the main reasons it has been criticised. Marxists likewise claim that societies are categorised by the means of production, hence producing class strata, and see race as a subset of class; while feminists in the 1990s routinely viewed whiteness as a form of social categorisation that produces privilege for Whites, their main efforts have been to politicise the experiences of women. Feminists of the 1970s, inspired by the US Black liberation movement, decided to put gender at the centre of their theorising and appropriated the term 'patriarchy' to describe a system of male domination, making gender subordination its starting idea.

It is clear, however, that Europe, Europeans and European settler-states dominate the planet, privileging Whites globally (Mills, 2009). The notion of whiteness, how it operates and impacts on Whites and non-Whites, is important in labour markets across Europe because of the heterogeneity of the stock of foreign workers from which labour market shortages are filled. This is because of the relational nature of race which is constructed and experienced where racial difference is perceived. Thus, the nature of the contact between the native white population and the mixed stock of foreign workers of white and black phenotype is an integral part of the discourse on labour market differentials both at a conceptual and an empirical level. Whiteness is also significant to racial stratification projects because hierarchical societies have pre-set strata for different groups to occupy or fit into. This suggests that some positions will be available at the top and some at the bottom. As a result, a predominantly white society will be enmeshed in white supremacy and controlled by the normativity of whiteness as the standard against which all other races are assessed.

Whiteness is often theorised from the standpoint of a norm that confers privilege rather than from the viewpoint of domination or superiority. Regarding seeing whiteness, white ideas and white culture as normative, feminists like Adrienne Rich (1979: 299) coined the phrase 'white solipsism' which refers to Whites' tendency 'to speak, imagine and think as if whiteness described the world'. Peggy McIntosh (1988), whose definition of white privilege was that of having a psychological existence rather than a structural one, viewed white privilege as an invisible package of unearned assets from which Whites could draw.[3] Though she hints at a power dimension to whiteness which guaranteed the privilege, she does not name power, nor does she credit it to white supremacy as do CRT theorists. She, however, states that 'whiteness protected me from many kinds of hostility, distress, and violence, which I was being subtly trained to visit in turn upon people of colour' (McIntosh, 1988: 9). We see a differentiation between two types of privilege: unearned power that simply confers dominance because of one's race, which works to systematically over-empower certain groups, and earned strength. McIntosh described unearned power as that which comes from unearned privilege and can look like strength when it is in fact permission to escape or to dominate. She saw this type of advantage as problematic and concedes that the presence of such negative types of advantages (privilege due to being white which over-empowered Whites) will always reify the hierarchies in the social order unless they are rejected.

Though privilege is supposedly something to be desired, McIntosh observed from her initial list of privileges enjoyed by White people in society that most of them appeared to over-empower Whites over Blacks. She then went on to suggest that Whites did not try to be privileged, but that rather white privilege was a phenomenon that came to them unintentionally, or without any personal cognisant effort. This is one area where her scholarship has been greatly critiqued, especially by non-White scholars and CRT theorists. To this point, Leonardo (2004) argues that to truly understand white privilege, one must look at white supremacy or the analysis of white racial domination. Although the two processes are related, the conditions of white supremacy make white privilege possible because 'In order for white racial hegemony to saturate everyday life, it has to be secured by a process of domination, or those acts, decisions, and policies that White subjects perpetrate on people of colour' (Leonardo 2004: 137). The problem with white privilege research, Leonardo explains, was in not looking at white supremacy, or not observing Whites who claimed ignorance to their privileged world. This is problematic because it means Whites can escape taking responsibility and pass it off as a few racist acts by a few racist people rather than the systemic problem that it is. He further argues that:

> The theme of privilege obscures the subject of domination, or the agent of actions, because the situation is described as happening almost without the knowledge of whites. It conjures up images of domination happening behind the backs of whites, rather than on the backs of people of colour. The study of white privilege begins to take on an image of domination without agents. It obfuscates the historical process of domination in exchange for a state of dominance. (Leonardo, 2004: 138)

Ruth Frankenberg touches on this conception of dominance and whiteness and how she learnt by proximity

> What it means to navigate through a largely hostile terrain, to deal with institutions that do not operate by one's own logic nor in one's own interest, and to need those institutions to function in one's favour if one is to survive, let alone achieve. I realised for almost the first time in my life the gulf of experience between individuals differentially positioned in relation to a system of domination, and the profundity of cultural difference. (Frankenberg, 2000: 449)

She argues that whiteness is a relational category which varies spatially and temporally and that it is constructed with a range of other racial and cultural categories, including class and gender. She introduces a connectivity between the prevailing racism in a particular time and place and how it determines the 'ways of living whiteness' for a White woman. Frankenberg articulates this 'co-construction' as being fundamentally asymmetrical, because 'the term "whiteness" signals the production and reproduction of dominance rather than subordination, normativity rather than marginality, privilege rather than disadvantage' (Frankenberg, 2000: 454). Similar to Peggy McIntosh, Frankenberg in her understanding of whiteness also focuses on dominance without acknowledging the subordination it (re)produces. Whereas Frankenberg focuses on the unifying characteristics for Whites and the resultant privileges they enjoy from being White, she appears to argue the oppo-site end of the same spectrum from Harris (1993) who focuses on the possession of whiteness and its functioning as the right to exclude non-Whites which in turn produces privilege. She writes that 'whiteness as a theoretical construct evolved for the very purpose of racial exclusion' (Harris, 1993: 1737). Thus, the concept of whiteness is built on both exclusion and racial subjugation.

Although both scholars agree that privileging Whites puts them at an advantage while it disadvantages non-Whites, Frankenberg (2000) does not identify or acknowledge the structures that maintain this hegemonic form of racial privilege. Cheryl Harris, on the other hand, names white supremacy as the underlying predicator and that 'the concept of white-ness was premised on white supremacy rather than mere difference' (Harris, 1993: 1737). A critical theory of white privilege describes it as 'An exercise of power that goes beyond notions of "white privilege" and can only be adequately understood through a language of power and domination: the issue goes beyond privilege, it is about supremacy' (Gillborn, 2006: 319). Thus, even as Peggy McIntosh's description of white privilege has been widely cited as an 'invisible weightless knap-sack', full of necessary supplies which she attests to as an unconscious, psychological process of being given the privileges whether the White person wants it or not, white supremacy on the other hand relates to the operation of forces that saturate the everyday, mundane actions and policies that shape the world in the interests of White people (Delgado and Stefancic, 1997). White supremacy suggests a power dynamic that controls the social order and provides and maintains such privileges. Indeed, the scholar W. E. B. Du Bois, in his examination of what it meant to be white in America, though he never actually used the term 'white privilege', inferred it in his writings as he notes that many Whites in America began to expect to be treated in certain ways because of their whiteness and the structural privileges being granted to them. He writes that,

> The consequences of [racist] thought were bad enough for coloured people the world over, but they were even worse when one considers what this attitude did to the [White] worker ... He began to want, not comfort for all men but power over other men ... He did not love humanity and he hated niggers. (Du Bois, 1965: 5)

Inherent in the concept of being White was 'the right to own or hold whiteness to the exclusion and subordination of Blacks' (Harris, 1993: 1737). At the individual level, such a position, of recognising oneself as 'White', necessarily assumes premises based on white supremacy: it assumes that black ancestry in any degree, extending to generations far removed, automatically disqualifies claims to white identity, thereby privileging 'white' as unadulterated, exclusive and rare (Harris, 1993: 1737).

The notion of 'white privilege' has become increasingly common as writers come to an awareness of the multitude of ways in which people who are identified as 'White' enjoy countless, often unrecognised, advantages in their daily lives (Gillborn, 2006). Like McIntosh, Gillborn identifies the 'invisibility of the world' and its whiteness, but he differs as he blames it on the racialised nature of politics, policing, education and every other sphere of public life being so deeply ingrained that it has become normalised – 'unremarked, and taken for granted' (Gillborn, 2006: 319). Despite the contentions associated with focusing on white supremacy to address race and racism (see Cole, 2009), Mills (2009) defends his initial charge that 'white supremacy' should be the overarching category for CRT even when different political and theoretical views are being employed in an interdisciplinary study. While he concedes that the modern world has more than one political system, the 'unnamed' among them continues to be race (Mills, 2009: 1).

Introducing the notion of white supremacy into race dynamics particularly in Europe continues to be problematic because it invokes old supremacist labels. One of the challenges when it comes to addressing race relations in society and in mainstream First World political philosophy, Mills (1998) notes in his book *Blackness Visible*, is that the issue of race barely exists. The situation has worsened today as race has almost fallen off the grid in Ireland and across Europe while it is covertly being employed to determine outcomes and access to all forms of resources. Theorists in the academic sphere still rather 'piggyback the problem of race onto the body of respectable theory', most especially within a Marxist paradigm where 'race is still really an afterthought' (Mills, 1998: 97–98). Like most critical race theorists, Mills insists the term 'white supremacy', which encompasses *de facto* as well as *de jure* white privilege, should be conceptualised as the overarching system for race, just as patriarchy is for gender struggles. This refers more broadly to the European domination of the world from where the racialised distribution of economic, political and cultural power as we have it today ensues. Mills calls this system 'global white supremacy'. While one might wonder why we need new systems when concepts such as racism already exist, the prevalence of racial inequality should be proof enough of their inability to adequately address the enormity of the problem of race. For example, colonial capitalism which is by definition restricted to the period of formal colonial rule, is 'not sufficiently focused on the racial dimension of European domination which needs to be highlighted' (Mills, 1998: 99). A similar argument can be put forward to debunk the ability of racism to address the issue of race, particularly with the abuse and often loose use of the term, which has acquired a 'semantic penumbra of unwelcome associations that unless a formal definition is given, no clear reference can be readily attached to it' (Mills, 1998: 99–100).

Charles Mills is not the only theorist who has highlighted the need to move to other forms of conceptualising race aside from racism. Bonilla-Silva (1997) similarly argues that the way racism is viewed currently as a complexity of values, attitudes and as institutionalised might deflect attention from the huge power differential that actually exists in the real world between non-White individuals on the one hand, and racist ideas and institutionalised white power on the other. He further notes that if the term 'white racism' were consistently used in reference to the conceptualisation of racism as 'institutionalized politico-economic structure', a new locution for race would have been unnecessary (Bonilla-Silva, 1997: 100). It is important to highlight that white supremacy is premised on 'non-white inferiority' (Mills, 1998: 110) and white privileging. It also involves white centrality – the notion that White people, and white culture in world history, are central – that is, they are most important. Whiteness is not simply a matter of appearance, or of having a particular skin colour, but is based on features other than the somatic, including cultural features. Whiteness in CRT is used in a sense that is broader than skin colour. Conceptualising white supremacy and global white supremacy has the semantic virtue of clearly signalling reference to a system, a particular kind of polity, so structured as to advantage Whites (Mills, 1998: 100).

An area of contention for advancing the concept of white supremacy as a central focus to addressing race stems from many European sociologists still working off the premise that only class stratification is real and that it produces race stratification. Despite arguments that white supremacy can 'direct attention away from the modes of production' (Cole, 2009: 248), white supremacy has not gone away, particularly with the resurgence of racism and anti-immigrant sentiments across Europe and in the United States. Though no longer overtly backed by law, it 'is maintained through inherited patterns of discrimination, exclusionary racial bonding, cultural stereotyping, and differential white power deriving from consolidated economic privilege' (Mills, 1998: 102). This claim from over two decades ago is even truer today in many First World nations where the modern form of white supremacy is commonplace and evident every time individuals self-identify as white in the way white is still being defined. It assumes the acceptance of the ideas behind white supremacy, including the superiority of Whites and the right to exclude and subordinate Blacks.

When Whites are exposed to scholarship on whiteness, it comes with responsibilities because describing white privilege makes them newly accountable as they will have to first give up the myth of meritocracy. Whites, however, learn not only to accept the privileges of whiteness but also demand its largesse as rights while maintaining ambivalence about it from the stories they believe and tell about their group and others (Joseph, forthcoming). This is a problematic complacency and ambivalence about race because 'when Whites who do not acknowledge they are privileged still accept and benefit from unearned public and private power they are given, they embody and enact White supremacy' (Pappas, 1996: 3). Racial scepticists, many organisations and individuals are resistant to talking about race because of fears that too much talk and focus on race reifies race. To this, scholars like Mills (2009: 275) argue that 'the White working-class's agency, and historic complicity in imperialism, colonialism, genocide, apartheid, the "colour bar" and Jim Crow, must be acknowledged and not minimized'. Kimberle Crenshaw (1995) also cautions that the mere rejection of white supremacy as a normative vision and a societal commitment to the eradication of the substantive conditions of Black subordination are different and it is vital to differentiate between them. Dyer (2000) and Frankenberg (2000) argue that exploring the issues of race, whether through whiteness studies or through CRT, is vital for true societal change. While central-ising race in mainstream, First World political philosophy is challeng-ing, Mills (1998: 104) insists 'one does not confront a history of racial domination by ignoring it'. This would mean giving away one's voice and ultimately one's power. A culture of silence around race knits racial domination more deeply into a system which is created and predisposed to take the white experience as normative.

Social stratification and inequality

Before launching fully into examining racial stratification, the next two sections will discuss both racial and social stratification and some key terminologies that frame the following chapters. Let me commence with a brief definition of social inequality. The condition whereby people have unequal access to valued resources, services and positions in a society is referred to as social inequality (Kerbo, 2000). It is influenced by how individuals and groups are themselves ranked and evaluated by others and the differing positions available within the social systems of nation states. Social inequality is a phenomenon that affects not only migrants or

newcomers in the state but all its populations. In the case of social stratification, the root word stratum in social stratification implies a ranking
of people or groups of people within a society. It signifies a system with
somewhat predictable rules and legitimation behind the ranking of individuals and groups. In his essay 'An analytical approach to the theory
of social stratification', Parsons (1940: 841), who was the first major
theorist to develop a theory of stratification, described social stratification as 'the differential ranking of the human individuals who compose
a given social system and their treatment as superior and inferior relative
to one another in certain socially important respects'. Stratification in this
light implies that people in a society are treated in one of two ways: as
inferior or superior. Parsons's use of the word 'ranking' infers an assessment process which supposes specific parameters that place people into
these categories. What becomes apparent here is that social stratification
is predicated on judgement. It is built on belief systems which justify
inequality and unequal ranking, without which it is unlikely that a
stratification system would remain stable over time (Kerbo, 2000).

Historically, the primary dimensions of stratification have been power,
wealth and status, while the way they are unequally distributed is defined
as social stratification. Various theorists in the social sciences have over
the years valued these three dimensions differently depending on their
theoretical leaning. Karl Marx, for example, was of the theoretical
view that wealth is the primary dimension of stratification while power
and status are derivatives, with property ownership being the relevant
empirical domain (Marx and Engels, 1848). On this basis, Marxists
categorise based on a materialist or class understanding of societal
development, where economic organisation or mode of production is
taken to be the basis from which most of the other social phenomena
such as race and gender are influenced (Kerbo, 2000). Weber (1922: 6),
on the other hand, claims that those who employ only a material economic factor to explain social actions are doomed to failure because the
subjective meanings and ideas by which people live frequently produce
effects different from those that a simple materialist theory would
predict. Weber was of the view that power, wealth and status are theoretically independent. However, his work on the evolution of rational
bureaucratic authority structures implicitly placed great emphasis on
the power dimension. Durkheim (1893), in contrast, placed social status
as the primary dimension of stratification, with income implying wealth
as derivative and occupational structure being the empirical domain or
site of action. Though all three theoretical leanings have different views
on which should be the primary focus – wealth, power or status[4] – they
have consensus about their connection with stratification and inequality.

The notion of social differentiation brings an added dimension to stratification and inequality. It is based on the meaning applied to people or groups having distinct individual qualities and social roles. While Marx linked social differentiation to increasing division of labour, the process does not necessarily suggest better or hierarchy, because differences can be noted and not ranked relative to each other. One reason why social inequality often emerges from social differentiation is that it is based on humans' capacity to apply meaning to events and things, and their ability to develop judgement of what is 'good', 'bad' or preferable (Kerbo, 2000: 11). This can lead to individual characteristics being ranked from superior to inferior. In such cases, social inequality is referred to in terms of prestige and honour. A second cause is when roles and social positions place some people in a position to acquire a greater share of valued goods and services, in which case inequality is referred to in terms of favoured positions in society. Many scholars and CRT theorists have indeed proffered arguments that suggest whiteness confers not just status but also favoured positions that can operate like a resource (McIntosh, 1988; Harris, 1995; Mills, 1997; Fanon, 2000; Frankenberg, 2000; Joseph, 2019). Though inequality may not be acceptable to all in society, it easily becomes de facto in that it becomes accepted as the way things are.

Let me give you an example from an exercise I carry out in lectures and inclusion presentations. It will illustrate how these two dimensions can interact. Imagine a manager comes into your office and asks everyone with glasses to move their workstation to the left side of the room and begin to work from that corner while those without glasses are to move to the right side of the room. Aside from a mild irritation that they have to give up their tables, there is usually little or no problem. Now imagine that as the manager, after that exercise, I declare that all those with glasses are better, more trustworthy and smarter than all those without glasses. Exactly! That initial reaction, angst, dissatisfaction, irritation, trying to reason with the irrationality of the statement and the inequality and inequity in such an action, is what happens every day to those at the bottom of the ladder. Note that the only difference between both scenarios I painted is that one has introduced judgement and placed a value of 'better' on the other. Now imagine if I go further to say that all those who wear glasses will be paid 40 per cent more than those without glasses because they are smarter; they get given the harder tasks, therefore it follows that they deserve more. This is an example of how stratification in any form is problematic. The lower down the ladder you are, the lower the value placed on the tasks you complete. This then becomes justification for how you are treated if you are at the bottom. Remember that your positioning at that point, as in the case of those with the glasses in my analogy, has nothing to do with your abilities. The next few chapters will help you see what the world is like from the perspective of those on the margins.

We see, then, that social stratification is not just about what happens to people who are stratified, it is also about the system that stratifies people. Just like the glasses in my example above, different factors influence the placement of individuals or groups on the strata. If it is influenced by hereditary factors, then strata placement is called ascription; for example, race and gender will fall under this category. When strata placement is due to qualities that can be controlled by individuals, it is called achievement, for example educational attainment. Stratification can prove to be problematic for two reasons: (i) If it is based on ascriptive factors such as race, then the idea that we can indeed have a truly meritocratic society becomes difficult as race (the way it is classified by society today) or even gender is not within individual control or power to change. (ii) The decision concerning which achievement attributes should have pre-eminence in the stratification process can also be problematic.

Social stratification is, however, predicated on judgement. This belief system justifies inequality and unequal ranking despite the level of human changes and advancement we have seen over time. Various belief systems in the popular domain have over the years affected where Blacks and non-Whites have been stratified in society; for example the well-known argument by Herrnstein and Murray (1994) that stratification outcome is determined by genetic and inherited intelligence. Similarly, the belief about whiteness which, though it had no genetic basis of superiority, stratified Whites higher than enslaved people during the slave era. It is evident that a person's location on the strata can give status which is not necessarily dependent on personal efforts or achievement alone. Even with majoritarian belief in meritocracy and equal opportunities, ascriptive factors such as race still impact on inequality in today's society. An understanding of the possible combinations of ascriptive and achievement factors and how they interact in the social world is fundamental to understanding the disparity in outcomes between groups.

Understanding racial stratification and inequality

Racial inequality in the labour market is real. CRT, through a racial stratification framework, locates its root cause within institutionalised racial systems (Bonilla-Silva, 1997, 2003). Societies stratify along a number of dimensions, resulting in a layering of categories of people with greater and lesser social power which forms hierarchies. When societies stratify along the lines of race, it is referred to as racial stratification. That is 'a system of structured inequality, where access to scarce and desired resources is based on ethnic or racial group membership' (Verdugo, 2008: 70). Similar to social stratification, racial stratification is predicated on two factors: (i) a belief system about the other; and (ii) the power to categorise and impute judgement on the other which can be either negative or positive.

Racial judgements are judgements about people's capacities and worth. They are 'based on what they [people] look like, where they come from, how they speak, even what they eat' (Dyer, 2000: 539). They inform the innumerable minute decisions that constitute the practices of the world as it is today. While race is not the only governing factor in racial inequality 'it [race] is never not a factor, never not in play' (Dyer, 2000: 539). Racial stratification is thus not simply a matter of how people are arranged in society, but rather it 'has implications for a person's life chances' (Zuberi and Bashi, 1997: 669); it signifies difference and structures inequality (Omi and Winant, 1994), which Wilkinson (2005: 24) insists 'is deeply corrosive'. Extensive evidence demonstrates that race continues to be an important basis of invidious treatment, limited economic opportunity and social exclusion (Bhattacharyya, Gabriel and Small, 2002).

Racial hierarchies are systems of stratification predicated on the belief that some racial groups are either superior or inferior to others (Harris, 1993; Du Bois, 1965; Mills, 1998). The natural conclusion is that racial systems must have mechanisms for determining a person's race, as that is what determines where people fit into the racial hierarchy. In the American system of racial stratification, immigrants entering the US are said to be assimilated into the dominant social organisation (Zuberi and Bashi, 1997). This includes a process of assimilation into the operating system of racial stratification. What is most interesting about Zuberi and Bashi's writings on the theory of immigration and racial stratification is that it implies a pre-existing hierarchy and positioning which new immigrants have to fit into; that racial groupings are real and they exist; and that there is some form of reconstruction through assimilation that takes place as a result of 'fitting' into the available strata. Indeed, they attest that 'immigrants lose their ethnic identifiers as they are reconstructed into races; therefore, the racial assimilation of immigrants of various ethnic groups is central to the construction of the racial hierarchy in the United States' (Zuberi and Bashi, 1997: 679–680). The validity of such a classification is open to contestation, considering 'there is not in existence or has there ever been a society or scientific community that made its racial classifications on the basis of genetic examination of the population' (Zuberi and Bashi, 1997: 671). Such a scheme is bound to fail as genetically there is more variability within populations than between them. Other race critical writers highlight the misleading nature of such a categorisation.[5] While racial stratification is real, biology or genes is not the root cause.[6]

The most influential approach to racial hierarchy in the US is the black–white or bipolar model of classification which is shown in a considerable body of research and theorising (Bell, 1995; Harris, 1995; Winant, 2001). This is a vertical location of racialised groups within a system of stratification (Gold, 2004: 953). This top-down or 'white-over-color ascendancy' (Delgado and Stefancic, 2004: 3) is a well-defined system that operates and has been identified by many CRT theorists in the United States. With global hegemony, first with Europe and then the US, Whites have long commanded respect being at the top of the racial hierarchy. Such a view of the world suggests that racist hierarchical structures govern very many political, economic and social domains, and still automatically privileges those it has defined as Whites and disadvantages those it has defined as non-Whites. Racial positioning unequivocally confers privilege throughout the world, be it Washington, Madrid, Paris, Dublin, Cape Town or Lagos. Scholarship in the US maintains that White Americans are at the top of the racial hierarchy and African-Americans at the bottom, with intermittent mention of Native Americans as an equally oppressed group, and then groups such as Asian-Americans and Latinos in between (Omi and Winant, 1994; Delgado and Stefancic, 2012). Though Sidanius and Pratto (1999) argue that the means by which group-based hierarchies, including racial and ethnic hierarchies, are established and maintained, and are similar across social systems, there doesn't seem to be a uniform definition or indicator of racial hierarchy or inequality in different states.

In more recent years, however, the bipolar bimodal hierarchy of 'White/Black' or 'White/non-White' in the United States has moved to one that has more than two levels, for example 'White/Asian/Hispanic/Black' (Bashi, 1998: 962). Meanwhile in the UK, until 1948 no racial distinctions were made in British law other than that between British national and foreign national or 'alien'. In the case of Ireland, it has been suggested (King-O'Riain, 2007: 523) that racialisation in the state had occurred, as the national Census from 2000 to 2006 asked a racial question which sought to categorise people into 'White', 'Black' or 'Chinese'. This indicates Ireland's progression from seeking an ethnic or national identifier to about being White, which is a racial designation. In fact, by

2006, the question Ireland asked had morphed into a combination of racial and ethnic meta categories such as 'White', 'Black', 'Black Irish', 'Asian' or Asian-Irish (King-O'Riain, 2007: 526). What is interesting about such racial categories in a society that barely acknowledges racial categorisation and by implication racial hierarchy, is that the society is presented with new racialised identities and categories into which old and new immigrants have to fit. Despite the dearth of scholarship on racial hierarchies in Ireland, its creation of new categories and subcategories is indicative of an existing racial hierarchy. Thus, in as much as understanding the process through which categories and subcategories are created increases knowledge about race dynamics, Zuberi and Bashi (1997), who problematise[7] the process, claim that it at the same time reifies race and ignores or denies ethnicity and forces people into racial identities. These developments continue to raise significant questions about the meaning of race, how migrants negotiate new identities and hierarchical spaces in Ireland.

Concerning visible difference, literary and theoretical expressions of racial identity today are described as social construction, which 'refers to a sense of group or collective identity based on one's perception that he or she shares a common heritage with a particular racial group' (Helms, 1994: 3). Although racial identity is a surface-level manifestation based on what we look like (Waters, 1990; Brettell, 2011: 269), it has deep implications for how people are treated. Skin colour has been identified as the main tool for racial identification. O'Hearn (1998) sees it as one of the strongest bases under which racial identity is categorised; Jacques (2003) described it as the universal calling card of difference. Jacques insists that colour is central to the global hierarchy that shapes the power and prejudices of each race for two reasons: first, because it is instantly recognisable, and secondly because it defines difference at the glance of an eye. Chávez, Guido-DiBrito and Mallory (2003) describe colour as one of the many labelling tools that allow individuals and groups to distance themselves from those they consider different. Indeed, 'racial classification is not value free'; rather, it leads to a dichotomous society with some at the top and others at the bottom (Zuberi and Bashi, 1997: 679). Race-based classification across the world leads to Eurocentrism which made Europe the model for the world, the norm against which all other races were to be measured (Zuberi, 2011). Many sociologists around the turn of the twentieth century assumed European racial superiority whereby the 'norm' became defined as 'White, heterosexual, bourgeois, male', and the inferior 'others' of colour as deviant (Bell, 1980; Asante, 1990; Zuberi and Bashi, 1997; Winant, 2004; Zuberi and Bonilla-Silva, 2008).

The proliferation of racial categorisation is partly due to the social sciences producing knowledge about 'others', particularly through misinterpretation of statistics (Zuberi and Bonilla-Silva, 2008; Zuberi, 2011: 1576). The assumed European racial and cultural superiority replaced the biological justifications of race. This was a move which brought about the assimilation and focus on unproductive behaviours of the 'unassimilated as a dominant perspective', again making the 'Negro a problem' (Zuberi, 2011: 1577). Despite the emancipation proclamation and amendments to the US Constitution on democracy as promoting human equality, the need for scientific justification of racial stratification could not be silenced, and the social sciences developed theories and methods of analysis that helped justify racial stratification (Zuberi, 2011: 1580). While 'racial identification' may be internalised and appear to be the result of self-designation, it 'is a result of the merging of self-imposed choice within an externally imposed context' (Zuberi and Bonilla-Silva, 2008: 7). We see this in contemporary times where the disproportionate over-representation of people of migrant descent in un(under)employment is often conflated with asylum seekers, deficit in communication in the English language, and residency rights or the lack thereof. The focus is typically about a migrant deficit and not the systemic organisation of people and bodies based on skin colour. When we forget or make slight of this point, social sciences become the justification for racial stratification.

Racial identification is thus not just about an appellative, neither is it simply a symbol of social status, but rather it plays a vital role in the maintenance of group differential. Although it seems to affect all racial groups within society in a similar fashion, the difference in implications makes it problematic. For example, the European American racial identification with 'whiteness' is a confirmation of positive self-esteem among Americans of European origin; however, for African-Americans this same cultural preference is a confirmation of their negative status within the society (Zuberi and Bashi, 1997: 672). Another instance is how the Irish became White. We see that even as for the first time Irish-Americans as a group were asked to choose between supporting and opposing the colour line, their response showed they moved from being racialised Irishmen to becoming White men with rights to take land off enslaved Black men and they cast their vote on the side against the abolition of Black enslavement. The Irish showed they had learned well the lesson that they would make their way in the US not as Irishmen but as Whites (Ignatiev, 1995). In Ireland, Whites today still choose a racial identification with whiteness over any other identity, as evidenced by migrant workers of white European descent who identify with their white identity over their immigrant identity as it gives them access to the primary segments of the labour market (Joseph, forthcoming). Whiteness also protects people of White heritage in Ireland from the migrant penalty and keeps them from the bottom of the economic ladder by elevating and advantaging them over their Black counterparts (Joseph, 2018, 2019).

While attributing racial identification to human differences might seem to be the logical course from these arguments, there is a growing school to the contrary. Asante (1990) contends that identity itself or difference have not been the problem in discovering the ideological basis of the enslavement of Africans; rather, it has been the idea of a racial hierarchy. In discussing the effects of race, Zuberi and Bonilla-Silva (2008: 7) suggest that 'race is about an individual's relationship to other people within the society' and not a question of how a person's race causes disadvantage and discrimination. In other words, the real issue is the way a society responds to an individual's racial identification. Race is thus not about an individual's skin colour. Neither is racial identity about shared individual characteristics but about shared social status. Racial stratification in essence is more to do with society itself than the innate makeup of individuals.

In the last two decades, globalisation and the increase of international migration and of diasporic communities have meant that groups within specific national locations are increasingly influenced by depictions of race, status and group membership that are not fixed in geographic space (Gold, 2004). Increasing diversity and significant demographic changes from intermarriage have added their own pressure to the changes experienced in the way groups are categorised, thereby unsettling long-standing understandings of hierarchy in many contemporary Western societies. One of the consequences of racial hierarchies is that desirable and undesirable; welcome and unwelcome people are produced. With the exception of the Irish, the Northern and Western Europeans were deemed the only desirable immigrants well beyond the first quarter of the twentieth century in the US, while others were assigned to races within the European model of racial hierarchy, which might have been quite different from the racial systems in their homelands. Sociologist Ronit Lentin refers to immigration to Ireland as having those it welcomes and those it does not (Lentin, 2007). Despite the years of Black presence in Europe, they are often seen as permanent strangers (Small, 2017). The enslavement of Africans impacts on their physical positioning and positionality. Racial stratification, which forces migrants to fit into available hierarchies as members of different racial groups, is a process which again seeks to homogenise ethnicity, culture and values.

Notes

1 Based on her work on unacknowledged male privilege as a phenomenon and the interlocking hierarchies in society, Peggy McIntosh carried out a similar analysis with Whites.

2 Though the concept of whiteness as property was first mentioned by Derrick Bell, an article in the *Harvard Law Review* gave the idea significance among CRT theorists. Drawing on the experiences of Blacks and minorities with slavery in the United States, Harris (1993) deconstructs the notion of whiteness by examining it through the lens of property and property law. She draws some very interesting parallels between whiteness and property and how its property value progressed. She starts by likening whiteness to a resource with protective abilities.

3 Using her own experiences of being White, Peggy McIntosh notes that while Whites like herself were 'being made confident, comfortable, and oblivious, other groups were likely being made unconfident, uncomfortable, and alienated' (1988: 9).

4 I refer to status as a position within a hierarchy.

5 Bonilla-Silva (1997: 469) insists 'races typically are identified by their phenotype' and the selection of certain human traits to designate a racial group is always socially rather than biologically based.

6 Zuberi and Bonilla-Silva (2008: 10), citing the work of Van den Oord and Rowe (2000) in their writing, challenge the misuse of statistical data in the analysis of race by social scientists. Though they agree that there are variations in human biology, they strongly disagree with Van den Oord and Rowe that race as a way of organising that variation is wrong. They also critique the use of data by Herrnstein and Murray (1994) in their very controversial book, *The Bell Curve*.

7 They further argue that the categorisation process presupposes the existence of a racial hierarchy into which the new categories are inserted. Because this process involves the creation of new meanings, groupings and associations between the hierarchy and the categories it comprises, a society's racial hierarchy by definition must change along with the racialisation process (see Zuberi and Bashi, 1997; Bashi, 1998: 963, for more in-depth reflections).

2

Migration, whiteness and Irish racism

Despite the ways whiteness has historically been invoked in the (re)positioning of the Irish on both sides of the Atlantic, the discourse on race in Ireland does not sufficiently focus on whiteness or colour-based racism. Rather, there is ongoing debate on the significance of skin colour, particularly as the racialisation of the Irish and the Irish Travellers is perpetrated from white bodies to white bodies. In order to introduce a CRT perspective to how we look at and talk about racism in Ireland, this chapter examines the symbolic use of colour in emphasising the perceived difference of racialised Irish people in their diaspora settings. It also discusses how whiteness has historically been mobilised to centralise Irish interests both at home and abroad. The cartography of the top tiers of the Irish labour market presents us with a false picture of a monocultural Ireland. This is in contradiction to Census data which demonstrate the presence of newcomers within its borders, including Ireland's indigenous ethnic minorities – the Irish Travellers. A key argument in the chapter is that rather than racism between white bodies invalidating skin colour as a locus of understanding racism, it shows how deviation from Eurocentric norms was employed to darken actors and influence the symbolic colour of the perceived difference ascribed to racialised Irish people, which provided significant justification for their racialisation on both sides of the Atlantic.

Although the possession of white phenotypic features is regularly invoked to benefit the Irish at home and abroad, a study of whiteness or white supremacy is rarely used to frame scholarship on racism in Ireland. Ireland, like the rest of Europe, is predominantly white in physiognomy. But the Irish, it would appear, have not always been seen as White; neither have they always enjoyed white privilege. This is evident from scholarship on 'how the Irish became White' as employed by Ignatiev

(1995), and in historical references to the Irish as 'White Negros' or 'Blacks turned inside-out' (Ignatiev, 1995). Despite a group's particular experiences, Brubaker (2001) insists it is not sufficient to refer to racial, ethnic or national groups as simply socially constructed entities without linking the macro-level outcomes with the micro-level processes. In other words, the ways, processes and when people identify themselves, perceive others, experience the world, understand their situation and act in racial, ethnic or national terms are significant. Zizek (1989: 56–57) similarly suggests that, in order to engage the multicultural, we need to work through 'the symbolic reality of the past, long forgotten traumatic event that can no longer evade interrogation'. One aspect that is often ignored is how reference to colour was employed in emphasising the projected difference of the Irish people in their racialisation, trajectory and changing identity. This, combined with a critical examination of Ireland's racialisation in its diaspora settings and how Ireland creates and responds to its racial others, provides validity for skin colour as a tenable locus of understanding racism in Ireland.

In accordance with the CRT tradition, the notion of whiteness and white supremacy, and the systems which empower and sustain them, is central to addressing race and its consequences by placing them in a broader perspective that includes economic and historical context (Delgado and Stefancic, 2012). Thus, the focus in this chapter is on the historical context in which whiteness has previously been mobilised to centralise White Irish interests both at home and abroad. Ireland's history, its encounters with whiteness and its process of becoming White are insightful in regard to how white supremacy crept into the nation. Many Irish people will, however, strongly oppose and reject any assertion of Ireland as a white supremacist nation. As an Irish researcher, I too find myself hesitant about the idea because white supremacy is typically equated with extremist forms such as the Ku Klux Klan, lynching of Blacks and other overt forms of racism. When we look at the non-extremist conception of white supremacy, as a comprehensive condition whereby the interests and perceptions of White subjects are continually placed centre stage and assumed as 'normal' (Delgado and Stefancic, 2001), the historical contexts in which whiteness has been influential in the changing Irish identity and positioning relative to other groups says otherwise. It is undeniable that the interests and perceptions of the White Irish population are central and that they constitute the assumed norm both in the labour market and how groups are positioned in the racial hierarchy. Thus, a historical look at Ireland, connecting the past and the present, in order to see the origins of our current national position about race, white supremacy, white privilege and racial inequality, is very telling. A comprehensive analysis would involve contextualising the political terrain, the socio-economic environment, Ireland's racialisation in its diasporic experience/s, and how Ireland creates and responds to its racial others within the state. The way Ireland presently rejects any claim to Irishness devoid of 'untainted' whiteness is the first indicator of how whiteness is normalised and centred in the scheme of things in Ireland. While it's not all doom and gloom, we cannot ignore how 2018 Presidential aspirant Peter Casey rose from a 1 per cent support rating to winning 23.3 per cent of the total valid poll within one week by riding on the backs of Irish Travellers after his anti-Traveller rhetoric. In the labour market, we see similar anti-Black sentiments in that, while the Central Statistics Office (CSO) unemployment figures for 2019 show that the economy is the best of the last ten years, with the national unemployment rate at 5.4 per cent, it seems workers have to be White to enjoy this windfall as the unemployment rate of Blacks is at its highest at 5–8 times that of the White Irish/European population.

Ireland: no longer a monocultural society

Ireland has, over the years, experienced differing migration flows in and out of the country. With its transformation from a country of emigration to one of in-migration, the ethnic diversity which challenges Ireland's status as monocultural has been well documented (Fanning, 2002; Garner, 2004; Lentin and McVeigh, 2006). While being mainly credited to the large flow of immigrants during the Celtic Tiger era from the late 1990s, the widely accepted narrative of in-migration in Ireland as a new phenomenon is often questioned (Ward, 1999; Kirby, 2002). The presence of large numbers of foreign medical students in Ireland, particularly from Nigeria and South Africa, was common during the late 1960s, around the time of the Biafra war. In fact, the abominable treatment of babies with Black African ancestry in Ireland dates as far back as the early 1960s according to groups like 'Mixed Race Ireland' and 'I am Irish'. These groups are fighting for the recognition of mixed-race people and the many survivors of institutional racial abuse. Their story is whitewashed out of Irish history despite their physical presence and documented suffering of racist abuse, as one of the first sets of people to grow up as visibly different in the then relatively homogeneous Ireland. This is to the extent that one wonders who to credit as the first generation of people of Black African descent in Ireland – that cohort or the 1990s arrivals?

The overwhelming 'flood' of newcomers, as it is more commonly described in public discourse, is routinely cited as the reason for the difficult relationship between Ireland and its racial others. This has also meant that Ireland has yet again had to manage differing migration flow rates and diversity. Ward (1999) for example insists that Scottish, English, Italian, Chinese, German, Jews, Huguenots and others came into Ireland in their droves. When we turn to the outflow from Ireland, from 1841 to 1851, the population of the country was said to have declined from 8 million to 6.5 million due to emigration and famine. Ruhs (2005: 7) observing that out-migration created a huge Irish diaspora, totalling almost 75 million around the world, with around 45 million people in the United States claiming Irish ancestry. It is no wonder that, Glynn, Kelly and MacÉinrí (2013: 1) insist, 'no other European country contributed as many emigrants per capita to the new world during the so-called age of mass migration … as did Ireland'. So, between the British imperial colonial government where the vast majority of Irish migrants went to British colonies or former colonies, and the great Irish Famine, when the nation lost over one-fifth of its citizens either to death or emigration, the Irish emigration status was born. The popular Irish expression that 'God sent the blight, but the British made the famine' is a reflection of the double catastrophe experienced by the Irish in these years.

The story of Ireland did not remain one of emigration; rather, the Celtic Tiger era witnessed many returning migrants from around the world which heralded yet another change in Irish status from emigration nursery to inward migration (Kirby, 2002). Ireland went from a country that was colonised to become part of the colonising force; from arriving in the Americas at the bottom of the ladder with Blacks to being able to vote against the abolitionists; and from being indentured servants to controlling various waterfronts in the United States. Consequently, what it meant to be Irish became racialised in new ways (McVeigh, 1996; Fanning, 2002; MacÉinrí, 2003; Lentin and McVeigh, 2006). Ireland has joined other countries classed as multicultural with over 15 per cent of its workforce being of migrant descent. The in/out migration story of Ireland has come full circle to one of emigration in the aftermath of the global economic crisis which heralded a new wave of emigration, different from the twentieth-century emigration of the 1950s and the 1980s (Glynn, Kelly and MacÉinrí, 2013). Today's (out)flow differs significantly from those of the past as a significant percentage of those leaving Ireland are immigrants returning to their home countries or migrating to the UK, Australia, Canada and the US as the top emigration destinations. Rather than unemployment being the motivation for the emigrating population, 47 per cent of recent emigrants were in full-time employment before leaving and underemployment was cited as one of the major driving forces (Glynn, Kelly and MacÉinrí, 2013).

The othering of the Irish at home and abroad

Although whiteness has been argued to confer privilege (McIntosh, 1988; Frankenberg, 2000) and property rights (Harris, 1993), the othering of the Irish occurred on both sides of the Atlantic, where the Catholic Irish who, though White, were portrayed negatively as 'savages' who needed to be rehabilitated and whitened. This centuries-long conception and portrayal of the Irish as homogeneously 'wild' and 'classless' appears in historical records from as far back as the seventeenth century and is linked to colonisation and emigration. The English colonisation of the Irish, which cast them as bestial and incapable of progress (Curtis, 1997), racialised and othered the Irish in ways which 'erased linguistic, religious, class and urban/rural heterogeneities' (Lentin, 2006: 3). Regarding racial stratification, the Irish, particularly the Catholic Irish, occupied the lowest rung of Britain's ethnic hierarchy and constituted an alien and inferior other routinely viewed with suspicion (Curtis, 1997). Racialisation, which is based on the idea that the object of study should not be 'race' itself but the processes by which 'race' becomes salient (Garner, 2009: 2), usually employs the assignment of negatively evaluated attributes to define, restrict and re/construct different groups (Miles and Brown, 2003). The exploitation of the Irish by the British, while racial, had economic consequences and was legitimised by projecting 'the cultural content of backwardness' onto the Catholic Gaelic in ways which Garner (2009: 9) described as racism without 'race'. This is because at an ideological and discursive level, all the elements of racism still occurred despite the absence of phenotypic difference between the Irish and English – the racialised and racialisers respectively. Rather than invalidating the ways racism is understood as being along the colour line, it is important to note that race is not fixed. Race is 'an unstable and "decentered" complex of social meanings constantly being transformed by political struggle' (Omi and Winant, 1994: 7). What we see in the Irish case in that era is that the culture, language, ascribed behaviours, religion, nationality and wealth of the English are set as the standard, while the perceived deviation from it by the Irish was employed to justify their othering, naming and repositioning lower down the social and racial strata than the English. Ní Shuinéar described othering:

> Denying equal legitimacy to individuals and cultures that do not conform to one's own arbitrary, ever-shifting criteria of normality – is a two-sided coin. On the one hand it creates a clearly defined, undifferentiated 'them' embodying every sort of negativity –including excess of essentially positive

traits. On the other, it forges a bond of solidarity between those who reject these aberrations: the fictive homogeneity of a constantly evoked but never defined 'us.' (Ní Shuinéar, 2002: 187)

Though phenotypically white, the Irish were homogenised and symbolically blackened in their encounters with those who sought to enslave them. For example, the English Crown's claim to superiority and supremacy over Ireland occurred through a process which homogenised the people and ascribed them a fictive imagery of 'Irish savagery' (Goldberg, 2001: 43). The Irish natives were also racially conceived as pre-modern and naturally incapable of progress, belonging to a backward culture and unfit to contribute anything beyond their labour to colonial development. They ended up often mistreated by biased judicial systems: 'imprisoned, publicly flogged, [and banished] for arbitrary or minor offences, labour unrest and other forms of resistance by the Irish, were swiftly and brutally suppressed' (Beckles, 1990: 513). Their suffering of slave-like working and living conditions often fuelled anti-English plots and rebellions. Cromwell's conquest of Ireland in the middle of the seventeenth century made slaves as well as subjects of the Irish people with 'over a hundred thousand men, women and children seized by the English troops and shipped to the West Indies, where they were sold into slavery' (George Novack, cited in Hoffman, 1993: 27). Contrary to general belief, Hoffman in his controversial book, *They were White and they were Slaves*, insists that White slavery predates Black slavery where from the eighth to the eleventh centuries 'the trade in White slaves was one of the few sources of foreign exchange for western European powers in a period when the East produced the goods that Europeans could not procure elsewhere'. He also records how during this period France was a major transfer point for White slaves 'with Rouen being the centre for the selling of Irish and Flemish slaves' (Hoffman, 1993: 4). While human slavery or indentured servitude as a whole was not based on racial difference, Black slavery from the end of the seventeenth century was deeply rooted in 'an ideology of exploitation based on racial logic – the establishment and maintenance of a "color line"' (Omi and Winant, 1994). It is interesting to note that all the attributes which were employed to justify the racialisation of White slaves and indentured servants were all ascribed to Blacks at the advent of racial slavery, and 'nativism was only effectively curbed by the institutionalisation of a racial order that drew the color line around, rather than within, Europe' (Omi and Winant, 1994: 5–6).

In Great Britain also, thousands of White children were forced to work as human brooms inside chimney flues living miserable lives and dying horrid deaths, while the disdain of the ruling class towards the surplus White poor was prevalent (Hoffman, 1993). This was further compounded by political captives being sold into slavery while some offered themselves as indentured slaves in the United States amidst slave hunting. During this period, 'the superior qualities of the English (or British) were extolled in respect, not just of distant peoples in Africa, Asia, but in relation to "white Negros" at home, the Irish' (Coakley, 2012: 36). Though the British shared a number of similarities with the Irish in that both groups are White and in close geographical location, their relationship exemplifies how 'historicism' elevates Europeans over those deemed primitive or underdeveloped others as a victory of progress (Goldberg, 2001: 43). Similarly, the Irish indentured servants, papists and colonists in Spanish colonial Puerto Rico who sought asylum in Puerto Rico, and who often arrived with little more than the shirts on their backs and gratefully repaid their Spanish hosts in a variety of ways (Chinea, 1997), did not help how the perceived lack of wealth (class) of the Irish was employed as justification for how they were racialised.

This 'symbolic use of blackness'[1] to classify the Irish as 'White Negroes' was not unique to them, as the Italians in the USA had the same experience (Guglielmo and Salerno, 2003). The process by which the Irish 'became White' was, however, a slow one, while the 'American melting pot'[2] absorbed other White migrant groups like the Germans much quicker. This process, which has been argued to have been facilitated by the phenotypic whiteness of the Irish, gave rise to a transition by which the White, Catholic Irish, an oppressed and colonised race in Ireland, became part of an oppressing class in America (Omi and Winant, 1994; Ignatiev, 1995). Despite these remarkable changes, the negative imaging of the Irish centuries afterwards appears to still influence their experience at home and abroad. The 'narratives of differentiation' between the Irish nation and England and their historical relationship frame the identities and positioning of the second-generation Irish population in England where the pejorative term 'plastic Paddy' is still employed to stereotype and undermine their processes 'of becoming' (Hickman et al., 2005: 174). This is not only from the British but is also experienced from the Irish at home. 'Irish denials of the authenticity of those same identities' conveys similar ambiguity towards the success story that is deemed to be the Irish-American experience in public discourses, through references to 'returned Yanks' (Hickman et al., 2005: 174). While there may be ongoing difficulties still experienced by some of the Irish diaspora, these terms which are used to deny and denigrate the second-generation Irish in Britain imply that their claim to Irishness lacks authenticity and can safely be ridiculed (Hickman, 2002). The 'injustices of recognition of the Irish community in Britain', according to O'Keeffe-Vigneron (2003: 33), are some of the consequences of the post-1945 Irish population in Britain, their migrant experience and cultural difference:

> Living in the country of the 'coloniser' and the negative imaging around the former 'colonised' have contributed to the difficult time the Irish have had asserting their identity, the unrest in Northern Ireland adding to the difficulties in promoting it as positive. The negative perception of Irishness throughout the years in Britain has created a lot of pressure on the Irish and their need to assert their identity and their difference has been largely ignored in mainstream British society. (O'Keeffe-Vigneron, 2003: 33)

The racial exploitation of the Irish had a strong link with skin colour, as their captors symbolically 'coloured' them to justify their racialisation, for example being categorised as non-Whites, Blacks turned inside out or in terms which in later years were employed symbolically to refer to Blacks, such as 'savage' (see Tsri, 2016). The interplay of binary opposites can be seen in the invoking of Black/White paradigms for the Irish at different times in their racialisation and the secondary binaries of good/bad, civilised/uncivilised and pure/evil. Other stereotypes ascribed to the Irish which seemed to be fuelled by anti-IRA fears also played a part in the ways they were categorised.

A historical look at the Irish case presents a typical example of how race influenced a group's positioning, considering that they arrived in the US and Britain at the bottom of the economic ladder as the enslaved Black population. Both groups were targets of racist stereotypes that usually drew on a debased Darwinism in which both Blacks and Irish were somehow perceived as nearer to apes than people of Anglo-Saxon origin (Curtis, 1997). However, the Irish were able to transition and change their de facto positioning at the bottom of the hierarchy. A similar argument obtains in Britain where the Irish were reported to have fared as badly as 'coloured immigrants', particularly regarding housing (Corbally, 2015), whereby signs such as 'Room for rent. No Irish. No Coloureds, no dogs' were hung on windows to deter prospective renters. But with the passage of time the Irish diasporans became accepted as White, such that today they are not considered outsiders to the white privilege enjoyed by White Europeans, particularly when it comes to status and employment. (It is important to note, however, that the situation in the UK is more nuanced than stated here due to the ongoing Northern Ireland situation and a persistence of anti-Irish racism – some of which is evident from the Brexit negotiations.) Regarding borders and movement, we also observe the Commonwealth Immigration Act of 1962 – a piece of legislation that substantially limited immigration for People of Colour but allowed the Irish freedom to move back and forth into the UK – a country that previously colonised them. While this special system is still in place today, none of the former Black African colonies of Britain is granted this access or free movement of persons or trade across its borders.

Historical evidence also suggests that the Irish were able to invoke whiteness and avoid the automatic positioning of 'inferior groups' at the bottom of the racial and economic ladder both in the US and Britain (Fanning, 2002). Their latter representation and acceptance as White thus exempted them from the restrictive immigration legislation that defined certain groups as ethnic. O'Keeffe-Vigneron (2003: 35), however, argues that this contributed to the subsequent 'invisibility' of the Irish in Britain in the 1950s and 1960s. Also, Corbally (2015: 106) argues that though 'they [the Irish] had, after all, moved due to a similar colonial relationship' as commonwealth migrants, and they resided in the same parts of the major cities, lived in similar conditions, laboured in similar jobs and met comparably derisory attitudes in their new country, 'the Irish were not quite immigrant enough'. Without downplaying the differential and, oftentimes, harsh treatment of the Irish in the diaspora, a black–white dichotomy was somewhat operational. In reality, the Irish were located some notches away from the bottom of the racial ladder, above Black Africans and non-English-speaking Whites, a point that is usually omitted in the discourse (Joseph, 2015).

Thus, on the one hand, it would appear that whiteness when it came to the Irish, failed them initially, as it did not protect them from enslavement at home or abroad, and neither did it provide them with a privileged status, making Irish whiteness and experience with racism open to contestation. However, concerning how the Irish were able to pitch camp with White America, Ignatiev (1995) notes that the Irish demonstrated that they had well understood that they could achieve upward mobility on the US racial ladder not as Irish but as Whites. In other words, they moved from being racialised Irish to becoming White with rights to vote (for men), own enslaved Black people and appropriate land belonging to them.

Ireland creates its own racial others: racist without racism

The notion that Ireland could be racial or a racist state did not feature in its public discourse until the late 1990s. With it being one of the first European countries to open its borders to the new migrant groups from the 2004 accession states, the idea of racism in Ireland seemed even more implausible. Ireland's shift since the early twentieth century, from out-migration to in-migration, from colonised to coloniser, from outsider to becoming part of fortress Europe keeping non-EU migrants out of its own borders, signifies an immense transformation in Irish history and identity such that Ireland has been argued to have created its own 'racial inferiors' (Lentin, 2007: 4). Though immigration to Ireland is not really new, it has heralded the return of 'the national repressed'[3] (Lentin, 2007: 4). The massive change from within is attributed to new residents and new communities who are transforming the country through their homemaking and civic habitation (Feldman et al., 2005). Other scholars (Fanning, 2002, 2007; Lentin and McVeigh, 2002, 2006) link it to Ireland's hegemonic relation with its own racial others within its national borders and across the sea. We have seen Ireland in its embryonic stages, battling with handling its newcomers and suppressing its not so 'accepted' Travelling community, combined with its struggle in re-imaging itself as part of the ruling class in Europe.

With attaining modern state status, the economic changes experienced by Ireland have seen a dramatic shift from high unemployment in the 1980s to a labour deficit, from emigration to immigration, from recession to boom and a new wave of recession in the latter part of 2008. The 2019 unemployment rate is three points below the euro zone average, at 5.4 per cent. It is the lowest in the last decade. The course of advancing the objectives of modernity does not come without a price, as economics, mobility and racism are fundamentally intertwined (Garner, 2004). According to Foucault (2003: 254), 'the modern State can scarcely function without becoming involved with racism at some point'. It carries out racial projects which keep the racialised others out through processes which favour its citizens and disfavour sojourners to varying degrees, thereby disguising racism (Goldberg, 2001). Though like most modern states, Ireland frames this way of treating those it views as different from a nationalist perspective (Coakley, 2012), a political system aiming to regulate bodies is racism (Hesse, 2001). Ronit Lentin also articulates how the Irish state is central to the construction of racism:

> Irish historicism creates its own 'racial inferiors'; firstly, through the ongoing racialisation of Irish Travellers, conceived as 'Irish national' though not always as 'White' ...; secondly, through governmental technologies of asylum and immigration controls, aiming to restore modernity's order just as all certainties – economic, civil, cultural, sexual – seem to be collapsing; and thirdly, through biopolitical governmental technologies regulating the lives of migrants, but also equality mechanisms, which reproduce racialised populations as ultimately unequal. (Lentin, 2007: 4)

Theorising Irish racism is incomplete without considering the White, indigenous Irish nomadic minority – Irish Travellers, who though conceived as 'Irish nationals' have been in Ireland for centuries and are not accorded the same status as the Catholic, White Irish. Ireland appears not only to have a colour-coded migrant penalty but also an intolerance of difference, as is evident in the racialisation of Irish Travellers (Hayes, 2006). This fact forms the basis of and reinforces the argument that Irish racism is not simply colour coded (Garner, 2009). Irish Travellers have been reported to fare worse on all socio-economic indicators and have faced various state projects aimed at assimilating them into the Irish national re-imaging of itself since the 1960s (McVeigh, 1996; Fanning, 2002; Lentin, 2007). Cultural imperialism in the education system has also been reported to precipitate Irish Travellers' early departure from education, further reinforcing their marginalised status in society (Hayes, 2006; Baker et al., 2009). They are subject to both increasing institutional racism – 'de facto apartheid of barring Travellers from pubs, schools and dances' – and those who do not conform to the stereotypes are 'suddenly redeemed from Traveller status ... "a former itinerant" ... a settled Traveller' (Ní Shuinéar, 1994: 59). While the Irish were naturalised by the English, the Irish are naturalising their own indigenous others, and popular images of Irish Travellers are merely the most extreme manifestation of an ancient Anglo-Saxon tradition of othering the Irish (Fanning, 2002; Ni Shuinéar, 2002; Feldman, 2007). Unlike the US, where non-Black minorities must compare their treatment to African-Americans' to redress their grievances, it would seem that in Ireland, Irish Travellers constitute the prototypical minority group. Nonetheless, it is important to note that part of the colonial tactics mobilised against the Irish and Irish Travellers involved similar cultural and symbolic representations of Blacks as 'dirty', 'poor', 'violent' and 'disruptive'.

Limerick's Jewish population seeking refuge in Ireland was another group othered in Ireland through the 1904 pogrom, which was no aberration but was framed by anti-Semitism at a national level (Fanning, 2002). Limerick at the time was reported as 'wretchedly poor' (Flynn, 2004: 32),[4] while the Jews in their demonisation were portrayed as treacherous and dishonourable, this being justified on the basis of 'putative cultural inability to assimilate and the threat posed by Jewish values for Catholic Ireland' (Garner, 2004: 143). The success of the 1904 Limerick pogrom is mainly attributed to an economic boycott against Jewish traders, where customers were urged to buy Irish and 'help stamp out sweated, Jewish labour, in the Tailoring Trade in Dublin' (Keogh, 1999: 54). That boycott, which was largely instigated by a Catholic priest, Fr Creagh (Fanning, 2002), finally took its toll on the livelihood of the Jews, many of whom were reported to have left Limerick. In the 1930s and 1940s, the Irish government also refused to take in Jewish refugees from Nazi Europe. The wave of global recession in the 2000s saw a return of the nationalist phrase 'Buy Irish and buy local, keep Irish businesses open', while simultaneously building the Irish economy on exports. Such nationalist trends are echoed across the Western world, from the American President, Donald Trump and his call to make America great again to Brexit and the far right's pursuit of Britain first.

Though the Limerick pogrom was seen by some as exceptional in Irish history, this strong sense of nationalism and seeing others (and others' difference) as a threat appears to be woven into the fabric of Irish society. Another group who experience racism and othering are asylum seekers – Ireland's quintessential racial others. There have been various governmental technologies of asylum and immigration controls with diverse impact which have been well documented by seasoned and upcoming researchers (see Crowley, Gilmartin and Kitchin, 2006; Thornton, 2014). This places Ireland with the rest of Europe guarding fortress Europe by its establishing of structures which ensure the (re) production of a homogeneous society in the face of a (perceived) aggressively advancing globalisation and multiculturalism. Resistance to heterogeneity in Ireland occurs not only through biopolitical governmental technologies regulating the lives of migrants, but also through equality mechanisms which reproduce racialised populations as ultimately unequal (Lentin, 2007). The arrival of asylum seekers on Irish shores put paid to the notion that a colonised and emigrating Ireland could not be both racial and racist. Ireland is no exception as responses to asylum seekers since 1997 have ranged from suspicion to hysteria (Fanning, 2009), and asylum seekers are at the bottom of the hierarchy when it comes to how migrants are categorised in relation to social rights and social policy (Considine and Dukelow, 2009: 419). This is evident from various Direct Provision measures which fail to recognise the human rights of asylum seekers and continue detaining families in limbo with various and severe psychological impacts (Thornton, 2014). Access to the labour market has been an area of contention in the Irish state when it comes to the integration of immigrants. Ireland's decision to opt into the EU directive (Reception Conditions Directive of 13 July 2016) in 2018 has placed asylum seekers in an almost impossible situation where, on the one hand, they have legal permission to seek employment, and, on the other hand, the conditions are almost impossible to meet.[5] It is like saying we will give you the right to find employment but we will make it impossible for you to find a job.

In the case of the Hungarian refugees in Ireland from 1956–1958, upon whom Article 17 of the UN Convention on the Rights of Refugees (1951), which Ireland had ratified, conferred the right to work (Fanning, 2002: 94), considerable efforts were made by the state to prevent them from seeking employment. Their confinement to the former army barracks in Co. Limerick for quarantine periods included the use of the state police to restrict their movements illegally. A worse fate is in fact faced by asylum seekers in twenty-first-century Ireland as they are confined to Direct Provision hostels pending decisions on their asylum claims, a process which oftentimes lasts as long as eight and sometimes ten years for individuals and families. This is amid the state's (and media) discourse which demonstrates the demonisation of those who seek refugee status as 'bogus refugees', 'economic migrants', 'illegal immigrants' and 'failed asylum seekers' while linking them to criminality and breach of state security (Schuster, 2003).

The othering of newcomers in Ireland also extends to migrant workers. This naturally became more pronounced during the resulting labour skills shortage and increased labour market mobility of the Celtic Tiger era where Irish workers had more opportunities to move to better paid jobs and between sectors. This also meant more opportunities for migrants who traditionally gravitate to places where economic activities are most vibrant, and Ireland post 1990 was no exception as large numbers arrived in the country. Some issues which affect this group include their work visa applications. Though its visa regime and border controls might be seen as flexible, Ireland 'aims at the German gastarbeiter model in that it seeks to keep the granting of residence and the right to work to a minimum period, and to enable the employer – rather than the employee – to control the visas' (Garner, 2009: 11). Only until recent policy change due to lobbying by advocacy groups have Irish work permit visas been given directly to the employee rather than the employer.

Ireland has been good to some migrant groups. The 2004 expansion of Europe saw Ireland in the lead as one of the first EU countries to allow the free movement of EU migrants from the accession states, granting them access to its labour market. However, it only favoured White European groups. Ireland's offer of uncontrolled entry and settlement to the citizens of other EU member states came at a cost borne by non-EU migrants as Ireland intensified efforts to control migration streams from outside the EU. This was part of a Europe-wide racialisation of immigration in which the most important border in terms of entry, residence, access to work and social security is nationality, split into two identities: EU and non-EU nationals (Garner, 2009). The direct consequence in

Ireland was mass reduction in numbers of the more 'unwelcome' non-EU migrants who formed the bulk of Irish stock of foreign workers prior to 2002. Interesting examples are migrants from Poland and Nigeria – the two countries with the largest increase in Ireland from Eastern Europe and Africa respectively. While immigration from Poland increased by 120,461 (5,671.4 per cent) between 2002 and 2011, Nigerian migrants only increased by 8,673 (96.7 per cent) for the same period, amid increased letters of threat of deportations and actual deportations of non-EU migrants and their Irish-born citizen children, despite their low numbers (see Lentin and McVeigh, 2006; Fanning, 2009; Joseph, 2018; Irish Naturalisation and Immigration Service, 2018).

The use of the law in racialising migrant populations was explicit in the state's dealings with a group categorised as Parents of Irish-Born Children.[6] Though they were subsequently granted residency permits in Ireland in 2005, this was only after the then Minister for Justice, Equality and Law Reform, Mr Michael McDowell's bulk issue of threat letters of the state's intention to deport them and their Irish citizen children – unless they chose to leave them behind. Fear mongering among citizens by government officials and some branches of the media branded migrant women as 'taking advantage' of the Irish citizenship 'loophole' to over-flood maternity hospitals with births through which they received residency permits, provoking a backlash that culminated in the 2004 citizenship referendum. So while the contemporaneous government decision in 2004 to engineer rapid large-scale immigration from predominantly White EU migrants barely caused a political ripple, during the same period there was an overwhelming vote against a clause in the Good Friday agreement resulting in the cancellation of the automatic rights to citizenship for all children born on the island of Ireland after 2004 unless one parent is an Irish citizen. While there had been a build-up in anti-immigrant sentiment which could also be seen across Europe, the political populism in support of the referendum was mostly directed against asylum seekers, African migrants and their children, and not against immigration per se (Fanning and Mutwarasibo, 2007). In the same vein, differential citizenship rights were rife at the deportation of Irish children with their non-EU parents, where failed asylum seekers and other non-EU migrants were accused of making bogus asylum claims during the 2002–2007 tenure of Michael McDowell. It is important to note that Eastern Europeans have also not been exempt from being othered in similar ways to the new second-class Irish citizens. Migrants that have become naturalised Irish citizens, it appears, are not quite Irish enough and are called 'New Irish' and experience more restrictions and conditions on their citizenship than the natives.

The currency of Irish whiteness

Without a doubt, being White in Ireland has currency. It has the power to influence whether or not you stand out, not to be nurtured but for negative treatment; if you will be derided or welcomed, if you will be automatically ascribed positive or derogatory attributes. It has an impact on what you can access in the labour market. Unlike the American context, where skin colour and the colour line feature prominently in the discourse on race, White on White racism experienced by the Irish raises crucial questions on whether a person's physiognomy is a key factor or the key factor in understanding race and how it influences outcomes in an Irish context. In order to address this issue, I will now turn to the ways in which whiteness has influenced the (re)positioning of the Irish in their diaspora settings and at home.

The ongoing debate about the Black and White paradigms for understanding race and racism is indicative of a problem with how the concept of race is applied to minorities of the same race. Garner (2009: 15) argues that Ireland's racialisation 'provides a more complex and nuanced way of understanding the evolution of "race" through racialisation' while also making it possible 'to avoid being side-tracked by colour as the only possible locus of whatever "race" means at a given time and place'. He makes this argument based on two key points, first by linking Irish enslavement by the British, and their mass shipment to the US and other Spanish colonies. He further argues that 'The case of Ireland demonstrates that the things that racism can do, such as control the movement of bodies, mark them as less human, and available for death, can also be done by reference solely to cultural distinctions in a colonial context' (Garner, 2009: 15). His second argument is that the Irish experience predates the discourse around the enlightenment and to some extent the establishment of the American colonies save the Spanish conquest of the now Latin America. While during the slave trade in America 'no White person could be a slave' as whiteness protects from the worst forms of slavery (Harris, 1993), Garner insists that 'the nineteenth century's obsession with somatic differences and the construction of pseudoscientific hierarchies based on particular differences has, I feel, distorted the discursive field and established body-centric racism as the norm' (Garner, 2009: 15). Research coming out of Europe in the last decade shows that skin colour significantly impacts on outcome and experience. For example, the 2014 report on immigrants in OECD countries discriminated against in the labour market shows Ireland as one of the countries with the highest level of discrimination against specific Black groups rather than the Irish being victims of discrimination

(Nisen and Panofsky, 2014; see also EU MIDIS 11, 2016). Irish reports also show increasing racism against people of African descent in Ireland (Michael, 2015; Joseph, 2019). While scholarship routinely points to the US as the prime example for colour-based racism, the study on which this book is based, which specifically focused on racial stratification in the Irish labour market, explicitly shows a White over Black ascendancy where Black workers are at the bottom of the hierarchy and White workers are at the top (Joseph, 2018). Irish history documents evidence of similar sentiments at a time when the Irish at home[7] in the 1840s and 1850s were willing to support the enslaved Blacks in the US in their quest to abolish slavery; whereas the encounters of the Irish abroad with colonised and aboriginal people in distinctly racist projects such as lynching and McCarthyism in a bid to escape the bottom of the hierarchy are well documented (see Ignatiev, 1995).

Another scholar, Mary Hickman (1998), has similarly argued that the Irish have been victims of the myth of a British homogeneous White society, that all people who were 'White' smoothly assimilated into the 'British way of life' (see also Modood et al., 1997). The distinctions between Whites are legitimised by, for example, place of birth and accent, which in turn influence their hierarchical positioning. The Irish-born in Britain are assumed to be distinguishable by their accent and place of origin (Hickman et al., 2005). Such racialised boundaries, Hickman argues, mask the hierarchy of belonging that constitutes Britishness and how the notion of white homogeneity operated on the premise that the 'problems' resided with those who migrated and possessed a different skin colour. While this 'myth of homogeneity' required the denial of differences among the White population (Hickman, 1998), it does not negate racism being colour-coded as is being suggested. Rather, it suggests that other factors such as country of descent and accent, as in the Irish case, operate along the hierarchy to darken even White subjects through the symbolic use of colour. It just goes to show that deviation from Eurocentric norms darkens actors, affecting their positioning on the hierarchy.

Not to downplay the differential and oftentimes harsh treatment of the Irish in the diaspora – part of the colonial tactic mobilised against the Irish involved cultural and symbolic representations of Black as poor, dirty, savage and uneducated among other such negative representations – it is clear that a black–white dichotomy was operational. In reality, the Irish were located some notches away from the bottom of the racial ladder, above Black Africans and non-English-speaking Whites, a point that is usually omitted in the discourse (Joseph, 2015). On this premise, I argue that the use of perceived difference in language, accent, religion and nationality of descent as a pretext to exploit and racialise the Irish conforms to the colour line, symbolically 'darkening' even White subjects with comparable consequences. Tsri (2016) discusses the symbolic use of the terms 'white' and 'black' to mean 'good' and 'evil' respectively. For example, angels are dressed in white while demons are dark and black. These colours are commonly constructed in binary opposition and accompanied, respectively, by disadvantage and privilege. As Tsri (2016: 5) states, 'Just as the use of the terms "black" and "white", both symbolically and categorically, serves to depreciate, stereotype and denigrate (i.e. blacken) those labelled black, it also, as the critics of "whiteness" argue, supports a privileged self-understanding of the people who label themselves as White' (see also Dalal, 2002).

Although critical race theory is sometimes criticised for placing race at the centre of its analysis, it does not simply see white supremacy as only involving extreme cases, but as systemic and everyday.

> [By] 'White supremacy' I do not mean to allude only to the self-conscious racism of white supremacist hate groups. I refer instead to a political, economic, and cultural system in which whites overwhelmingly control power and material resources, conscious and unconscious ideas of white superiority and entitlement are widespread, and relations of white dominance and non-white subordination are daily re-enacted across a broad array of institutions and social settings. (Ansley, 1997: 592)

Whiteness has benefited the Irish despite their sufferings. In the Caribbean, a special dispensation which was granted to landowners, where they were allowed to contract a fixed number of agricultural specialists from nearby non-Hispanic Caribbeans to assist them in establishing and running their plantations, insisted the experts had to be both White and Catholic – a requirement which was reported to have appealed to Irish planters, overseers and skilled craftsmen residing in the nearby British and Danish colonies (Chinea, 2007: 175). Another case in Irish history is the Longshoremen's United Benevolent Society, formed in the US in 1852, where all the members, who were exclusively White Irish, employed whiteness as a criterion for exclusion. They decided that 'work upon the docks ... shall be attended to solely and absolutely by members of the Longshoremen's Association, and such White labourers as they see fit to permit upon the premises' (Ignatiev, 1995: 120). The Irish workers and the Association, while excluding non-Whites, pitched their tents with other groups with whom they shared whiteness, as demonstrated by their flag. Their allegiance to White European America was evident in their banner, which was decorated with the flags of France, Germany, the Netherlands, Sweden, Ireland, Denmark, Hungary and Italy, under the American flag and the word 'unity'. At the top of the banner was the inscription 'We know no distinction but that of merit'. This de facto privileged opportunity enjoyed by many of the White Irish diaspora in the US, which was not readily available to their Black counterparts, 'conjures up images of domination happening on the backs of people of colour' (Leonardo, 2004: 138).

While many agree that racism exists in Ireland, scholarship concerning identity and diversity in Ireland has been limited primarily to the areas of ethno-nationalism and racism. There is little focus on how the nation encourages homogeneity or how it invokes and partakes of white privilege by identifying with whiteness. The belief in the early 1990s was that, in addition to there not being Black people in Ireland, 'Irish experience of anti-Irish racism' meant the Irish lacked the power to be racist (Lentin and McVeigh, 2002: 17). Though such sentiments point to the significance of not just ethnic but racial difference, Lentin and McVeigh argue that 'race cannot be theorised [only] in terms of skin colour or other visible differences'. By employing similar arguments to Bonilla-Silva's race without racism, Garner (2009) described Ireland's racialisation as the colonial setting for proto-racism, where the colonisation and settlement of Ireland by the English, and later the Scots, constitutes the birth of 'race' as a political category that inscribes inequality on the bodies and cultures of the actors. He states that 'In a paradoxical historical circle, contemporary Ireland has become home to "racism without racists" – an economic and social space organized by neo-liberal principles of governance and the movement of capital and labour, whose results are to racialize immigrants and Irish nationals alike, regardless of whether or not they are ostensibly "white"' (Garner, 2009: 3).

While racialisation entails discursively attaching bodies to a fixed culture, the Irish, English, Scots and all of white Europe distinguish each other by religion, class, language but not physical appearance. Bryne (2016) found among her former Irish professional peers evidence of biological/phenotypical racism in Ireland which supports both Bonilla-Silva's 'racism without race' and Garner's 'racism without racists' ideas. Racial stratification as it operates in the Irish labour market is a white over black ascendancy where whiteness is not only the possession of white skin colour, but other attributes which are Eurocentric, including being male, Christian, able-bodied and heterosexual. Any deviation from these Eurocentric norms symbolically 'blackens' human subjects, affecting their positioning on the racial strata (I return to this in further chapters).

Although skin colour is not the only possible explanation for the change in positioning of the Irish in their diaspora settings, the mobilisation of phenotypic whiteness by the Irish is indisputable. Amid intense competition among different groups of newcomers, Ignatiev (1995: 98) maintains that workers contracting for the sale of their labour ideally compete as individuals, not as groups, giving rise to animosity among them but also its opposite – unity. The idea that the absence of free competition leads to enduring animosity was evident in the case of the Irish in the US during slavery where the most intense and desperate labour competition was not between Irish and free Negroes, but within each of the two groups (Ignatiev, 1995). In other words, race becomes a social fact at the moment 'racial' identification begins to impose barriers to free competition among atomised and otherwise interchangeable individuals such that the greatest individual competition takes place not between groups but within each group (Ignatiev, 1995). While it can be argued that such conflict was more economic than racial with little to do with the colour line, we know that despite the harsh reality recorded among the groups the Irish were still able to band together in a way they did not with the Blacks in the US:

> If the experience of Cork and Longford men killing each other on the canal projects taught them that it was to their mutual advantage to come together, and if the rivalry among Irish and Germans eventually gave way to cooperative relations, why did the competition among Irish- and Afro-American labourers fail to lead to a mutual appreciation of the need for unity? The answer is that the competition among these two groups did not take place under normal circumstances, but was distorted by the colour line, what O'Connell called something in the 'atmosphere' of America. (Ignatiev, 1999: 99)

Race and ethnicity are defined as separate concepts, yet they do not have very clearly defined delineations in the everyday lives of people and are often conflated and used interchangeably. In the US the social construct of race has been argued to overlap with ethnicity (Rodríquez, 2000). Aranda and Rebollo-Gil (2004: 913), in their article 'sandwiched' minorities, argue that 'the racial continuum that privileges whiteness over blackness is indeed a social fact ... and ... the racialisation of ethnicity has resulted in ethnoracism'. They insist that 'The presence of national minority oppression does not signify the absence of racial oppression ... In a land where the national identity is white, nationality and race become interchangeable. We live with a white definition of citizenship, which generates a racist dynamic' (Martinez, 1998, cited in Aranda and Rebollo-Gil, 2004: 910). Even as they argue that race in twentieth-century America is not colour coded, they do not take cognisance of how symbolic colour can be assigned to various attributes or a coloured interpretation assigned to them. In the social construction of race, both the ethnic and global dimensions such as class, nationality of descent, culture, language, religion and geographical location are attributes which are assigned symbolic colours that affect the positioning of human subjects on a nation's racial hierarchy.

Conclusion

The black–white binary is a paradigm that suggests that Blacks 'constitute the prototypical minority group' (Delgado and Stefancic, 2012: 75). While such thinking is undeniably contentious and divisive, the continued pernicious use of race in lived experiences of Black and White workers warrants its use (Winant, 2000). The incongruence between Ireland the land of a thousand welcomes and the Ireland that between 2002 and 2010 exchanged its stock of foreign workers from non-EU to EU migrants after the 2004 accession, signalling a transition to more 'acceptable' migrants, raises crucial questions not just about whether a person's physiognomy is a key factor in understanding race, but also how much it influences labour market outcomes. The racialisation of the Irish at home and abroad and the experience of Irish Travellers indeed raise questions on the validity of skin colour as a locus of understanding racisms. However, the ways whiteness has been invoked by White Irish populations indicates that skin colour is employed in assigning access to both economic resources and status. The seemingly non-colour-coded racism experienced by the Irish can be seen to have a symbolic colour assigned where their deviation or perceived deviation from the Eurocentric norms of whiteness darkened them and influenced their initial experience. Exploring the historical contexts in which whiteness influenced the changing Irish identity and positioning relative to other groups from the bottom to the top, and from unwelcome to welcome migrants, shows Ireland's experience and response to difference has been a racially oriented one where the country's law and national policies have been initiated to homogenise its workforce even in the face of mass globalisation and immigration. Despite the numbers of immigrants coming to Ireland increasing exponentially in the last two decades, neither racism nor the presence of immigrants in Ireland is a new phenomenon.

Ireland's response to its Traveller community is indeed problematic for how race and racism are understood and is often seen to counter the claim that racism is colour based. Thus, while the Irish experience, which is ethnoracism, is different from the racism experienced by People of Colour, it was also colour coded, and thus colour based. This is because while whiteness was given a central position and seen as English, Christian, wealthy and educated/enlightened, the projected difference of the Irish people was attributes which are symbolically represented as 'black', such as savage, uneducated and apelike, among many others. The Irish themselves in the US, Spain, the UK and at home routinely invoked whiteness to separate themselves from the bottom of the social, racial and economic ladder. They have also used both cultural and physical whiteness as a criterion to determine who is acceptable and who is not, who is a true citizen and who is not, who is new Irish or simply Irish, who is entitled to the state's resources and who is not. Ireland has proved to be not just a racial state but also racist in its response to people who deviate from the more acceptable forms of whiteness represented as White, English speaking, heterosexual, able-bodied, male and Christian. Its integration strategies, which have targeted cultural rather than structural changes, have involved the diet, dress and dance of others.[8] These are surface-level interventions which, though important, are clearly unbeneficial, and absolutely inadequate for improving the outcomes of marginalised groups who encounter discrimination in the labour market. This is particularly true in Ireland with its historical bias towards nationalism, where policies and the law are invoked to protect the rights of White Irish citizens. In this way, Irish whiteness acts as property which confers rights and privilege on its possessors. Its very presence automatically discriminates against non-Whites and non-citizens. Every day white supremacy proliferates in the Irish labour market. Rather than Irish racism being non-colour coded, the othering of the Irish is built on the back of cultural non-whiteness which in addition to skin colour includes perceived class, behaviours, religion, accent and culture which can darken Whites generally, and the Irish, more specifically, in these instances.

Notes

1 See Tsri (2016) for in-depth discussion on the symbolic use of 'Black'. He argues that the term 'Black' has to be abandoned for referring to Africans.

2 This theory on American identity is centred on the assimilation of White immigrant groups and how they merge into the cultural melting pot, adopting American lifestyles.

3 Sociologist Ronit Lentin argues that the national repressed is the pain of emigration, returning to haunt the Irish, through the presence of the immigrant 'other' and in its wake invoking the unseemly presence of 'less than fully Irish' indigenous and non-indigenous racialised ethnic groups, such as the Traveller, the Asian, the Black and the Jew (Lentin, 2002: 233).

4 Poverty levels were high in Limerick. The Jewish population grew and became moneylenders, and significant numbers became indebted to the Jews. A sermon by Fr Creagh moved large numbers from the Arch Confraternity to attack the Jewish sector of the city, pelting them with mud and stones and breaking windows. The boycott hit the Jews' means of livelihood, with some people openly reneging on their debts, which the Jews were unable to collect because of threats (Flynn, 2004: 31–33).

5 Under the directive, asylum seekers will have access to the labour market nine months from the date when their protection application was lodged, if they have yet to receive a first instance recommendation from the International Protection Office, and if they have cooperated with the process. Eligible applicants may apply to the Minister for Justice and Equality for a labour market permission, which covers both employment and self-employment and is renewable every six months. Those who have received a judgement within the previous nine months are not eligible to apply. This access to the labour market does not take into account the migrant penalty, where non-EU migrants have a higher unemployment rate than their EU counterparts.

6 Children born in Ireland to non-citizen parents were assigned a new category, that of 'Irish-Born Children', and racially differentiated from children born in Ireland to citizen parents.

7 In 1845, Frederick Douglass, one of the great anti-slavery activists in the US, made a five-week lecture tour of Ireland giving a series of fiery anti-slavery lectures where he was reported to sometimes draw parallels between Irish and American slave experiences and more often distinguishing between them as forms of oppression.

8 For example, despite the higher unemployment rate of people of African descent in Ireland (CSO, 2016), and higher discrimination in employment reported by the group (EU MIDIS 11, 2016), Ireland's submission to the United Nations Committee for the Elimination of Racial Discrimination in 2018 presents Africa Day celebration of the continent's culture as its intervention for this group rather than a comprehensive inclusion strategy which would look at education, representation and labour market access.

3

Evidence of racial stratification in Ireland: comparing the labour market outcomes of Spanish, Polish and Nigerian migrants

Racial inequality in the labour market is not new in Ireland, Europe or anywhere in the world. What many grapple with is how best to represent these data. In the last decade the plight of Black workers, despite worsening across Europe, has almost fallen off the agenda and is subsumed under labels like 'Diversity and inclusion' in Ireland and 'Widening participation' in the UK. A racial hierarchy framework can make racial inequalities and group differential in experiences explicit. In a special issue which examined racial inequality in the USA and Britain, Song (2004) addressed the question of whether a racial hierarchy framework helps in explaining racial inequalities and group differential experiences in those two Western multi-ethnic societies. Regardless of the position we take, the reality is that every European country and institution still structures access to its resources and residency rights around race and nationality. With the increasing racial categories operational in Ireland, there is barely any acknowledgement of racial categorisation and by implication racial hierarchy. Yet the society is presented with new racialised identities and categories into which citizens and newcomers are meant to fit. The idea that migration affects socio-economic outcomes and labour market experiences is widely accepted. What is problematic, however, is the disparity in the way it affects different migrant groups, how this is presented and, more importantly, where the responsibility lies. Several Irish scholars (Fanning, 2009; Michael, 2015; Kelly et al., 2016; McGinnity et al., 2017) suggest that Ireland has increasingly become hostile and intolerant to its migrant population.

The racial order in Ireland is a white over black ascendancy. What this means is that White Europeans are stratified at the top of the economic ladder and Blacks at the bottom. White Europeans outperform people of Black African descent even when controlling for education and right to work. Ireland also has a hierarchical placement through inter-/intra-group ordering of its migrant population which becomes evident when race is centred when comparing the outcomes of migrant groups. Although there is little mention of whiteness in the public discourse on differentials in labour market outcomes, inequality and discrimination, whiteness continues to be a silent but key factor in recruitment, promotion and labour market experiences. Suffice it to say that all Whites are not treated the same in the labour market, nor are Blacks treated the same as Whites. The racialised economic landscape in Ireland is evident from a colour- and nationality-based differential in outcome among migrant groups and their segregation into paid and unpaid labour.

Profile of migrants in Ireland

Migration is a fast-growing feature of many countries, with considerable variation in the growth trends and profile of migrant populations. There are currently more than 127 million people who were foreign-born in OECD-member countries, which accounts for about 13 per cent of its total population. This is according to the 2018 International Migration Outlook report which records China, Romania, Syria, India, Poland and Mexico as the main countries of origin, with 7.6 per cent of the new migrants being from China. Since the 1960s many receiving countries have experienced considerable diversity in inflow and migration categories, such as labour migration, family migration and humanitarian migration. For the purpose of this book, I mainly focus on the profile of migrants in Ireland in relation to labour market participation.

As an English-speaking country in the EU, one would have expected Ireland's conversion to a receiving nation to have occurred much earlier than the 1990s. However, Ireland was one of the last of the EU15[1] countries to become recognised as a receiving country of migrants. Despite this slow uptake, there has been a steady increase of migrants coming into Ireland to live and work. The Republic of Ireland 2011 Census[2] of Population data published by the Central Statistics Office (CSO) records that 12.2 per cent of those ordinarily resident in the country were of migrant descent. This figure fell to 11.6 per cent according to 2016 Census figures (this decrease is to some degree attributable to the 87.4 per cent increase in dual Irish nationality; people who are classified as Irish in the Census). While migrants hail from as many as 199 countries in total, the overwhelming majority (74.4 per cent in 2011, and 73.6 per cent in 2016) of 'non-Irish nationals'[3] come from just 12 countries. The EU accounted for 71 per cent of all non-Irish residents in Ireland in 2011. This increases to just less than three-quarters

(74 per cent) when the rest of Europe is included. The second largest category was Asia at 12 per cent, followed by Africa at 7.6 per cent. When the 2011 Census data are examined in terms of country of origin, just two countries, namely Poland (at 30.6 per cent) and the UK (at 28 per cent) accounted for 58.6 per cent of all non-Irish residents living in Ireland. None of the remaining ten countries forms a proportionate share larger than 10 per cent. In terms of Africa, Nigerians represent the single largest category, at 42.4 per cent of the total for this region (41,642). The 2016 Census records a rise in people of African descent at 1.2 per cent of the total Irish population. Regarding the specific nationalities of the studied populations, the April 2011 Census recorded 122,585 Polish migrants, 17,642 from Nigeria and 6,794 from Spain.

Concerning change in the population for the studied groups by nationality and continent for 2002, 2006 and 2011, the changes reflect the increased labour mobility within the EU following its enlargements of 2004 and 2007 from the EU15 to EU25[4] and now EU28.[5] One striking observation is that while these figures represent the increased allocation of Personal Public Service Numbers (a unique reference for accessing public services in Ireland) to EU25 citizens, the group categorised as 'other'[6] nationalities recorded a decrease, signalling a shift from non-EU migration to EU citizens migrating to Ireland. Although this might be accounted for as a reduction in non-EU migrants arriving in the state, the visa restrictions and concerted effort around 'fortress Europe' and its restrictions on non-EU migrants vis-à-vis EU migrants suggest otherwise. Increases in the migrant population in Ireland between 2002 and 2011 were mainly accounted for by EU citizens. Polish and Slovakian immigrants represent the two largest groups, showing an increase over the decade of more than 5,000 and 3,000 per cent respectively (5,671 and 3,536 per cent). Correspondingly, the percentage increase of Hungarians, Lithuanians and Latvians all exceeded 1,000 per cent (specifically 1,864, 1,643 and 1,046).[7] Apart from the UK, Italy recorded the highest increase of all EU15 countries in this period, with an increase of over 103 per cent; this compares to an increase of 56 per cent from Germany and 53.2 per cent from Spain and France. Looking at migrants of African descent coming to Ireland, Nigerians had the largest increase of over 96 per cent. The peak period for Nigerian migrants moving to Ireland occurred between 2002 and 2006, when the numbers increased from 8,969 to 16,300, followed by a much smaller increase to 17,642 by 2011. While this group (and other non-EU migrants) all recorded increases between 2002 and 2006, with India, Philippines and Brazil recording the highest numbers, there was a noticeable decrease in their intake post-2006 compared with the increases recorded for the

EU25 accession states. The US also recorded a decrease, of 3.5 per cent for that period.

Labour market outcomes and disparity

Although race has been widely acknowledged as an illusion that is socially constructed, skin colour and nationality of descent continue to influence socio-economic outcomes. Various studies across Europe that measure the experience of discrimination indicate that the highest levels of discrimination based on ethnic or immigrant background are in the area of employment, and are higher for non-White minorities (EU MIDIS 11, 2016; McGinnity et al., 2017; Zschirnt and Ruedin, 2016). These studies show that skin colour, foreign-sounding first or second names, accent and nationality of origin were the main reasons cited by respondents for their experience of discrimination. Unlike the American context, where skin colour features prominently in everyday discourse, any other attribute but race is centred in Ireland, particularly one of a migrant deficit. These theories attribute differentials in outcome to some form of deficit among marginalised groups. A migrant deficit approach is counterproductive and should be discouraged as it perpetuates racial stereotypes and presupposes that labour markets are meritocratic socio-economic environments, contrary to evidence which shows they continue to be loaded with structural barriers in which groups encounter and contest their marginalisation.

With over 15 per cent of Ireland's workforce being of migrant descent, the country has earned the right to be described as a multicultural society. Ireland was also one of the first three EU states to open its labour market to migrants from the EU accession states in 2004 without restrictions. Despite the interest in diversifying the workplace, the top tiers of both the public and the private sectors of the Irish labour market remain predominately White (Joseph, 2018). To help readers understand the data source in this book, I present summaries of the employment programme[8] and the Irish Census statistics for 2011 and how different migrant groups performed in the labour market. In accordance with the CRT tradition, race is first of all centred in the analysis of both data sources to highlight outcomes by nationality of descent, skin colour and race. By controlling for nationality, gender and the highest educational attainment, analysis from the two sources of secondary data reveals a differential in outcomes among migrants. While all the migrant groups in the study fared worse than the host community, both sources of data showed the occurrence of economic inequality among migrants consistent with a Black–White dichotomy where, depending on nationality and race, certain groups in the Irish labour market were more likely to be at the bottom and others at the top of the labour market. For ease of understanding, the data are presented sequentially. The data from analysing EP's database are presented first, followed by the analysis from the Irish 2011 Census data using a stratification framework.

The employment programme

Profile of selected EP participants

The EP 2009–2011 programme recorded that 639 unique individuals participated in the programme, including 241 persons from the selected countries (Nigeria, Poland and Spain). Migrants of Nigerian descent recorded the highest uptake, totalling 85 persons, with migrants of Polish and Spanish descent recording similar participation levels at 77 and 79 persons respectively. These three groups make up over a third (37.7 per cent) of all migrants who participated in EP during the three-year period under consideration. Concerning the gender breakdown, the research population records a remarkably higher female participation in the programme than male. Polish and Nigerian groups recorded similarly gendered participation rates, with two-thirds of Nigerian participants (67 per cent) female, and a similar female proportion within the Polish group (65 per cent). The migrants from Spain had an almost equal participation rate between males at (46 per cent) and females (54 per cent). Among the research population, Nigerian females had the highest number of participants who accessed EP at 38 per cent (57 persons). This might be interpreted to mean that Nigerian women are more open to seek assistance from support services. However, the 2016 Census shows that 56 per cent of Nigerian homes in Ireland are one-parent families and female led. This means the responsibility to provide both financial and emotional care rests on these Nigerian females. It might also be a strong indication that the high level of discrimination this group encounters serves as a driver for them to seek extra support in their career journey.

In relation to age distribution, the migrants from Eastern and Western Europe recorded a younger age range of participants in the programme within the 20–29 and 30–39 ranges (see Table 3.1). The Spanish migrants were particularly highly represented in a younger age range, with over half of the participants (57 per cent) within the 20–29 age range. The Nigerians were more represented in the older age range, with over half (52 per cent) aged 30–39 and a further 31 per cent between the ages of

Table 3.1   Distribution of programme participants by country of descent and age

Country	Under 20 (%)	20–29 (%)	30–39 (%)	40–49 (%)	Over 50 (%)	Total (N)
Nigeria	2	14	52	31	1	85
Poland	0	43	43	12	2	77
Spain	0	57	37	6	0	79
All countries of descent	1	37	44	17	1	241

Source: Generated by the author from CSO (2011), July 2014.

40 and 49. The Polish were evenly distributed, recording 43 per cent for both the 20–29 and 30–39 age ranges. These age differences throw up significant questions, particularly on how age interlocks with other attributes in influencing outcomes. Eighty-three per cent of Nigerian migrants who accessed EP were over thirty years of age while 57 per cent of Spanish and 43 per cent of Polish migrants were under thirty.

Regarding the levels of educational attainment, more than half (63 per cent) of the programme participants were reported to have a university degree or higher, with 15 per cent recording second- level education or lower.[9] The migrants of Spanish descent recorded the highest educational level, with 91 per cent having a university degree or higher, compared with the Polish at 62 per cent, while the Nigerians recorded the lowest proportionate to their population at 36 per cent. Almost half (44 per cent) of the Nigerians recorded their highest educational attainment in further education,[10] which includes vocational and technical qualifications,[11] indicating a high level of practical skills (see Table 3.2, p. 93). These figures do not correspond with the distribution of migrants as recorded in the national Census, which records Nigerian[12] migrants as having a higher third-level education than their Polish counterparts compared with the much lower levels recorded in EP (Table 3.2). It also records a much higher percentage of Spanish migrants with third-level degrees compared with their profile in the Census figures for migrants for the same period in Ireland. This might be indicative of the kind of people who access employment support programmes like EP.

In the distribution by gender and highest educational level, males and females recorded similar representation at 65 and 62 per cent respectively for participants with a university degree or higher (Figure 3.1). Males were more represented at the lower end of the educational level,

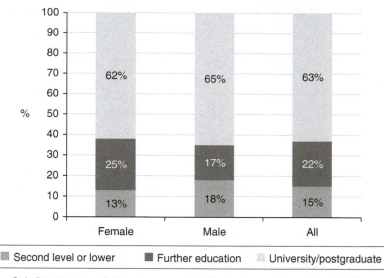

Figure 3.1 Distribution of all programme participants by gender and highest level of education

with almost 1 in 5 having their highest educational attainment at second level or lower. For females, on the other hand, 1 in 4 had their highest educational attainment at the further education level.

Here we see significant differences within the groups in their distribution by highest level of education and gender. This differentiation enabled the comparison of their labour market outcomes. It provided insight on whether educational attainment is the key determinant of labour market outcomes. The Spanish women in the study recorded the highest level of educational attainment, based on the database sample, with 95 per cent having a university degree or higher. They also had a higher level of education than their male counterparts, who recorded 86 per cent with a university degree or higher. Within the Polish group, women recorded a significantly higher level of education (70 per cent with university degree or higher) than their male counterparts, while the Polish men were over-represented at second-level education or lower (37 per cent). The Nigerian group were over-represented in further education, with more than half of the women (51 per cent) having further education training as their highest level of educational attainment (this accounts for the higher representation of females in further education than males, as shown in Figure 3.1). While the Nigerian women recorded the lowest representation in tertiary education at 28 per cent, they recorded high vocational skills qualifications. One important observation is that they were the only group who recorded a lower third-level education than their male

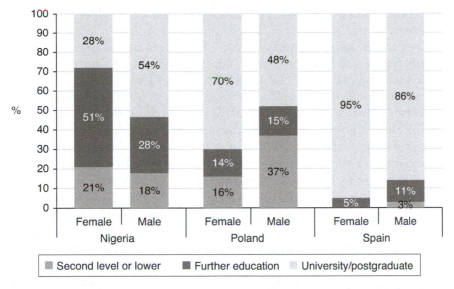

Figure 3.2 Distribution of programme participants by country, gender and highest level of education

counterparts. Nigerian men recorded a higher educational level (54 per cent) compared with the Polish men (48 per cent) proportional to their population (Figure 3.2). These differences helped to explore whether education is the primary determinant of labour market disparity among migrants.

While the top of the educational ladder tells a particular type of story, the bottom tells a different story. The Spanish migrants' representation at the bottom at 1 per cent was insignificant, thus reflecting the high educational attainment of the participants who accessed EP. For the Nigerian migrants, the bottom of the educational ladder records 20 per cent of their total population who accessed EP, that is 1 in 5 of them, had a second-level education or lower. For the Polish 1 in 4 (25 per cent of their representative population in EP) had a second level or lower. When educational attainment is centred while controlling for gender (Figure 3.2), the Nigerian migrants have a higher educational level than their Polish counterparts when third-level and vocational training are combined. When taking vocational training into consideration, the Nigerian migrants recorded 80 per cent with vocational training or above, versus 76 per cent of Polish migrants and 99 per cent of Spanish migrants. When controlling for gender, the story changes. While fewer than 1 in 5 Nigerian males had a second-level education as their highest educational attainment, 1 out of every 3 male persons of the Polish participants on the EP database had a second-level education or lower.

Concerning lone parenthood, just 11 per cent of the selected population are in this category, with Nigerian women accounting for the overwhelming majority (21 out of 26 persons). This correlates with the over-representation of women recorded in the national statistics figures (Central Statistics Office, 2011, 2016), which show that females make up the highest number of people whose socio-economic status is looking after the home or family. Polish women recorded 11.2 per cent and Nigerians 11.5 per cent in this category. This might also account for why these two groups had the highest number of females who accessed the programme in the 2009–2011 period covered by the study.

With regard to the profile of the Nigerian, Polish and Spanish migrants on the EP database, its demographics suggest some particularities of each group. Concerning education, the Spanish migrants have a generally higher level of education while Nigerian women have a higher representation in vocational training. The Polish men had the lowest level of education. Although the study did not specifically focus on age, some basic deductions concerning age can be made from the database figures. Eighty-three per cent of Nigerian migrants who accessed EP were thirty years of age and over, while 57 per cent of Spanish and 43 per cent of Polish migrants were below thirty. Some of the implications are that the older migrants of Nigerian descent might be competing with a younger cohort of migrants for the same jobs. With ageism on the increase (Butler, 1969; Cantillon and Vasquez del Aguila, 2011), they are more likely to be affected not just by their race and nationality but also by their age. Similarly, an older cohort will have its particularities, such as family demands and dual relationships, as against a younger group with fewer or different kinds of demands.

Disparity in outcome: when migration affects groups differently

In the three-year period studied, the EP database recorded high placement rates (progression to employment, training or education) for the selected populations of the study. Migrants of Nigerian descent recorded the highest rate proportionate to their population (at 89 per cent), compared with Poland (84 per cent) and Spain (85 per cent) (Figure 3.3). However, when placements are categorised into paid[13] and unpaid[14] employment, the Nigerian group recorded the lowest progression rate into paid employment (at 40 per cent), as against Poland (60 per cent) and Spain (69 per cent). This outcome correlates with the CSO (2011) statistics in which migrants from Nigeria recorded an unemployment

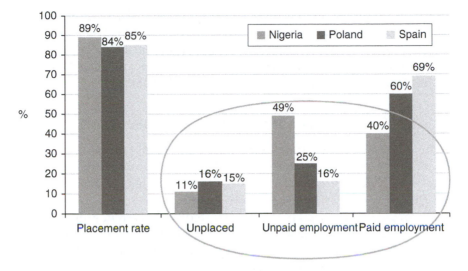

Figure 3.3 Labour market outcome of programme participants by country

rate of 38.5 per cent (which rose to 43 per cent according to the 2016 Census figures). A similar outcome was recorded in the CSO 2010 Quarterly National Household Survey, where migrants of Black African descent had the lowest employment rate.[15]

Even when the extent of the disparity in labour market outcomes is unclear, we must remember that all groups are not treated the same. These data are a prime example of some remarkable inconsistencies in outcomes among groups. One of the most noticeable differences is the over-representation of migrants of Nigerian descent in unpaid employment at 49 per cent, representing over half (55 per cent) of the total labour market placements recorded for this group. Meanwhile, the migrants from Poland and Spain recorded much lower figures in unpaid employment, at 25 per cent and 16 per cent respectively, representing less than a quarter of their placements (Figure 3.3). This shows that the labour market participation of a high proportion of Nigerian actors is without financial remuneration. This is problematic for the Nigerian group members on a micro level for two reasons. First, the data show that over three-quarters of Nigerian migrants who accessed the EP were in the 30–50 age range (Table 3.1). Drawing on developmental psychology theorists, including Freud (1905), Kohlberg (1969), Maslow (1970) and Erikson (1980), unmet expectations around career establishment and development are likely to be rampant among this group and to have long-lasting negative impacts in terms of self-esteem and confidence. Secondly, this group is also affected by their intersectionality, specifically race with other vectors. The vast majority of lone parents in the study, albeit a minority overall, are Nigerians and overwhelmingly female. Here too it is the case that lone parenthood exerts great financial demands and also results in additional costs in terms of childcare when Nigerian-Irish women are attempting to enter paid employment.

Volunteering as a holding place for marginalised migrants

Here are key questions to consider about the implications of the data which show that in Ireland over half of the labour participation of Black workers is in unpaid roles. Would these Nigerian-Irish workers have decided to take up unpaid work if they could access/obtain paid employment? Do societal mechanism/s predispose certain groups to the limited choice of unpaid work? Interrogating the various elements of EP's 2009–2011 database, allows insight into the outcomes of migrants on the Irish labour market. The picture provided by the statistical data is, however, insufficient as a standalone method to show how these disparities are produced. It is also unable to present, even anecdotally, the perspectives of those most affected by the system. This is one of the disadvantages of relying solely on a quantitative analysis when human lives and experiences are involved. Consequently, I am going to draw from the stories of interviewees to proffer explanations for some of the observed discrepancies (see chapter 4).

First, let's consider the notion of choice implied by how the term 'volunteering' is loosely applied. My informants show that the high uptake and recourse to unpaid work recorded among the Nigerian migrants, and by implication Black Africans, is born out of necessity rather than choice. While unpaid work in the form of internships, work placements, retraining or upskilling seemed beneficial for career progression, the lived experience of Black Africans proves otherwise. Unpaid work did not serve the same purpose or yield the same result for all the groups in the research population. The Nigerian migrants in my study 'progressed' to unpaid work because it was the sector where they experienced the least resistance to their labour market mobility (by this I mean where they encountered fewer discriminatory practices and less labour market closure; see Joseph, 2019 for detailed discussion). While it seemed to produce a similitude of movement or labour market mobility, volunteering is experienced as a place of marginalisation exacerbated by a person's racial identity.

> The inference is that you tended to move into community development and do some voluntary work to gain experience because that was the only way anyone would talk to you. Once it is volunteer, you are good, everything

about you is perfect, but once it is for a paid role, no, you are not good enough. So you tended to move into the volunteering sector and once there, you realise the extent of your marginalisation and position and those there are also the marginalised and you feel they will share your concern but no, worse mistake. (BnFemale[16])

The barriers encountered in accessing paid employment are common stories among the Nigerian migrants. This cohort of workers engage in volunteering in order to obtain Irish work experience – despite the level of work experience from their home countries; to be noticed by potential employers, show their motivation to work; create opportunities for conversation and to develop social capital, among other reasons. While volunteering is highly recommended for all these reasons, in Ireland it is a space which exacerbates the marginalisation of its more unwelcome population. Migrants retraining on arrival in Ireland is evidenced by their high uptake of further education courses; however, this retraining is mainly a 'down-skilling' rather than an 'upskilling' process in order for them to be able to access 'low-skilled' jobs. Migrants try to access employment areas with the least resistance. Rather than being a pathway to paid employment, volunteering unfortunately becomes a holding place for Ireland's surplus labour that produces a similitude of movement without actual mobility or change of place. This occurs to the extent that some migrants become professional students going from one education programme to the other. They are surplus not in the real sense of the definition, but because they are a cohort of unwanted and unwelcome groups in the labour market. This is worrying as Blacks have historically been exploited in the labour market and their bodies consumed in slavery – a form of unpaid work. Despite claims in some media quarters and from some political opportunists in Ireland that Blacks are 'freeloaders' who are unwilling to work, the data show that Nigerian migrants had a higher participation rate in the labour market than any other group when paid and unpaid work are considered as participation. This is in spite of the difficulties and racial discrimination reported by the Black interviewees in navigating the labour market.

The recourse by Nigerian-Irish workers to unpaid work is intricately linked to the closure in the labour market which is influenced by their nationality of descent. It is a systemic and specific experience of the group and group members. Many of the interviewees expressed their frustration that it seemed they are only to be used for unpaid work, internships/apprenticeships or voluntary work.

You find that where it even comes to education and work placement, you can only be taken when there is no financial incentive. Even some of the work placements that have the possibility of turning into a job, they will not take you for it. (HnMale)

The expectation that unpaid work and retraining would reduce the gap between gaining paid employment, improving their chances and providing advantage in the job market, is often unrealised. The gaps they identified which operated like impenetrable barriers include lack of/limited experience in Ireland; lack of trust and bias by employers against their foreign credentials (qualifications, skills and experience); limited contact with professionals and officials in the top tiers of the labour market, and work references from Ireland. Black migrants in Ireland face a dilemma where, on the one hand, they gain the Irish work experience required for progression into paid employment, but on the other hand they are trapped in a continuous circle of unpaid work. For instance, HnMale said:

> They [the Irish state] are happy in this country for people to take you for voluntary service and work that you should be paid for, they allow you [to] do it for free. … Yes, I am not being paid and the work I am doing now, I designed it and set it up and I have been running it for them for free. I had accounting as a first degree and was working in the banking industry when I first came. It is not recognised in Ireland until you go through an evaluation process. You have to go through the process of retraining. … I had to have a shift from where I was and even after retraining based on one's own calculations ends up not being the right one. For example, I moved from financial services to community development sector. After graduating from the HR course I did, I found it difficult to get work in the field. Then I tried customer service but it was a short contract and it didn't last. … So I had to go back to college again and since then, I have been going from course to course. (HnMale)

Migrants are stuck in volunteering because progression into paid employment is determined by factors other than education, experience, language of the host community and Irish work references which are the usual reasons cited for migrants not progressing into paid employment. While Black workers are more affected than Whites, the problem is not the idea of volunteering itself but Black workers being stuck in those unpaid roles, which serves to hold them in the stereotypes held about their group. BnFemale said:

> I feel there has been a lot of negativity right from arrival [in Ireland as a migrant] and the only way to have your foot in the door was volunteering and you volunteer for many years. I will be hard put to find a Black person who didn't start as a volunteer except maybe the medical doctors. In any other sector, you would have started as a volunteer or you were ready to do the jobs where there was no one to do them. (BnFemale)

One dynamic which clearly emerged in thinking through this problematic of how not only migrants of Nigerian descent but Africans generally are over-represented in unpaid work through a number of cases in the study, is the prejudgement/stereotyping which is hinged on race and which undermines the efforts of African migrants navigating the labour market. This becomes explicit from the interviewees of Spanish and Polish descent who reported a different experience of unpaid work and training, as it was linked to their initial goals for coming to Ireland which included learning the English language. For this cohort, their recourse to training and unpaid work was a choice, rather than compulsion due to limited options. The following reports support this view:

> Basically, what I did when I came to Ireland was in the first month I attended a language course for 3–4 months to familiarise myself with the language. After that, I started to access two different courses, EP and Jobcare. In the meantime, I did some volunteer work which also helped me keep in touch with the Irish society. (EsMale)

AsFemale said:

> When I came here [Ireland], I came to improve my English two years ago. I couldn't speak English properly and when I went to interview, they told me, okay you are good and confident, and from your CV, I know you have skills but your English is not enough. (AsFemale)

Similarly, BpFemale states:

> I was looking for a new role to change the current job two months ago, but my level of English when I came in here [Ireland] was not so good when I compare with the other people. I had to improve my level of English. That's why I couldn't get that kind of job. (BpFemale)

CsMale noted, 'for me, my job is like a school as my main goal is to learn English'.

What do these reports tell us about the different progression rates and routes of migrant groups in the labour market? They clearly demonstrate that some migrant groups, particularly of White European descent, find volunteering a useful path to career progression. They do not typically encounter exploitation or a prolonged stay in unpaid labour market activities, such as continuous training and/or retraining at a lower academic level than their prior learning. This is unlike their Black counterparts, represented by the Nigerian-Irish migrants in the study, who were compelled to engage in volunteering – which is an extremely slow means to bridge the gap in achieving their employment goal.

This slow outcome is evident from the study, where on average it took two to six months for clients of the EP programme of Spanish descent to find paid employment, the Polish migrants six to nine months, and Nigerians nine to eighteen months. While similar time-frames emerged from the semi-structured interviews for the White European groups, for the Nigerian-Irish migrants, it took them an average of over twenty-four months. Nigerian migrants, and by inference Black workers, experience a closure in the labour market which is linked to a prevalence of racially motivated bias and stereotypes. While accessing unpaid work is part of the pragmatic choice made by the Eastern and Western European migrants as a necessary part of their career progression, the over-representation of the Nigerian migrants in unpaid employment is not due to personal choice. It is linked to limited access to paid employment and a way of exercising their agency to tackle their limited employment options.[17] On a macro level, it suggests a growing[18] unpaid segment in the labour market which appears to function like a holding place for marginalised groups but is in reality a form of economic exploitation of the skills of Black workers. This sort of exploitation is commonly found in research in Ireland, where Black workers are routinely invited in as research subjects to be exploited for their knowledge and experience and are not seen as the source to produce that knowledge. In contrast the expertise of White 'experts' is often developed from having a series of conversations with marginalised groups, and producing documentaries and espousing knowledge on those groups. I strongly caution against what Alice Feldman (2020) describes as knowledge epistemicide – the exclusion and killing of knowledge systems other than those created by White European male scientists. This paternalistic positioning is again an exploitation, a form, albeit more covert, of modern-day slavery, where the labour, skills, knowledge and expertise of Blacks and marginalised groups are exploited for the gains of the White population.

Correlations between employment and educational attainment

Although immigrants are often categorised as one group, they do not all occupy the same positioning in the labour market. Some are closer to the top while some groups are found at the bottom of the economic and racial ladder. Being at the top is a power(ful) position which many are not willing to give up. And when we present the outcomes of immigrants in Ireland as one group, it obfuscates the differentials among and between groups and the experiences of the most marginalised. To give more visibility to the experiences of foreign-born workers in Ireland, the labour market outcomes of migrants is compared to illustrate the hierarchical nature of Irish society and the impact on those at the bottom and top.

Concerning the influence of education on the mobility of migrants in the Irish labour market, the most remarkable difference became apparent when comparing the overall outcomes across groups based on their highest education level and progression to paid employment; in other words, comparing 'like' with 'like', based on highest recorded educational attainment. Eighty per cent of the programme participants from Spain whose highest education was university level or higher progressed to paid employment, while the equivalent figure for Polish migrants was 70 per cent and Nigerian migrants 52 per cent (Figure 3.4). Among those with further education, 83 per cent of those from Spain progressed to paid employment, while everyone from Poland with further education gained paid employment. Though Nigerian migrants recorded the highest number with further education, they recorded the lowest progression into paid employment at 43 per cent. A similar situation occurred for the unskilled whose highest level of education was second level or lower, where Nigerians fared the worst of all the groups. In all three educational levels, Nigerian migrants fared worse than all the other groups.

The levels of education recorded for the groups may be said to account for the difference in outcome among them. This migrant deficit approach

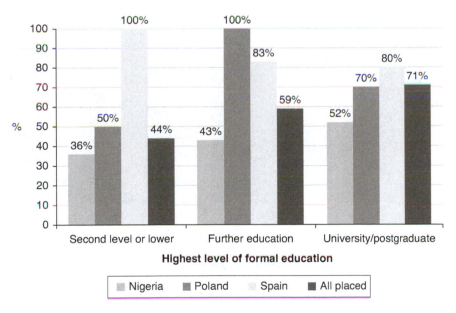

Figure 3.4 Percentage of programme participants placed in paid employment by country and highest level of education attained

can lead to erroneous conclusions, such as those drawn by the authors of *The Bell Curve*, who asserted that people of African descent have lower academic capacity and that this might account for the differential socioeconomic outcomes between them and others (Herrnstein and Murray, 1994). Some interesting observations suggest otherwise. The first difference observed is within groups, whereby Polish and Spanish females recorded largely higher levels of education than their male counterparts. However, Spanish males are shown to have the best employment outcomes by far (Figure 3.5). A similar observation can be made when outcomes across the groups are revealed and where educational attainment did not produce corresponding results in terms of progression to paid employment. For example, the Polish males, despite being less qualified in educational terms compared with their Nigerian male counterparts, recorded a more positive employment outcome (at 68 per cent) than the Nigerian males (at 48 per cent). When further education is considered, the Polish females and Nigerian males are almost at par in their educational attainment, yet there is a marked difference in outcome, with the Polish females and males outperforming the Nigerian migrants. Similarly, the Spanish males recorded almost double the performance of the Nigerian males. The most striking outcome differential occurred with the Polish

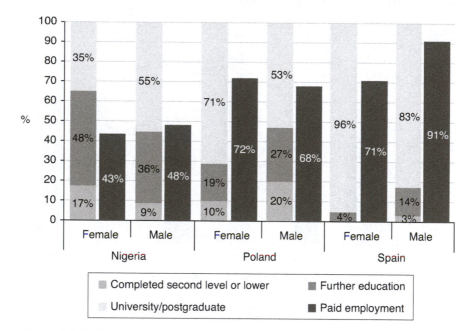

Figure 3.5 Paid employment outcome by country, gender and highest level of education attained

males who, among those who progressed into paid employment, had the highest representation of those with a second-level or lower education (20 per cent or 1 in 5 persons), and still outperformed the Nigerian males and females.

The employment programme's database demonstrates some cogent facts. The first is that education has an impact on the labour market outcomes of migrants. This is evident in Figure 3.4, where the highest progression into paid employment by the migrants in the study was from those who had third-level degree or higher (71 per cent), while migrants with further education recorded the next highest (59 per cent) and then second level or lower (44 per cent). While there are secondary issues which might have had an influence on the differential in outcomes,[19] it does not, however, nullify the fact that there are significant differences in outcome and some obvious variables that influence this outcome. In this regard, the argument that the level of educational qualifications is responsible for limited employment chances for migrants was not supported by the data in EP's database. While qualifications were relevant, they were not the main determinants. Rather, both race and gender in the case of the migrant groups had a bigger impact on their economic outcomes.

Evidence of a colour-coded hierarchy in the Irish labour market

The hierarchical nature of the Irish labour market can also be seen through the inter-/intra-group ordering of migrant groups in the study. The first observation is on the inter-group layering. The data show that the European groups had a better outcome than the African group, even when comparing 'like with like' in terms of highest educational level attained. Thus, regarding group stratification the Europeans are stratified over Africans in the Irish labour market in terms of economic outcomes. Another very interesting observation is that all Whites are not treated the same in the labour market; neither are they positioned on the same strata. Rather, there is an intra-White gradation within the group which is dependent on the perceived class of each 'White' country/ continent (I discuss this further under classed race). This intra-group stratification is seen where despite Spanish and Polish migrants having white physiognomy, the Spanish migrants had a better outcome than the Polish, who in turn had a better outcome than the Nigerians. So, while gender affects the intra-group layering of workers as evidenced across all groups where the male groups outperformed their female counterparts within each group (see Figure 3.5), gender does not buffer the impact of racial difference as all the male groups did not perform better than all the female groups. In other words, all the African and

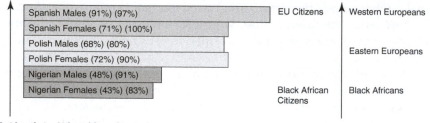

First bracket = % in paid employment
Second bracket = % with third-level and further education

See Figure 3.5 for breakdown

Figure 3.6 Diagrammatic illustration of the labour market outcomes of migrants from the research population based on the employment programme's 2009–2011 database

European males are not stratified above all the African and European females. Rather, the layering is broadly connected to racial difference, and more specifically difference in nationality of descent and skin colour. My data show that Spanish females still fared better than the Polish and Nigerian males; and Polish females in turn fared better than their Nigerian male counterparts. This structuring is illustrated in Figure 3.6. It shows a stratification in the Irish labour market which is linked to race and nationality. There is a clear distinction between the labour market outcomes of Spanish migrants from Western Europe and Polish migrants from Eastern Europe despite both groups being White Europeans. In other words, while there is a stratification among races, where Whites are stratified over Blacks, there is also an inter-group stratification where people from richer white countries (perceived or actual) are stratified over people from countries with a lower GDP.

Census 2011 confirms a racial hierarchy in Ireland

The whiteness of the top tiers of the labour market in Ireland

The centring of race in analysing the 2011 Census figures similarly illuminates the organisation of racial inequality in Ireland and its racial hierarchies along the labour supply chain to unveil the whiteness of the top tiers of the Irish labour market. The main criteria used in locating the groups in this study along a racial hierarchy from the 2011 Irish Census data include the employment rate of migrants, the percentage of managers, those seeking their first job and the percentage of those who had lost or given up their job as at 2011 relative to their population. The Census data show EU migrants as recording an overall employment rate of 52 per cent, with 56 per cent among Polish nationals and 66 per cent of Spanish nationals in paid employment. For Africans, the employment rates decreased sharply, with a 31 per cent employment rate recorded for Africans generally and a 32 per cent rate for 'Nigerian nationals' (Table 3.2). In terms of those who had become unemployed either from having lost their job or given up their previous employment, the group most affected were Nigerians, at 17 per cent, contrasting with Polish nationals at 14 per cent and 7 per cent among Spanish nationals. Also, though only a very small percentage of migrants were recorded as looking for their first regular job, there was a substantial difference in outcomes between Africans and Europeans within the broad categories (Table 3.3) and within the research populations (Table 3.2). From both tables, we see that 1 per cent of EU migrants compared with 4.5 per cent of Black Africans were recorded as looking for their first jobs, while the research populations mirrored the broad groups, with Nigerian migrants recording 3 per cent as still looking for their first regular job compared with 1 per cent among Spanish and Polish migrants.

When the Census data are further explored based on ethnicity, there is an even greater distinction in outcomes between White and Black migrants. The data show that 344,962 persons were recorded as White who were not 'White Irish' or 'White Traveller', of which 60 per cent were recorded as being in employment in 2011 (Table 3.3). Out of the

Table 3.2   Summary of the labour force outcome and participation for the research populations at April 2011

	Spanish (%)	Polish (%)	Nigerian (%)
Principal economic status	66.0	56.0	32.0
Lost/given up first job	7.0	14.0	17.0
Assigned to managers	15.0	6.5	4.5
Third-level education or higher	62.7	22.3	39.4
Looking for their first job	1.0	1.0	3.0
Communicate well in English	Not available	30.6	82.0

Table 3.3   Labour force outcome by race and ethnicity at April 2011

	White Europeans (%)	Black African (%)	Black not African (%)
% in employment	60.0	37.0	50.0
Lost/given up first job	14.0	21.0	14.0
Looking for first job	1.0	4.5	2.3

total number of persons categorised as Black or Black Irish-African, a much lower rate of 37 per cent (of all those aged fifteen and over) was recorded for those in paid employment. Similar to the disparity in outcome for EU migrants, White Europeans recorded only 1 per cent of their population as looking for their first regular job, with 14 per cent in that group becoming unemployed from losing their job or having given up a previous employment. Much higher figures were recorded in the case of Blacks or Black Irish linked to Africa, where 4.5 per cent were recorded as looking for their first regular job and 21 per cent of their total population recorded as unemployed from having lost or given up a previous job.

According to the Census figures, the group with the lowest economic outcome in the Irish labour market were those in the Black or Black Irish-African category. While the findings from EP did not explicitly indicate race in the labour market differential, the ethnicity questions introduced into the Irish Census from 2006 onwards allowed the collection of data on differential in outcomes based on race. These differences are significant as they make the direct link between labour market differential and race undeniable. They also reveal a racial hierarchy in the Irish labour market with Europeans at the top and Black Africans at the bottom of the labour supply chain. The three independent data sets in the study – the Irish 2011 Census, the EP database and the interviewees' perspectives from thirty-two semi-structured interviews – all present a similar landscape of the racial hierarchy in Ireland of a White over Black; European over African ascendancy. Together, they provide triangulations for the study from which the data in this book are taken.

Generalisability of the data[20]

Can the data generated in this study be extended to a wider population at large, is there room for generalisability and are there areas for comparison? Figure 3.7 shows the population distribution of all EP participants from 2009–2011, comprising 639 unique individuals, while Figure 3.8 shows the distribution of participants who obtained paid employment by the broad groups and their highest level of educational qualification. The labour market outcomes show similar patterns between the three nationalities selected for this study – Spanish, Polish and Nigerians, which represent the broad groups Western Europe, Eastern Europe and Africa respectively. The three largest populations that accessed EP were EU25 and African migrants, both at 28 per cent of all participants of the programme for the three-year period, and EU15 migrants at 22 per cent (Figure 3.7).

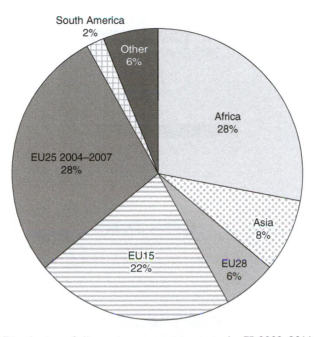

Figure 3.7 Distribution of all programme participants in the EP 2009–2011 database (N = 639)

While the migrants from South America had a better outcome than other migrant groups, the EU15 migrants in turn had a better outcome than the EU25 migrants. Out of the three groups, the African migrants recorded the worst labour market outcome, with a placement rate of just 36 per cent (Figure 3.8). From the broad groups, the African migrants have a greater risk of being at the bottom of the labour market ladder. The discrepancies uncovered in this study raise questions, particularly whether the similarity in outcome among the research populations and the broad groups is related to abilities such as achievement factors (skills, experience and education), or other causal factors.

A comparison of the outcomes of all the group members who progressed onto paid employment showed a clear distinction among the groups which was not simply based on educational abilities. First, more than half of all the EU15, EU25 and South American migrants attained paid employment across all levels of their highest education. By this I mean that, when comparing like with like, 69 per cent of all EU15 migrants who had a third-level degree attained paid employment, while the African migrants proportionate to their population recorded that 43 per cent attained paid employment. Concerning the lowest level of educational attainment recorded on the database, 50 per cent of EU15

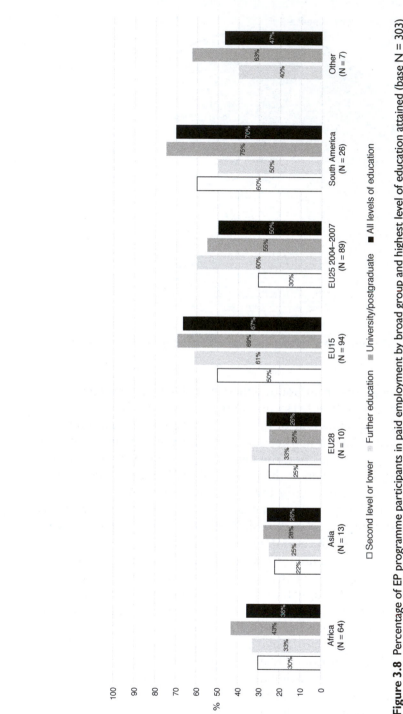

Figure 3.8 Percentage of EP programme participants in paid employment by broad group and highest level of education attained (base N = 303)

migrants and 60 per cent of South Americans with second-level education or lower attained paid employment compared with just 30 per cent of Africans (Figure 3.8). Thus, the results among the research populations are reproduced among the broad categories, forming an established pattern with no irregularities. These figures also highlight that Asian and EU28 migrants are at an even higher risk of marginalisation, as the database figures show they fare even worse than the African migrants in the labour market (this might however also be due to their very low numbers that accessed EP compared with other groups).

Ireland has a racial hierarchy where Whites are positioned at the top and Blacks at the bottom. Despite claims that Ireland does not have a colonial history like that of America, Blacks in Ireland experience a stratification similar to the US where they are most likely to be at the bottom of both the racial and economic ladder. This is not because they have lower academic levels, skills or abilities, but because the system is racially structured in ways that advantage Whites and guarantee their success over Blacks. The whiteness of the top tiers of the labour market which becomes evident when race is centred and a stratification framework employed means that not only is the system racialised to keep groups in their place, but, as argued by Bonilla-Silva and Baiocchi (2008: 146), its 'social networks' and 'norms of behaviours' will also be racialised.

Notes

1 The EU15 includes Ireland, the UK and all the EU countries before the enlargement on 1 May 2004, that is, Austria, Belgium, Denmark, Finland, France, Germany, Greece, Italy, Luxembourg, Netherlands, Spain, Sweden and Portugal. UK definition: England, Scotland, Wales, Northern Ireland, Isle of Man, Guernsey, Jersey.

2 I use the data from the 2011 Census instead of the 2016 data as the employment programme which was analysed covered the same period of 2009–2011.

3 I have used the terms 'non-Irish nationals', 'foreign nationals', 'Black Irish – any other background' to reflect the phraseology used in the CSO statistical reports. I have, however, put them in inverted commas to emphasise the difference from the terminology which I have decided to employ in this book – namely, 'migrants', 'immigrant' people of a particular 'descent', that is, African descent, Spanish descent, Polish descent.

4 EU25: defined as the EU15 plus the ten countries that joined on 1 May 2004 (i.e. Cyprus, Czech Republic, Estonia, Hungary, Latvia, Lithuania, Malta, Poland, Slovakia, Slovenia).

5 EU28: defined as the EU25, plus Bulgaria and Romania, which joined the EU on 1 January 2007, and Croatia, which joined on 1 July 2013.

6   All nationalities excluding EU27 and America (US).
7   All population percentages calculated as a proportion of their total population in the corresponding Census.
8   EP is an employability programme which supports migrants legally resident in Ireland to be able to compete in the labour market by improving their employability. Its placement is described to mean progression of participants into paid or unpaid employment, internship, work placement (including all forms of voluntary work) or progression into education or training courses.

In EP, all clients of the programme are voluntary participants who are mainly referred by previous participants of the programme through word of mouth, self-directed internet searches or referrals from voluntary and statutory agencies. The organisation is located in Dublin city centre and its service is available only to migrants who are resident in Dublin and the greater Dublin area. EP carries out CV preparations, six weeks' training on living and working in Ireland, and provides individual support to its clients in applying for jobs including interview preparation, and gives clients individual employment advice.

9   The Irish Qualifications Framework (NFQ), which goes from levels 1–10, describes the qualifications of the Irish education system and how they interlink. Levels 1–5 prepare learners to meet the minimum entry requirements for a range of higher education institutions and for employment. The Advanced certificate (level 6) is for advanced vocational/occupational skills, which enables Certificate holders to work independently or to progress to higher education and training. The Ordinary Bachelor Degree (level 7) is normally awarded after a three-year programme; Honours Bachelor Degree (level 8) after a four-year programme; and Master's degree (level 9) has the Taught and Research Masters which is awarded following a one- to two-year programme. Doctoral Degree is awarded level 10.
10 Education received after secondary further education that is distinct from university education.
11 Combining the further education and vocational training with third-level education put the educational attainment of all the groups almost at par with each other. It places the Nigerian migrants at 80 per cent, Polish migrants at 76 per cent and Spanish at 99 per cent.
12 From my interactions with Nigerian migrants, upskilling in Ireland often means down-skilling from level 8 degree courses to level 5 courses in order to access jobs with higher chances of being employed. These educational courses are not available to people with a prior degree. In the same vein, some experience employer rejection because they are overqualified. Many thus end up denying their university degrees to circumvent these limiting circumstances.
13 'Paid' employment is used to represent any employment opportunity with financial remuneration which is not a volunteering role.
14 'Unpaid' employment represents any career progression opportunity which does not receive financial remuneration. This includes voluntary work, internships, work placements, education and training. This term is deliberately applied to emphasise the change in the labour market where workers carry out essential work without financial remuneration.

15 The Economic and Social Research Institute (ESRI) and the Equality Authority on the Central Statistics Office's 2010 Quarterly National Household Survey showed that Black Africans and ethnic minority EU individuals had much lower labour force participation rates than Asians and White individuals from the EU countries. Employment rates were lower among Black African and ethnic minority EU individuals, at 38 per cent and 51 per cent respectively compared with an average employment rate of 61 per cent for the sample population (White Irish individuals). Black Africans were reported to be four times more likely to be unemployed than White Irish individuals (McGinnity, Watson and Kingston, 2012b).

16 The first letter represents a unique person; the second letter the nationality of descent of the participant (where s=Spain; n=Nigeria; p=Poland); male or female is given as the self-identified gender of the interviewee.

17 Other potential factors which could be at play (which the scope of the study did not cover) include ageism, considering that the Nigerian migrants were generally older than the European migrants. This might be a reflection of the kind of work and the level of work they were looking for, as entry-level work might suit the younger cohort from Europe.

18 This feeds into the outcry in 2017–18, where young people were seen to be moved into unpaid work via labour activation projects.

19 Some other issues which, due to the limited data available on EP's database, could not be compared include the types of jobs for which migrants were competing; if they were different between males and females, or between people from different nationalities in terms of language roles; or if the Polish men were seeking construction jobs. The age difference between groups might also influence the stage in their human development they were at, and hence the job types and levels they were seeking (whether entry level, middle or top management roles).

20 The terms EU15, EU25 and EU28 have been defined previously; however, there are slight variations in how they are applied in this section. Here, EU25 refers to the ten new member states post 2004 and EU28 refers to the three new member states post 2007 (Bulgaria, Romania and Croatia).

4

A framework for exposing racial stratification: theory and methodology

Do you think society is equal or unequal? Every time I ask that question, I get the same answer – that society is unequivocally unequal, from Blacks, Whites, males and females. Critical race theorists likewise insist that society is hierarchical. What this means in plain and practical terms is that some people in our society are at the top and some are at the bottom of the society. Who, then, is at the top and who is at the bottom? More importantly, how do we determine which group/s are at the top and which at the bottom? Although statistical data give a picture of inequality in Europe, very few projects focus on the racial hierarchies in society. In this chapter, I present key considerations for researching racial stratification by discussing how I examined the racial order in Ireland. It is advisable to read chapters 4 and 5 together.

Researching racial stratification in the labour market

What can CRT tell us about racial stratification? To investigate racial stratification in Ireland, two issues become immediately important: first, to identify if there is a racial order in Ireland and secondly, how to scientifically investigate the racial order to establish it is not just an anecdotal claim. To achieve this, a CRT methodology and a mixed-method research design are recommended. At a paradigmatic and methodological level, Silverman (2001: 25) recommends the use of qualitative methods if people's 'life history' or 'everyday life' is being explored. Until 2015, when this study was completed, while we knew Ireland like other modern states to be an unequal state, there was no clear scientific delineation of how groups are aligned. From the theoretical framework and the main tenets of CRT provided, I will now outline the key considerations and steps in the process.

Since the research sought to answer the question 'why', an explanatory study was chosen. The design consists of a two-stage process as part of a mixed method. Stage one consisted of secondary data analysis, while stage two was semi-structured interviews. The three sources of data utilised in the study included an employability programme (N = 639), Ireland's 2011 national Census statistics and thirty-two semi-structured interviews with migrants of Spanish, Polish and Nigerian descent living and working in Ireland. This chapter presents the detailed steps utilised in the study and how I converted theory to practice in researching racial stratification.

Defining the extent of the problem

Although many CRT theorists recognise racial stratification as the causal factor of racial inequality in the labour market in the United States, the difference in the US's relationship with its immigrant populations, enslavement and citizenship makes one question the relevance of such a framework in Europe. Defining the presence of a racial problem in any country is heavily dependent on being able to provide statistical evidence. While personal stories either through interviews or focus groups are admissible, providing statistical evidence is always more compelling and not easily refuted. This has to be carried out using a framework like CRT that centres race. The guiding question then is to determine who is at the top and who is at the bottom of the economic ladder. They are usually the same group/s at the top and bottom of the racial ladder. To determine the extent of the problem, the researcher must have an initial observation, typically from secondary data analysis. One very rich data source is the national Census data. You can also draw on data from an employability programme like EP[1] which provides services and targeted interventions for migrants.

If you have established that there is a differential in outcomes among people of different races, the second phase of researching racial stratification is to investigate/eliminate the usual suspects, such as educational attainment, gender, age, race, nationality of descent, language of the host community, right to work and other such factors. Secondary data analysis is also advisable here. In Europe, educational attainment and route of entry or immigration status are typically blamed for the disparity in outcome among groups, particularly between non-European and EU migrants. In order to eliminate the conflating of the outcomes of asylum seekers and undocumented migrants with people with a legal right to work in the country, all data sources must be of people with the legal right to live and work in the country without a work permit or restriction.[2] In Ireland, that would be a stamp 4 permit holder, or EU family or European citizenship. Concerning education, analysis of the statistical data should compare like with like, that is is there a differential in outcomes among groups with university or school-leaving qualifications while controlling for race, nationality of descent or age, or any of the possible intersecting axes that the researcher chooses.

Designing the research method

To determine the research method, your deductions after the initial analysis should create or leave the researcher with some 'why' questions. Examples of the 'why' questions in my study include:

1 Why were the Black workers in EP and the 2011 Census statistics at the bottom of the economic ladder in Ireland despite their levels of education and ability to communicate in English, the language of the host community?
2 If the disparity in labour market outcomes is due to migration, then all migrants with equivalent educational attainment should have the same/similar labour market outcomes. This was not the case. Why?

This means the researcher needs to answer a 'why' question and find a theoretical framework that explicitly centres race or racial inequality. CRT is a good choice as the only theoretical framework that foregrounds racial inequality in a racial stratification framework. Next is developing a research question and method that can explain the initial statistical result and observations. Remember, you first need to make an observation which may or may not be a problem, before you begin the research. This observation is very important as it is linked to the question you want to answer – your research question. For a racial stratification study, an explanatory design (see Creswell et al., 2006) is advisable because your research will have two strands, the first of which is a quantitative strand that comes from the quantitative data analysis of either an organisation's database (like EP's) and/or the Census data. The second strand is qualitative data collection that could be through semi-structured interviews with selected informants. A primary mixing strategy is required in your research design where the quantitative strand is sequentially followed by the qualitative one. The qualitative result can in part be employed to explain the quantitative observation. This kind of explanatory design answers the 'causal why question' and occurs in two distinct interactive phases (Vaus, 2001; Mathews and Ross, 2010). The quantitative result serves a dual purpose – it provides statistical data of how groups fare in the economy; and it is also used to make decisions about the qualitative research questions, sample size, groupings and data collection in Phase two of the study. Creswell et al. (2006) describe studies involving these types of processes as explanatory design because the qualitative phase is implemented for the purposes of explaining the initial results in more depth. Morse (1991) called it sequential triangulation, while Morgan (1998) referred to this as the qualitative follow-up approach.

This design is beneficial for a number of reasons. First, it enables the researcher to decide which groups to investigate. Secondly, the fact that the quantitative and qualitative strands are carried out in two different phases and only one type of data are collected at a time is an advantage, as it makes the design easy to implement. Thirdly, the final report in this design can be written with a quantitative section followed by a qualitative section, which makes it straightforward to write with a clear delineation for readers (Creswell et al., 2006).

Choosing the research population in racial stratification research

There are a number of sources from which data can be gathered. These could include members of the host community, who are a data-rich source on how they recognise the racial category of migrants and how that influences their responses; while employers and human resource managers could be data-rich informants on how they select suitable candidates and promote staff. However, Zuberi and Bashi (1997: 679) state that 'racial stratification is a dichotomous hierarchy' where some are located at the bottom and some at the top, and to properly study it 'one must look at the social relations between and the socioeconomic outcomes for both the group that comes out on top and the one that is on the bottom'. A comparison of this nature enriches the extent to which your research findings can be applied, particularly in determining if the findings are unique to a specific group or a societal problem, that is, if there is a systemic problem or one that is due to individual deficit. From these three possible information sources, the narratives of migrants, whose racial stratification is being investigated, is recommended. This means the groups with the largest representation at the top and bottom will be your best data source for purposes of comparison. In this study, the largest groups with the best and worst outcomes in EP were chosen as the data source. They indeed proved to be very rich informants, with counterstories on the labour market experience of migrants, how they recognised the racial strata, and the pragmatic steps they took in negotiating the various social and politico-economic systems. Having groups at opposite ends of the spectrum provides opportunities to compare how the same economic system treats its migrant populations differently in the same study.

The three data sources I employed in this study include thirty-two semi-structured interviews conducted between October 2014 and February 2015. All the interviews were recorded, transcribed and subsequently thematically analysed. The second data source was the EP 2009–2011 database of 639 unique individuals, which was analysed using SPSS statistical analysis software. The third source was the Irish 2011 Census statistics. In this case, the CSO 2011 database search engine was employed to generate specific tables, and Excel spreadsheets were utilised to display the data. The rationale for choosing the three migrant populations, Spanish, Polish and Nigerians, is that at 241 out of 639 persons (37.7 per cent), they formed the largest groups that accessed EP between 2009 and 2011.[3] Respectively, they also represented Western Europeans, Eastern Europeans and Africans generally, and Black Africans more specifically. In addition to this, the Census statistics show Black Africans are at the bottom of the economic ladder and White Europeans at the top. This fulfilled the theoretical position of comparing the outcome of those at the bottom with those at the top.

Researching the racial order in Ireland

We have urged analysts to search for alternative methodologies to comprehend how racial stratification produces racial inequality' (Zuberi and Bonilla-Silva, 2008: 335)

As Zuberi and Bonilla-Silva have suggested, I indeed devised a means of scientifically researching racial stratification in Ireland. This simple process directly converts theory to practice by interpreting the theory of immigration and racial stratification proffered by Zuberi and Bashi (1997). Despite the value of quantitative data in researching racial stratification, the human element is invaluable to its interpretation. This human element can be attained in research through qualitative methods such as interviews and focus groups, asking interviewees questions in a way that honours the values and theoretical understanding of CRT. Collaborating with research participants by providing the possibility to accommodate their ideas and suggestions (Creswell et al., 2006) can make the process transformative for the participants and curtail the possibility of further marginalising research participants. This section provides a step-by-step account of how I researched the racial order in Ireland and the key consideration.

Basic interview procedure

To maintain good research ethics, the basic procedures for conducting in-depth interviews are universal. This includes setting the criteria for selecting research informants and obtaining the participants' consent. During the interview process itself, adequate consideration must be given to confidentiality and participants' safety; offer the possibility for interviewees to withdraw from the process. If audio-recording is involved, offer to turn off or erase the recording at any point; and offer access to the transcript for correction or acceptance if so requested by the interviewees. All the interviews in my study were recorded, labelled with code numbers and transcribed afterwards. To guarantee the anonymity of the interviewees, the names of the informants and all identifiable references to their employers and colleagues were deleted or altered where necessary in the transcripts.

Semi-structured interviews

Thirty-two semi-structured face-to-face interviews which lasted from forty-five minutes to one hour were conducted at a suitable time in comfortable, confidential settings. Although saturation can occur during interviews, where new data are not being generated from the interview (Glaser and Strauss, 2009), I carried out ten interviews per group as each new narrative added a different perspective. Twelve interviews were conducted for the Nigerians because of the higher uptake from the group.

Selection criteria

The primary selection criteria for the participants included legal residency right to live and work in Ireland without a work permit; current employment either in paid or unpaid work; and being a first-generation migrant from one of the three selected research populations – Poland, Spain and Nigeria. The sample size was determined based on employment status projection for each selected group and a gender balance of one male and one female for each criterion. This included participants in senior management, middle management, minimum waged occupations and unpaid work. Sixty per cent of the participants in the study were anonymously invited from EP via an email invitation to past participants who were no longer users of the service. The other 40 per cent were directly invited from outside EP in order to access participants in senior management roles.

Interview guide

An initial questionnaire with two sections was developed to collate biographical, non-identifiable data including age, gender, current nationality and nationality on arrival in Ireland, family composition, salary, length of residency in the state and migration route into Ireland.[4] Section two of the questionnaire addressed migrants' understanding of racial stratification in Ireland. The questions were grounded in a CRT understanding of racial stratification. In this case, I made particular reference to the scholarship on immigration and racial stratification by Zuberi and Bashi (1997). First, from their claim that 'new arrivals may not know their race when they arrive, but they certainly learn it eventually' (Zuberi and Bashi, 1997: 676), it was important to find out what immigrants in Ireland know about racial stratification, how they knew it and the racial order they recognised in Ireland. To achieve this goal, interviewees were presented with a blank page and asked to give a diagrammatic representation of how they saw members of four nationalities positioned in Ireland relative to each other – Spanish, Polish, Nigerian and Irish (see Figure 4.1, p. 111). This question is based on the theoretical understanding that race is relational (Fanon, 2000; Goldberg, 2000). Thus, the selected newcomers must be compared with the host community.

Let me address one question I am always asked at conferences, and always by White people who critique my data: they ask why I do not compare Nigerians with other African countries. The question I ask them is, what will that do for a racial stratification research? Some White people are interested in showing/proving a migrant deficit in the labour market rather than acknowledging that systemic racism might be endemic. Only comparing among migrants from the same group (i.e. Black Africans against Black Africans) will help them achieve that outcome. It can only show intra-group layering and not the inter-group layering. And racial stratification is about how races are stratified relative to other racial categories. To satisfy that question, however, the evidence of racial stratification in Ireland presented in chapter 3 shows that other Black migrant groups from EP have similar labour market outcomes as the representative group. Also, the 2016 Census shows that Congolese migrants have a 63 per cent unemployment rate compared with Nigerian migrants in Ireland at 42.5 per cent. So to that question, I say here that I have not compared the African group with the worst labour market outcome with the White Europeans, but rather I have compared the largest Black African population in Ireland with the largest European group in Ireland. However, to limit this challenge in a racial stratification research, ensure the secondary data analysis of the initial problem incorporates other groups. You can then carry out the individual interviews/surveys or focus groups with the representative groups to enable you to drill down to micro-level analysis.

Questions in racial stratification research

Where is CRT in these questions?

The success of your research hinges on how you phrase your questions. Many young researchers and those new to CRT wonder how they can practically carry out CRT research. First, you would need to know why CRT research is different from other forms of research. How can you show that your research is different? What key features of CRT have you incorporated into your research? CRT theorists recognise that the framework is growing. The call for new methods meant I could directly interpret and convert theory to practice. But how can CRT researchers access those harder-to-reach human subjective feelings and inner truths which are important to the authenticity of a CRT study? A light bulb moment in developing this method of researching racial stratification came from sociologist, Alice Feldman, who viewed my initial interview questions and asked 'where is your CRT in these questions?' What makes a CRT narrative different from other narratives? Is it the interview questions, the researcher's interpretations or the insider/outsider status of the researcher to the research subject? The following theory sharpened my critical thinking about the racial order in Ireland and raised questions on whether Ireland has similar racial categorisation and order to the United States. Zuberi and Bashi state that 'migrants of various national origins are "forced" to assimilate as members of different racial groups because of racial stratification'. They add that 'immigrants lose their ethnic identifiers as they are reconstructed into races; therefore racial assimilation of immigrants of various ethnic groups is central to the construction of the racial hierarchy in the United States' (Zuberi and Bashi, (1997: 769). These theoretical ideas are discussed in the interview guide which I adopted for the semi-structured interviews. It consists of the following five sections.

1 Commence with an open invitation to the interviewees to recount their trajectory in the Irish labour market from arrival up to their present roles; use three sub-questions to help probe if needed. These questions are relative to changes in the migrants' career goal from arrival in Ireland until the present time; whether it had changed; the influencers and attempts they had made to change their jobs. This was particularly useful in my study as it revealed stories many of the

interviewees reported they had not shared with anyone previously. A leading or normal research question is often an invitation to talk about any discrimination they have encountered or if they have ever experienced racism. A CRT research question should ask interviewees if they had every tried to change their jobs and why. This would unlock many of the experiences of discontent they had encountered in the workplace and recruitment process. By asking why people want to change their jobs, the researcher will uncover more depth, those often untold stories that people refrain from telling in a bid to be politically correct and appear grateful.

2 Section two covers migrants' trajectory into the country. This is to establish how status and racial identities are imposed by categories or subcategories, presented for new migrants to fit into, the changes and conflict that arise for migrants as a result of conflicting status from their home countries or previous location to Ireland. This allows the researcher to identify migrants who are down-skilling or upskilling in their career trajectory. When Zuberi and Bashi (1997) say new migrants are given new categories to fit into, how do we as CRT researchers know that and how do we research it? These theoretical understandings offer researchers ways to think with a CRT consciousness when developing interview questions.

3 Section three will help you examine migrants' experience of race, dominance and/or privilege in the workplace. At this point, first refer the interviewees to the initial question in the questionnaire and discuss how they placed the four groups in the diagram in the format they did. Secondly, ask the participants how they know where groups are placed in Ireland; at the top, bottom, in between or if absent. This section is the most insightful and extremely useful for a study of this nature because it initiates conversation about the diagrams drawn by interviewees (Figure 4.1) and how groups position different nationalities on the strata. In my study, it proved that migrants indeed have a way of knowing the racial order not only in the US but in Ireland also. It also provided insight about how migrants know their place and how intersecting identities affect the way actors are layered on the strata even when of the same race (see details in chapter 5).

4 Section four is on managing difference in the workplace. It is important to keep asking questions that honour the CRT tradition. Take the opportunity to be innovative in your questions to stimulate deeper reflections from research participants. In my own study, I asked the following questions: What makes you feel (un)comfortable at work? Are there aspects of yourself you do not show all the time at work? What are they and why? I was also particularly interested in gaining

insight about 'acceptance'. Thus, a number of questions were asked about how they know if they are accepted or not in the workplace; and how they would define or recognise acceptance.

5 Section five gives voice to the marginalised and often silenced people, to make the research subjects part of the research. It is made up of statements usually bandied about by the general public about people of migrant descent. In a CRT thesis, giving voice to the silenced is important. When well managed, it creates an opportunity for groups to develop their counterstory to the dominant narrative. The statements in this study covered three significant areas that were in the public domain between 2009 and 2011. The method is to repeat each statement one at a time to the research subjects, who are then given time to respond. Note these are not questions but statements. The three statements utilised in my study were:

a) meritocracy – 'If you work hard enough you will get a job';
b) relationship between the natives and newcomers – 'Immigrants are taking our jobs' and;
c) colour blindness – 'Race is no longer an issue.'

Racial stratification in Ireland

You will by now agree that it matters who is at the bottom and top of the economic ladder; if not, no one would be trying to avoid the bottom. But is such a conversation useful or is it aimed at gaining what Song (2004: 859) calls 'moral and material capital'? Or does it allow the telling of the story of marginalised bodies by 'opening a window onto ignored or alternative realities' (Delgado and Stefancic, 2012: 45). The three independent data sets show a White over Black ascendancy in Ireland. This means that Ireland is not only a racial state (Goldberg, 2001) and a racist state (Lentin and McVeigh, 2006), but Ireland is also a heavily racially stratified state.

Similar to the migrants in the US, migrants in Ireland are able to recognise the racial order, their position and the position of others within the strata. In their theory of immigration, Zuberi and Bashi (1997: 670) insist that 'racial systems must have mechanisms for determining who is in which race as it is what determines where people, families and other groups fit into the racial hierarchy'. They also maintain that immigrants in the US who do not know their race on arrival eventually know it because a racial identity is imposed by the racial stratification system which operates in the United States. These ideas represent my starting point for investigating racial stratification in Ireland and the process of converting theory to practice.

To determine the racial structure in Ireland, a questionnaire was devised to help address racial stratification in the Irish labour market and the extent to which the data generated supported this argument, as discussed in earlier sections. In response to the question, 'how do you think society is arranged?' 100 per cent of respondents agreed that Irish society is hierarchical. Next, they were asked to represent diagrammatically how the Spanish, Polish, Nigerian and Irish people are positioned in society.[5] Twenty-eight interviewees drew a stair-like or hierarchical structure (Figure 4.1).[6] With varying degrees of hesitation, all respondents positioned the Irish at the top and Nigerians at the bottom, except for one who said he would have placed the Nigerians at the bottom as well, if he had not heard more negative comments about the Polish than the Nigerians. From this, a hierarchical structuring of groups in Ireland and the order in which actors are arranged became evident. This supports the claim of Zuberi and Bashi (1997) that migrants know and have a way of knowing the racial order in their host country. It is important to reiterate that race was centred in this study as the primary stratifier (racial differentiator), with nationality of descent and skin colour as ways in which race was expressed and identified. Note the following important factors and indicators. Gender was not specified in the exercise; and three of the nationalities (Irish, Polish and Spanish) have the commonalities of typically being White European Union citizens; both the Spanish and Polish groups are migrant groups relative to the Irish in Ireland. It is significant that the respondents were nonetheless able to separate these hypothetical persons onto different strata. This means there are other factors through which race is nuanced. What are they?

The Irish were mainly positioned at the top of the hierarchy because they are members of the host country. In the case of the Spanish and Polish, where both groups are of migrant descent relative to Ireland, 72 per cent of the interviewees placed the Spanish second on the strata from the pinnacle, with the Polish on the third rung, while 19 per cent placed the Polish second and the Spanish third. A very small number (3 per cent) placed the Nigerians third above the Polish, and 6 per cent placed both the Spanish and Polish second on the strata with Nigerians at the bottom. In terms of the diagrammatic representation, Figure 4.1 shows the four basic structures drawn by the interviewees. For ease of explanation and to discuss the impact of racial stratification, the various diagrams have been interpreted and combined in Figure 4.2.

From here, a picture of an Ireland that is racially stratified in a vertical or top-down order signifying a dichotomous hierarchy becomes evident. This supports Zuberi and Bashi (1997) that 'racial stratification is a dichotomous hierarchy' where some are located at the bottom

The Question:
Place the following nationalities on a diagram to represent how you see them positioned in society

1 = Nigerian   2 = Spanish   3 = Polish   4 = Irish

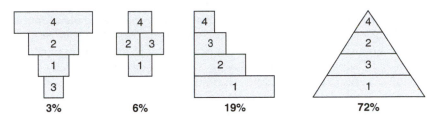

3%   6%   19%   72%

This suggests
✓ A dichotomous nature of society
✓ Top-down/vertical arrangement of society
✓ White–Black ascendancy with White at the top and Black at the bottom

Figure 4.1 Percentage response by interviewees of the racial order in Ireland

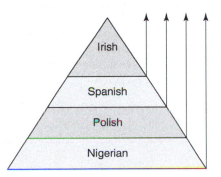

Figure 4.2 Summary of how Irish society is racially stratified

and some at the top. In this case, White is at the top and Black at the bottom. Delgado and Stefancic (2004: 3) described this as a 'white-over-colour ascendancy'. This racial order in Ireland can also be framed as a vertical location of racialised groups within its system of stratification (Gold, 2004: 953). It produces the exact same hierarchical picture of the Irish 2011 and 2016 Census data and the 2009–2011 EP database (639 unique individuals), with Black Africans at the bottom and White Irish and White Europeans at the top. Despite the small sample size of the interviews, the statistical evidence provides validity for these findings through triangulation which unveils similar hierarchical structures from three independent sources. This simple yet theoretically based method is reproducible with larger groups and across other European countries to determine the racial order.

Notes

1 See note 8 of chapter 3.
2 Student visas only allow twenty hours of work during term time. It is not advisable to include this group in determining the racial hierarchy.
3 EP employment officers have routinely mentioned experiencing more difficulty for clients of African descent than their counterparts from the EU in placement progression into paid employment, and professional or higher managerial roles. An initial analysis of EP's database seemed to disagree with this view, as there appeared to be no significant difference in the rates of placement for clients from these three population groups. However, controlling for employment revealed significant differences where Nigerians had the lowest rate of progression. Also, it took more than one year to place 40 per cent of Nigerian clients, as compared with 21 per cent for Poles and 17 per cent for Spaniards (in-depth analysis of these data is available in Joseph, 2015, 2018).
4 The questionnaire design was premised on the theory of immigration and racial stratification (Zuberi and Bashi, 1997).
5 Native Irish citizens were added to the questionnaire because race is relational. In other words, difference is experienced relative to others. As the host community, it is important to compare the positioning of others relative to Irish natives.
6 Initially, the first four interviewees were presented with two diagrams. However, this idea was abandoned and the remaining twenty-eight interviewees were then asked to give their personal interpretation.

5

Knowing your place: racial stratification as a 'default' starting position

In a country with racial groups like White, Black or Black Irish, Asian or Asian-Irish, it suggests that racial groups are created and categorised as they become visible in society. While these have some very useful purposes like collation of Census data and the provision of public services, it becomes problematic when we consider who categorises people, the power dynamics involved, and the meaning associated with the categories in terms of where, how and with whom individuals are categorised. All of these have implications, for example, if a person is categorised as EU or non-EU; from the Third World, developing or developed world. Other pertinent concerns include the arrangement of the categories: if flat – signalling racial equality, or top-down – signifying a hierarchical ranking; the status, privileges or negative judgements attached to each category; and the challenges they present to the categorised group or group members when exercising their agency. Let's be clear, there are racial categories with value implications, and the following questions then arise: can group members choose or change their racial categories? More importantly, how do members of the host community and newcomers know their categories?

In Ireland, racial hierarchies exist where some are at the top and some at the bottom. Based on extensive empirical evidence from labour market outcomes of migrants in Ireland and analysis of semi-structured interviews, this chapter discusses the racial categorisation of migrants through a racial stratification framework and how it is experienced as a 'default' starting position by migrants. The key features of racial stratification discussed within this chapter include its homogenising attributes, the inter- and intra-group layering of group members, and the available hierarchies and how migrants fit into them as members of racial groups. The chapter provides insight on how immigrants know and occupy their place on the racial strata. It concludes with a discussion of the implications of racial stratification on the socio-economic outcomes of Black and White workers and how it differs along colour lines.

The impact of racial stratification in Ireland

Living and working in racially stratified societies directly and indirectly affects the lives of all their inhabitants because all groups do not have the same starting point. Although the biological existence of race has no scientific merit, race is implicated in the way Black and White workers in the Irish labour market are separated at the bottom and top of the economic ladder. Figure 5.1 shows a representation of the four nationalities in the study and the varied distances they would have to negotiate to attain the same result/outcome in the labour market. It immediately presents three interesting interpretations about how racial hierarchies impact on the lives of those on the strata. The first obvious implication is that groups stratified higher up on the racial ladder will have easier access to their labour market objectives than those lower down. The second is the converse of the first: the level of difficulty and distance to attain the same economic goals as those at the top gets progressively more difficult and more competitive as you move down the ladder. In essence, groups at the very bottom of the ladder have to work at least three times as hard as groups stratified at the top to achieve the same results. This is not because such opportunities/jobs demand more, but because those at the bottom have to start from a lower position on the strata. They have to contend with secondary issues which those stratified above them do not have to face. One respondent explained it thus:

> My interpretation is that if they [Polish, Spanish, Nigerian and Irish nationality] want the same position, if they start from the same point,

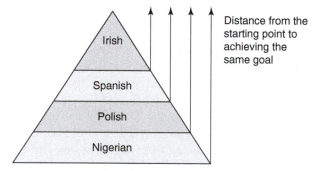

Figure 5.1 The implications of racial stratification in the Irish labour market

some already have privileges. ... In my opinion, Nigerians have to be even more prepared to demonstrate their value and that is why in this ranking they have the worst position. ... It is completely possible but harder. (EsMale)

The distance to attain the same goal for the Spanish migrants in Ireland is definitely longer than for the host, but shorter than for their Polish counterparts, and the Polish likewise will have a shorter distance to reach the same goal than the Nigerians.

While belief in a top-down hierarchy can also shape group relations, public policy formation and political alliances (Song, 2004: 859), it also calls into question our taken-for-granted belief in meritocracy and equal opportunity. Living in a racially stratified society invariably means, first, that if every migrant puts in the same effort, the labour market strata will remain unchanged. Those at the bottom would have to put in much more effort to attain the same result as those stratified above them. Secondly, those at the bottom, in this case Black migrants, are at a higher risk of being marginalised due to their race; and thirdly, while inter-/intra-group mobility on the labour market strata is affected by race and gender, race has a greater impact on labour market outcomes across groups than within groups. What I mean by this is that among White males and females from the same group, race is not an issue in their positioning on the economic or racial strata. However, gender will be an issue. To address a question I am frequently asked: among people of African descent in Western society, race will have a bigger impact on your outcome than your gender. This does not mean that gender is insignificant; to the contrary, Blacks are affected by their intersectionality, for example, a Black woman or a Black, gay, Muslim, male. In the case of a White Irish person, race does not come into the mix, as males and females occupy the same strata when it comes to race. A White Irish woman's gender, sexuality, religion or any of the protected characteristics will be employed to symbolically 'colour' her and locate her lower than a heterosexual, White, Christian, able-bodied male. A White male will be symbolically 'coloured' as well by any of those characteristics. While every group is impacted by race, the effect is more pronounced along colour lines based on nationality, race and skin colour. The Black African migrants, who are on all counts over-represented at the bottom of the labour market, are also the group at the bottom of the racial ladder in Ireland. White European migrants, while not at the pinnacle are also not at the bottom. They fare better than their Black African counterparts in terms of employment opportunities. The point of this conclusion is not just to show how Blacks in the Irish labour market are more marginalised than other migrants, but also to highlight the structural nature of racial inequality.

Racial stratification in the labour market is not a personal or individual matter; neither is it an accidental outcome. It is endemic to the structure of the labour market system but largely unacknowledged by those in power as the colour-coded hierarchy of the labour market order is not called into question or publicly challenged. In fact, groups stratified at the top of the racial order do not readily admit to the advantages it provides, and neither do they recognise the distance their automatic positioning at/close to the pinnacle of the racial ladder imposes on groups positioned below. The racial stratification of Whites over non-Whites is the unacknowledged affirmative action for Whites that advantage them over those categorised as Blacks and non-Whites all over the world. It is like a visible national identity card that is carried everywhere because it is attached to individuals. It affects the labour market outcomes of migrant groups in a manner over which they have no personal control. By this I mean that assigned racial strata are unchangeable. Group members can, however, change their position on the economic ladder through minority agency and personal action (see discussion in chapter 7). Although race also interacts with other expressions of difference, such as gender and class through the *classed race* (see below) to influence the labour market outcomes of actors and their inter-/intra-group positioning, the impact of racial stratification is more common and has become the de facto way society is organised. Notwithstanding Ireland's or Europe's claim of commitment to diversity, inclusion, integration and equality, many of its actions and policies function in ways which guarantee stratification and maintain this present racial order. Racial stratification is not about where you end up – though it impacts it; rather, it is about where you start.

Ways of knowing the racial position

Our understanding of racial stratification, and where one is located, is socially constructed and transferred by the outcome of people of similar racial identification. This became evident when I asked the interviewees how they knew where each of the four groups in the study were positioned. They identified six main ways through which groups know where they and other groups are located on the racial strata. Each of these will be described by text extracted from the interviewees' narratives.

1 *Share of the state's resources available to each group*. People are often evaluated based on their resources. One of the ways interviewees in

the study were able to separate groups into different strata was based on the share of the state's resources available to each group. This is observable by the representation of people of each nationality of descent in management roles, as noted here by ApFemale:

It is what I see around me, ... that more Polish or Spanish people are in higher positions than maybe Nigerians. ... I see less people from Nigeria in the hotel in higher positions. Maybe not all as you can meet people from Nigeria in better position too but what I mean is that it is not very often like other nationalities. For example in the bar, we have all nationalities but in the senior position, you find more Spanish, Polish or Germans than Nigerians. (ApFemale)

Another observable difference in access to income comes from the total population of each group in the country and the geographical location where they stay:

I don't know how I am going to explain this. I put it in the way we are positioned in the City. The Irish usually live in the nice areas, in nice houses and places with gardens. I know they are more in numbers, ... I know there are poor Irish people but they have more money. The total number of them as well is more. My GP is a Polish in a Polish clinic so I feel the Polish are well integrated here. The Nigerians, well some of them have businesses on Moore Street, I don't know if they are Nigerian shops but they are Africans. ... Oh I feel embarrassed now. (DsFemale)

2 *Status of each group, including public opinion, the respect they receive in public spaces and the media representation of the groups.* In terms of public opinion held about each group, DpFemale states, 'it is from the way my colleagues talk about the different groups, how they work and it is about their character as well.' GnFemale cites the media and the general mistrust directed towards certain groups:

For the Nigerians, people generally have this mistrust of them. Most of the times, I hear people say are you from Nigeria, umm ... mm Nigerians. For the Polish, they feel the Polish are getting their jobs. For Black people, the way they are portrayed in the media, people think we are from the jungle! (GnFemale)

While this negativity towards the Black African groups was named by the participants, DpFemale reminds us that:

It is not only happening to Black people. I don't see a lot of respect for the Polish. (DpFemale)

3 *Their historical position*, which results in groups being homogenised and group bias held about them. The interviewees who positioned

migrants of Spanish descent higher than the Nigerian and Polish migrants mainly attributed it to their perceived national wealth. This wealth is not directly linked to individual wealth, but to the real/perceived historical wealth of each race and nationality. In this instance, race and nationality are conflated, and then viewed as homogeneous groups. The group becomes a classed race (see discussion on classed race in the next section), thus allowing the ascription of stereotypes to whole populations. KnFemale makes an interesting observation about how the stereotypical image of Nigerians in the public domain mainly portrays negativity about the group, further worsening their racial positioning at the bottom of the ladder:

To be honest now, you won't even be able to do a blame game here because the kind of bias out there about Nigerians ... it is on the street. If you say you are a Nigerian, the first thing you hear is that they are spongers and they've come to live off others, to be on the dole [social welfare] to take the country's money, they are lazy. So can you blame anybody? If a Spanish person says I am Spanish, they don't go 'oh sponger'. Those phrases out there go before you. And you can add to the list that Nigerians are fraudulent. They never think Nigerians have entrepreneurial skills; they are highly educated or enlightened. You don't hear people saying things like that. (KnFemale)

4 *Response of the host community to different groups – if and how the groups are accepted, respected, liked or disliked.* This concerns the response of the host community to its newcomers and it is seen as an indicator of the racial positioning of each group:

Some Irish people don't like the Polish people, maybe because their migration to Ireland is many years old. Maybe after a while, they will change about Spanish people. Maybe they will start to hate the Spanish people, I don't know. I hear bad things about Polish people that lots of Polish people came here. For the Nigerians, I don't hear bad things about them because of the immigration from Nigeria, there are not many from Nigeria. (CsMale)

The response of members of the host community is also evaluated in terms of the respect and dignity with which group members are treated:

The other day, I was on the queue for a taxi and the next person was a Black taxi driver and there was a middle aged White man who came and he didn't want to get in that taxi because he was a Black driver and he went to the next taxi. ... I was waiting at the queue in the supermarket, the way they received me I feel is better and different than the way they receive others and they are usually darker skin people. Only a few times but I observe that. (BsFemale)

Although the differential treatment of Black and White bodies in Ireland in these instances might direct attention to human differences as the problem, it is important to bear in mind that the problem is not the difference itself but in how the difference is treated. The attitude of the host is also reflected in their willingness to engage with the different cultures, languages or aspects of the lives of the migrant groups within its borders. This attitude is seen as an indicator of the racial positioning of actors. For example, the interviewees observed that many Irish people travel to countries like Spain frequently while barely visiting African countries like Nigeria. Many who do, go on humanitarian or aid programmes. There is also a higher uptake from members of the host community in learning languages like Spanish and French over Polish or any of the African languages.

5 *Exhibited similarities and closeness to the host, including physical and social distance* (hereafter referred to as 'sameness'). The similarities shared between the White European respondents and the native Irish population are taken as a matter of fact without the group acknowledging its advantageous properties. The Black African respondents from Nigeria who interestingly also named whiteness highlighted the automatic rights it provides for its possessors. This sameness occurs in terms of being EU citizens, of phenotypic and cultural whiteness, of a commonly recognised official EU language, and of cultural, ethnic and geographical closeness. The responses of members of the host community (the native Irish) to groups exhibiting attributes close to theirs are seen as indicators of the racial order in the state, as possession of attributes similar to the host guarantee groups a positioning closer to the pinnacle. While the majoritarian story justifies the differential access to state resources based on citizenship rights, the fact still remains that EU citizenship automatically stratifies EU over non-EU citizens, disadvantaging the latter and creating inequality by making the playing field uneven. For example, CsMale stated:

Because I am from Europe, it is easier to get a job. I have better rights. I know people who are from Brazil and they will need visas, things I don't have to worry about. I think that is a way to do that stratification. But it is like that in every country. ... I think that when countries treat different visas differently, then that stratification will happen. (CsMale)

Concerning the reason/s why cultural difference and social and geographical distance are indicators of the racial order, EsMale's narrative describes it aptly:

The Irish, Spanish and Polish are ranked higher because they are European countries. The Polish are a very big community that is established in Ireland in the past 20 years. The Spanish community has also become big. They have the facilities that some European citizens can have. Also, their culture is similar. There are fewer differences in the culture between Polish, Spanish and Irish. At the bottom, I will say Nigerians because you move from a Continent, so I guess the cultural differences are bigger and there are less opportunities for Nigerians because companies are not looking for people to cover African markets. (EsMale)

6 *The de facto racial advantaging of certain groups over others.* The observation of the de facto positioning of Nigerians and Blacks at the bottom of the racial strata in Ireland:

I don't like to place one set of people above the other so for me it is really difficult. But I chose that because here in Ireland, *that is how it is.* I put Polish last and Nigeria third. If not that I had heard bad things about Polish people, I will put Nigerians last. (CsMale)

Similarly, BpFemale placed the Nigerians at the bottom of the strata while automatically ascribing a nationality to the Nigerians which located them outside the EU and its privileges. What becomes clear from this is the way people are automatically categorised based on their nationality of descent. The European migrants in the study did not at any point consider that the hypothetical Nigerian could be mixed race, a dual citizen or in fact represent individuals with European background either by birth, marriage or descent:

Irish I chose in the first position because they are quite nice and very polite, well most of them. The Spanish and Polish, because we are from other countries, and because we have EU status. We will *always* be in the second position and it will be the same in other countries if you are an immigrant there. I chose Nigeria at the bottom position. (BpFemale) (emphasis added)

The migrants of Nigerian descent recognised the racial order from how meritocracy is counterpoised by social structures that guarantee racially unequal outcomes in the labour market in favour of White Europeans – as a matter of rights:

However you look at it, if I was competing with an Irish person for a role, qualification will not be the benchmark. The first thing will be that she has a right. She has been here and you just came in so it is hers. (BnFemale)

Black Africans are intensely aware of the disadvantage experienced by their group. They view meritocracy as a myth:

In any scheme or organisation, you will see the Irish at the top, whether they know it [the job] or not. They are always at the top and I have not seen an organisation with a Nigerian at the top. The Polish are next irrespective of their level of communication. You will see in many offices that you are being managed by someone who is not able to communicate as well as you. (FnFemale)

What I am trying to buttress is that regarding opportunities, the beneficiaries, regardless of their peculiar characteristics, qualification, ability, whatever ... I see the Spanish as being valued at a higher level. The Polish are next before any other African or Nigerian. (InFemale)

There is a de facto positioning of White EU citizens over 'others'. This is a colour- and race-based differential treatment that serves as a structural barrier in the labour market, producing marginalisation and economic inequality for Blacks and economic dominance for Whites. It is common knowledge that for many job opportunities, native Irish persons are considered first because of racial rules that guarantee that race and nationality of descent affect people and make it thrice as hard for some groups. HnMale, a medical registrar of Nigerian descent who placed Nigerians at the bottom of the strata, states in response to the question:

In every aspect, statistics have many Nigerians in the social welfare bracket, not by choice but as the only option left to them. Secondly, in the private market, because the other three groups are within the EU, you find it difficult for them [Nigerians] to fit in and also looking at the colour [skin]. So the EU places the others above Nigerians. There is also the issue of accent even when you are very educated, many people can pretend they don't understand you. (HnMale)

AnFemale and CsMale further reinforced these words:

In terms of the Nigerians, the colour, the accent, everything puts them at the bottom in terms of competing in an even market. So in the labour market, even the Polish, in as much as they are disrespected between the three, I think the Polish will be preferred to Nigerians. So even the policy within the European Union which says who to employ, says the EU before non-EU already guarantees the rearrangement of people and that those groups get the job. (AnFemale)

I think it is something related to our background. Racism maybe 60 years ago was something normal. Today, if someone is racist, they are going to hide that. I think that is good that it is not so normal and people have to hide it now. So hopefully in the next 20, 30 years it might be different again. Though I think the older generations like my grandparents were very racist. I think that even now, I say I have not heard bad things about Nigerians but I place them at third [on the drawn strata], why didn't I place them first? I think I am racist and that makes me feel bad. I think if I was to come home with a Black girl today as the person whom I want to marry, how will my parents feel and react? (CsMale)

With the post-2016 proliferation of freedom to express racist comments unchallenged with increased anti-immigrant sentiments, CsMale might not make this comment today. The experience of Black workers in the study highlights how response to visible difference, including skin colour and accent, continues to be a major determinant of outcomes in the labour market, and hence a signifier of where actors are located on the racial ladder. It also indicates that social systems controlled by human factors can potentially exacerbate inequalities, as victims of the system become blamed and racial states continue to be key players in the perpetuation of racial inequality. It is undeniable that the labour market outcomes of migrants are affected by more than their individual ability and educational outcomes.

Classed race as a pre-existing racial positioning

I will now turn to how class interacts with race to influence the positioning and outcome of migrants in the labour market. Whiteness is not just about skin colour. It is about a tangible possession and the power such positions hold. Those who possess phenotypic whiteness typically see the world from the perspective of class because their race is not a problem and neither does it disadvantage them; rather, they are beneficiaries of its largesse (Joseph, forthcoming). Many of the proponents of race, on the other hand, typically see the world and how it is structured through race-conscious lenses. As important as class is to Marxists, Black and White migrants in Ireland do not directly identify class as a determinant of outcome in their labour market trajectory. Class, however, is an indirect determinant of the ascribed status and positioning of migrants on the racial strata on arrival in Ireland. From my study, the first indication that social class is an important factor in the racial stratification of migrants occurred when the interviewees who positioned the migrants of Spanish descent higher than the Nigerian and Polish migrants mainly attributed it to their perceived wealth. This wealth is not directly linked to individual wealth but to the perceived historical wealth of each race and nationality. In other words, rather than the individuals being classed, the historical social class of the group is by default attributed to the whole group, which I describe as a *classed race*. And unless there is an active intervention,[1] each race is classed and then ascribed to group members on arrival in the labour market as their default racial status and starting position, irrespective of individual achievement or attainment factors such as education or personally accumulated wealth.

One might wonder about groups that have similarity in skin colour. If skin colour operated in isolation, then every white skinned person would start at the same level in life. In the study, it should mean that Spanish, Polish and Irish groups are stratified on the same level. This is not the case, as they are nonetheless separable onto different rungs on the racial ladder based on five factors, further buttressing the argument that the races are classed or that people are seen as of a classed race. First, a group's positioning is drawn from the economic status of the represented nationalities rather than the individual's wealth. The national wealth position from a country's GDP is then ascribed to the general group and employed to separate the White EU groups onto different layers on the racial ladder. Groups from historically poorer countries are assigned positions at the bottom while those from historically richer nations with a higher GDP are assigned a stratum at the top. This is possible because society conflates race with nationality and skin colour. Phenotypic whiteness is automatically ascribed to EU groups without taking cognisance of a growing population of Black Europeans.[2] Rather, Black Irish/Black Europeans are treated as permanent strangers. The migrants of Spanish descent are positioned higher up than the Polish because they are from Western Europe, or the old EU as many respondents liked to describe it. This is because a Polish background is seen as poor or poorer, and that status is employed to place them lower on the ladder. It is important to reiterate that the classed race is not about personal attributes or individual achievement, but is due to nationality and how the country's historical wealth is perceived. Thus, even when for example a group's language ability in English was worse than the Black group, it was still stratified higher because it is not primarily about individuals but about groups and systemic inequality.

This idea of a 'classed race' which operates through the imputing of the historical status and class of each group to current groups is in consonance with the CRT tradition, which insists on taking a historical perspective of race. This is reflected in the stories of many of the interviewees where those whose race is classed higher are stratified higher in the labour market, benefiting from similarity with in-group members and subsequently attaining greater labour market mobility vis-à-vis those whose race is classed lower. In a similar manner, the class ascribed to the African continent is used to evaluate people of African descent. Many indigenous White Europeans have scant knowledge about the African continent and the African people, and views are typically characterised by stereotypes and negative perceptions. This stems from the definitions and teachings about Africa in Europe as 'Third World', Global South, 'developing' or 'underdeveloped'; speaking about 'slaves' rather than enslaved people. The way in which race is classed and ascribed to groups is not simply due to historical influences but also reflects current views held about group members. Negative publicity and stereotyping of not just migrants coming to take Irish jobs, but specifically of Black Africans as 'free loaders', 'spongers', 'lazy', 'slaves' and other historical imaging have infused society, with much negativity about people of Black African descent right from (and before) their arrival on Irish shores.

The 'classed race' is also predicated on the homogenisation of group members, where they are all expected to be the same, act the same and have the same labour market outcome. This can be a challenge, particularly when group members either resist or deviate from such expected group norms. It allows group members to be held accountable for their race and nationality of descent, as we see reflected for example in my study, where a medical practitioner who expressed shock that a patient refused to be treated by him because the patient got a 'tummy bug' during a visit to Nigeria. Other incidents include recruitment professionals assuming Nigerians speak French, or Black workers contending with insubordination from new intakes because they automatically assume the Black worker can only be junior staff. The real question you ask to get to the crux of such incidences is, what is it about this Black person that automatically makes visitors to the office or new intakes assume that they must be junior staff? This is a very common occurrence, with for example Black guest speakers at conferences being mistaken for doorkeepers or other services workers. Such experiences are insightful when you centre race in your understanding. We see that the ascribed default identity from a person's classed race is invoked on contact with the other despite their personal achievement until they have either proved to be different from the expected identity or they are known individually. It also means that active interventions, such as accurate information, can change the response to difference. A recent study on the recruitment of migrants suggests that employers fill in missing information they don't have about different groups from stereotypes (Kingston, McGinnity O'Connell, 2015). Although group members strive towards achieving positive distinctiveness through their individual mobility (Tajfel and Turner, 1979), the impermeability of the different strata makes that a challenge, particularly with the prejudgement employed to categorise actors. While many people do not openly perform racist acts, and the response to race might be expected to be different, the historical racial positioning and prejudgement of different groups is still pervasive though covertly perpetrated. It still functions as the way in which society automatically assigns its citizens and newcomers their racial positions. This is evident in Ireland from national Census statistics showing that many Black migrants are assigned to care work and are racialised into caring roles such as healthcare assistants, home support workers, nursing and social care workers. This is somehow too close to the era where Blacks were exploited during their enslavement, and presented as people who were only good and too happy to clean homes and care for others' families through the popular 'big mama' image and representation of enslaved Black people. Polish migrants themselves are automatically ascribed the attribute of being hardworking in physical strenuous roles like hotel operatives, construction workers and retail.

In summary, the racially structured hierarchy in the Irish labour market operates through a *classed race* system. Black actors, their countries, continents, culture and credentials are judged negatively, and are utilised to assign them to the bottom of the racial ladder, thus influencing their socio-economic outcomes. White European countries, culture and credentials, on the other hand, are judged positively and employed to assign them a default positioning which automatically stratifies them higher.[3] Concerning the layering of actors within the broad categories of the White-over-Black, European-over-non-European ascendancy, it is through classed race that groups that are similar are separated onto different rungs of the strata. If we take the case of the three migrant groups in the research population, the classed race of each nationality is employed within the black–white dichotomy to stratify the three White European groups on to different strata, such that the group seen as the 'poorest' is stratified lower. Here, actual or perceived wealth (social class) operates as a 'darkener' as those perceived as poorer-country nationals are stratified lower. Through the interaction of the classed race of each group, their default positioning in the labour market is assigned and the layering of groups is affected as more levels of difference are employed to ascribe migrants a racialised positioning on the strata. The classed race and the socio-historical status ascribed to different groups not only affect where their members stand on the racial order, but also influence the share of the resources and social status available to them within their new country. If, like me, you have ever wondered how the Western world is able to keep its Black population stratified at the bottom of both the economic and racial ladder, considering that race is not biological, this is the answer. It is because the Black race, continent, countries, culture and their by-products are all classed lower than the White race, and whiteness serves as an affirmative action for Whites guaranteeing them a position away from the bottom of the ladder.

Racial stratification as a default starting position

Scholarship on racial stratification is typically discussed in terms of access to resources and the positioning of groups and group members. Positioning on the strata invariably means all groups do not start from the same position in attaining their labour market goals. It differs depending on race, skin colour and nationality of descent. The different starting position serves the purpose of homogenising the inhabitants by rewarding possessors of similar attributes in the labour market, thus giving them a head start which advantages them over those who exhibit difference. From Figure 5.1, the positioning of the four groups means some groups are given a head start in their labour market pursuit when going towards the same goal. It is this starting position I describe as a 'default starting position'. It is based on a person's racial category which is employed to assign a starting position to different groups through their race being classed (see above). There is a correlation between the racial stratification of actors and their labour market outcome because the racial position is a position of power, dominance or subjugation. Let's not forget that race is a racial formation project that was set up to distinguish Europeans from others. Statistical data and the experience of Black migrants show they are automatically assigned to the bottom of the strata in the labour market, while White European migrants, though not at the pinnacle, automatically avoid the bottom of the ladder as they are ascribed a higher starting position than migrants of Black African descent.

This default starting position, though restrictive, is fluid and changeable through personal effort and minority agency. It is the key mechanism through which the racial stratification of actors is established in the labour market. On arrival, immigrants are assigned a racial group based on their racial category, which then determines where they fit within the politico-economic system in their new country. This in turn determines their access to wealth and status, which are socially constructed as suitable for the different levels on the strata. For example, arrival as an asylum seeker in Ireland means access to only €38.80 weekly in 2019; denial of access to paid employment (this was only introduced in 2019); restricted movement and rights; and no access to third-level education. Arrival as an EU migrant means freedom of movement, immediate access to the labour market, healthcare services and the child benefit system for those who accessed them in other EU countries. Many people of Black African descent spend two to ten years regularising their visa status, right to work and retraining to European education while White migrants have immediate access to education and the job market without restrictions. Let me paint a more vivid picture. Racial stratification is like someone holding you down for two to ten years with all manner of barriers and chains while others just like yourself but from different parts of the world are allowed and encouraged to run towards the goal. You are then released and asked to compete for the same opportunities as them. My work on racial stratification is not on whether the barriers set in the path of people of Black African descent in the name of nationalism are right or wrong. The alt-right will argue 'citizens first'. What I do here is highlight the impact of those processes and how it affects human lives. Those at the top are entitled to more and those at the bottom less. Racial stratification defines where a person stands on the racial stratum which in turn affects the labour market outcome when the macro variable is race. While this process may appear deterministic, that is not the case, as there is evidence of a dialectic relationship between the systems and individual agency which I describe in chapter 7 as 'minority agency'.

It would be simplistic to assume that racial stratification is value free. It is not simply where a person is placed; rather, it determines what status they are ascribed, what they can and cannot get, where they can and cannot go, how they are treated and how people respond to them. In other words, it is not a physical position but a socially constructed one; it is not about a physical position but an outcome. The combination of whiteness and European citizenship which imputes, for example, 'trust'[4] of White people's educational standards, abilities and right to work in Ireland gives White European migrants a head start in their labour market trajectory. The in(up)ward mobility of the Black African migrants from, for example, Nigeria, who in the study coincidentally were all naturalised Irish citizens at the time, is on the other hand severely handicapped by race. In this case, visas, country and continent of origin, rather than naturalisation, and racial markers such as skin colour, all serve as racialised gatekeepers restricting access to higher rungs by protecting and imputing rights to those deemed to have access – White migrants and White Irish natives. Actors located at the bottom of the racial ladder are more likely to be the same at the bottom of the labour market strata. Similar to the time in racist America where Harris (1995) argued that whiteness protected Whites and Blacks who successfully 'passed' from slavery, Blacks and those categorised as Black in Ireland are at a much higher risk of exclusion in the labour market, stratification at the bottom of the racial order, ill-treatment, colour-based racism, exclusion from automatic acknowledgement as part of the human race, being seen as guilty of incompetence and only suitable for menial and unpaid work, and, ultimately, exposure to cultural and symbolic harm (Joseph, 2019).

Ascribing a default racial positioning to actors on the hierarchical structure invariably means migrants are returned to that default positioning when they change space, or encounter new contact with organisations or people, especially if they are personally unknown to them. This is noteworthy because the impediment or head-start associated with a person's racial identity can be facilely re-enacted on an ongoing basis. Thus, Black migrants are at a higher risk of experiencing microaggression due to race, even after they have moved up the economic ladder because their default racial positioning remains unchanged. A classic example is Oprah Winfrey's racism row in the Swiss shop incident, where despite the wealth and respect she has gained in the US, in a place where she was unknown she was just another Black woman whom the shopkeeper assumed could not afford a designer bag. While inter-(intra-) group mobility on the labour market strata is relatively fluid, mobility on the racial strata is more restricted. It is for these reasons that I describe racial stratification as a homogenising system of structured inequality, where an assigned default starting position determines access to scarce and desired resources based on racial group membership.

Notes

1 By 'intervention', I mean actions taken to alter a person's default positioning to attain individual mobility, which can include programmes like EP. In racist American parlance, racial 'passing' was a way to alter a person's positioning or assimilation into the dominant culture. Studies have shown that marrying up was one of the mechanisms used by Japanese-Americans where they married into a white racial group (see King and DaCosta, 1996).

2 There is ongoing debate in Ireland of what it means to be Irish; if whiteness determines a person's Irishness. Afua Hirsch also recently published a book *Brit-ish*.

3 This idea of White Europeans being stratified higher than Black Africans also correlates with the analysis of the outcomes of the EP programme participants (2009–2011).

4 I use 'trust' here rather than recognition of their credentials, as the experiences of Black workers showed that, though having their qualifications recognised and being assigned an equivalent value to Irish education helped, it was more about trust in the quality of non-European education and Western education in Black bodies.

6

Intersecting stratifiers: how migrants change their place on the labour supply chain

Despite the difficulty experienced by migrant groups in the labour market, there is always mobility. This can go in a number of directions: upward, downward or lateral. Meanwhile, some migrant groups stagnate, remaining stuck. Whites enjoy better mobility in the system and thus dominate, while darker-skinned workers are known to be over-represented in unpaid and low-paid labour sectors, thus forming racialised ghettos in the labour market. Based on micro-level analysis of the everyday experiences of migrants, this chapter discusses how migrants change their place in the labour supply chain. When migrants negotiate their way through the racial hierarchy in racially stratified societies in the Western world like Ireland, they employ one of three means: interest convergence – between the host community and prospective employees (Bell, 1980), gaining access to social capital (Bourdieu, 1986) and the equal opportunity of a meritocratic system. The way the labour market experiences of migrants align to any of these concepts has long-term implications for everyone. It also shows the extent of integration and inclusiveness in the society. This is further compounded by the segmented nature of the twenty-first-century labour market which is presented in this chapter as tripartite and with intersecting vulnerabilities such as gender, age, religion, sexuality and others, that foster (inter-) intra-group layering within the racial strata.

Gender, race and other vulnerabilities in the labour market

Migrants can erroneously be seen as a group of people who experience migration in the same way. However, inter- and intra-group differences abound in how overlapping forces structure their lives, positioning and outcome. Gender is one of the many other vectors which interact with race to influence socio-economic outcome and group performance. These interactions mean there are myriad expressions of the self which are available to migrant people, and multiple layers to how they are seen and perceived in the labour market. This further compounds an already complex situation of how racial stratification operates in the lifeworld and positioning of people of migrant descent who simultaneously occupy different positions in different societies. When multiple forms of dominations converge in a person's life, it is described in CRT as 'intersectionality'. As much as gender, race or any of the other characteristics impact on a person's outcome, it is difficult to separate a person's race from all the other aspects of their lives when we look at the outcome. The reality of intersectionality in our daily encounters debunks the idea that there is a monolithic identity detached from other forms of identities. Thus, to truly talk of racial domination, it is imperative to examine how race interacts with other forms of domination including gender, sexuality, class, religion and all forms of disadvantaging identities (Crenshaw, 1989; Fraser, 1995; Collins, 2000).

Gender is a site of multiple disadvantages not only for White Europeans as we might perceive from arguments about the gender pay gap. Although the study did not set out with gender as its focus, the intersectionality of people's lives was evident in the lives of the migrant women in Ireland. The female migrants in my interviews fared worse than their male counterparts in the labour market, even when controlling for achievement factors such as education.[1] Migration affects females and males differently as 'immigrant women may also be vulnerable to spousal violence because many of them depend on their husbands for information regarding their legal status' (Crenshaw, 1991: 1249). This is more prevalent among groups from patriarchal societies. Due to gender roles and family circumstances, many women of migrant descent do not make their career decisions wholly based on economic ambition. This is because the automatic role assignment of primary carers of the home in the twenty-first century, while slightly reduced, still falls primarily on women (CSO, 2011, 2016). This is further exacerbated by being newcomers in Ireland, and far from their home countries and support networks. The temporary use of women's bodies in child-bearing also negatively affects their labour market mobility because becoming pregnant, while a happy occasion for many, also results in lost time, altered career goals and increased susceptibility to marginalisation in ways which affect their positioning on the strata. For example, one of my interviewees was threatened with redundancy when pregnant, while another was actually made redundant. Although the latter reported winning a legal case against her employers, she insists money did not compensate for the emotional impact. Discrimination against pregnant women is part of a growing general problem, as indicated by a recent report which estimates that over 54,000 new mothers are losing their jobs across Britain every year – almost twice the number identified in similar research undertaken in 2005 by the Equal Opportunities Commission.[2]

As with many studies on gender, this study made no distinction for migrant women. Arguments that migrant women are discriminated against based on gender alone without centring race will silence their racial identity and how it exacerbates such issues. This is the very essence of intersectionality in CRT, in that covert forms of discrimination are not simply directed at a woman's identity but at her interlocking identity as a migrant woman. Crenshaw makes the argument that

> Feminist efforts to politicize experiences of women and antiracist efforts to politicize experiences of 'people of color' have frequently proceeded as though the issues and experiences they each detail occur on mutually exclusive terrains. Although racism and sexism readily intersect in the lives of real people, they seldom do in feminist and antiracist practices. And so, when the practices expound identity as 'woman' or 'person of color' as an either/or proposition, they relegate the identity of women of color to a location that resists telling. (Crenshaw, 1991: 1242)

Unless there is an awareness of how race, gender, class (directly or indirectly due to the classed race) and even age interact to produce intersecting disadvantage, and thus domination, many migrant women's sufferings remain obscured and silenced. In one particular case, a female respondent of Polish descent stated that 'being a woman took six years from me but my husband is starting to help now'. This is an example of how more females than males grapple with gendered roles. Though both sexes are in various ways attributed some gender-specific roles, different cultures, races and nationalities perform gender differently, and the responsibilities expected of them are also different.[3] Gender interacts with secondary issues that accompany migration, such as ageing, settling in a new country, regularising residency permits and increased family size/composition. These issues have a way of influencing employment chances as people who most often relocate as single or unwed, without family ties or responsibilities, often end up in relationships, managing a family, their personal lives and careers. Family responsibility influences many women's choices to stay in safe jobs, not seeking new sectors where they can be promoted, or they may take the more prevalent option – seeking out part-time jobs. Gendered roles place the onus on many women with young children to seek to stay with their children. This is justified by emotive sentiments such as 'it is their time', 'career can be done another time', 'I am forty now and I had my kids when I was at the last circle for women to have kids'. From these statements, issues other than race and gender become evident as we see the positioning of women being influenced by biology and age. These kinds of vulnerabilities interact with race and gender; for example, the age of active child-bearing, interest in marriage and looking after a young family all come with their own challenges, creating extra difficulties. This 'intersectional subordination' is not intentionally produced, but an imposition of burdens that interacts with pre-existing vulnerabilities to create yet another dimension of disempowerment (Crenshaw, 1991: 1249).

The differential treatment of women of migrant descent is compounded by economic pressure. In Ireland, some of my interviewees with young children reported being compelled to return to employment by welfare officers who they reported treated them as if they were fleecing the economy and welfare frauds. Others were personally pressured to return to work despite not having family support with childcare or enough income to afford the cost of childcare. These women experienced pressure to return to work with young children below four years of age, despite being in a social system that allows single mothers to stay at home to care for their young children until the age of seven. Such situations create a dilemma where migrant women have to choose between performing their gendered role in supporting a young family or succumbing to economic pressures and returning to work. Though this is not unique to migrant women, the pull is experienced differently by native Irish women, White migrant women from Europe and Black African migrant women because of the availability of support networks in the form of extended families, their intersecting identities and how race affects their positioning. This cannot be fully addressed from a single perspective as an either/or of race, gender, age or even patriarchy, which are all active in these situations.

Many of the experiences of Black women in accessing employment are not fully accounted for within the boundaries of racism and sexism as they are currently understood. One interviewee who seriously deliberated about having children because of economic pressures and her family network being far away from Ireland, shows that being of migrant descent influences an issue as vital as having children. The labour market mobility of many migrant women presents them with a dilemma between the social expectations associated with their gendered roles of being primary family carers and that of career advancement. To fully understand how gender affects a woman's life as a female migrant, we need to reflect on the gendered considerations which influence their labour market mobility and how intricately it is linked with their identity as migrants. Political intersectionality arises from the conflict between gender (where status is linked to family) and race (where status is achieved through individual mobility).[4] This conflictual process of managing status as a woman and a migrant can also be illustrated by many women negotiating later starting hours at work in order to get their young children to school. This is more prevalent among single parents with limited support networks, parents, grandparents or neighbours with long-standing family relationships. You find many women of African descent, although from dual-parent families, regularly take on jobs with adverse and strenuous working conditions to suit their gendered role. For example, the job choice of one interviewee turned her life into a twenty-four-hour working day. She took on a twelve-hour night shift contract so she could manage her childcare responsibilities during the day, despite not being what she described as a 'night person'. Other differences which come into play in these cases include family size, which definitely differs across communities, and the duty of care which is typically assigned to women, particularly those from patriarchal societies. The cultural differences between different groups intersect with gender to exacerbate the challenges of accessing secure paid employment. This can also account for inter-group disparity in labour market outcome.

The intersectionalities in people's lives also influence the types of roles migrant women are assigned in the workplace. The study reported allocation of gendered duties where males are assigned roles that are seemingly more 'male', such as driving the forklift to pick up goods, and supervising and quality checks of packages, while female migrants are assigned more menial or 'girls'' tasks, such as packing boxes and order picking. Intervention in such situations can be quite complex, as covert differential treatments cannot be challenged on the grounds of racism as male migrants are employed by the company; neither can it be proven on gender grounds as it also employs White Irish women, who are given more responsibilities and are provided with better working conditions. These kinds of cases exemplify how intersectionality can affect actors differently and influence their outcome in the labour market. Though Black women are the quintessential cases for intersectionality, any form of difference from the norm (male, White, heterosexual, Christian, settled and able-bodied) produces intersecting axes of oppression for different groups and will be experienced differently.

Gender stratification of migrants is linked to the classed race of each group which produces a White over Black ascendancy, with Blacks at the bottom and Whites at the top. This means that within each group an intra-group layering by gender obtains where, for example, the bottom will have Black males stratified higher than Black females, and, within the upper strata, White males stratified higher than White females; likely Christians over non-Christians; heterosexuals over LGBTQ persons. Although these characteristics were not centred in the study, they are possibilities of how intersectionality is reflected in the racial order. Other vulnerabilities include migrants' age and its impact on outcomes when race is centred. It is important to mention that intersectionality also affects other marginalised categories and racialised identities such as Black African men, White Muslim women, Travellers and various other combinations (Akpoveta, 2010).[5]

How migrants change their place in the labour market

Although migrants cannot change their racial category, as in where they are positioned on the racial strata, they are able to change their position on the economic ladder in the labour market. They can somehow negotiate their way through the racial hierarchy in racially stratified societies. The main determinant of access to paid employment opportunities in an egalitarian society based on meritocracy should be a person's qualifications and ability. This makes it crucial that access to qualifications and assessment of abilities is not a system of privilege to advantage certain groups over others. This is reflected in the Employment Equality Act 1998, which came into operation in Ireland in October 1999 and replaced the Anti-Discrimination (Pay) Act 1974 and the Employment Equality Act 1977. The 1998 Act outlaws discrimination in employment in Ireland on nine distinct grounds.[6]

The in(up)ward labour market mobility of individual migrants in Ireland is attributable to one of three concepts: interest convergence between the host community and prospective employees (Bell, 1980), access to social capital (Bourdieu, 1986) and equal opportunity. The ideologies of these concepts provide insight into how migrants negotiate the Irish labour market. They also, however, indicate a wider societal and egalitarian challenge because race was the only variable which accounted for any significant difference in my study in how some groups were more likely to attain mobility through one of those routes than the others. The long-term outcome and implication are problematic for group members if left unchecked.

Interest convergence: the downward mobility and economic exploitation of migrants

The convergence between the need for cheap but skilled labour and access to resources by migrants accounts for many of the success stories in the labour market, rather than individual merit within a meritocratic system. Interest convergence is a tenet of CRT discussed in chapter 4. As an analytical tool, it allows for the micro-level exploration of how certain groups end up at the bottom and others at the top; it aids the investigation of the power imbalance between groups; the privileged and disadvantaged; gainers and losers, and the criteria that promote this convergence of interest. Although at 5.4 per cent, unemployment in Ireland in 2019 is at its lowest since January 2007, this positive turn in the economy only applies to Ireland's White population. In the 2016 Census, the unemployment rate of migrants stood at 15.4 per cent against the natives at 12.6 per cent. This figure, which gives the impression that the outcome for migrants is comparable with that for Irish natives, also obscures sharp disparities which become evident when viewed by race and nationality. For example, Western Europeans recorded the lowest unemployment rate (French 6.7 per cent, Germans 7.8 per cent, Italians 8.5 per cent, Spanish 9.2 per cent), followed by Eastern Europeans (Polish 13.1 per cent, Lithuanians 14.7 per cent, Latvians 17.2 per cent), with Africans recording the highest unemployment rate at over five times that of Western Europeans at 42.9 per cent (Kenyans 38.7 per cent, Nigerians 42.9 per cent, Ghanaians 52.2 per cent, Congolese 63 per cent). Despite the seeming success story, the reality is that of a very sharp divide, with Whites at the top and Blacks at the bottom of the economic ladder.

Interest convergence,[7] advanced by Derrick Bell (1980), originated from the scepticism within communities of colour towards civil rights gains in the 1960s US. Though the notion of employment equality should lead to equality of opportunity on meritocratic grounds,[8] the gains by minorities have been argued to be concessions that are offered, to the extent that they are not seen as a major disruption to a 'normal' way of life for the majority of Whites (DeCuir and Dixson, 2004: 29). For many migrants from Eastern Europe or from the continent of Africa, the pull to the convergence table which makes their exploitation possible is mainly economic; while for the Spanish migrants who migrate at a much younger age, it is the need to learn the English language. The varying degrees of difficulty experienced by all migrant groups in accessing paid employment at their educational level results in their subsequent gravitation to sectors and jobs that offer them the least resistance. Some migrant workers pursue menial or voluntary work to acquire relevant work experience and Irish references or once their initial savings start to deplete. For others, it is to avoid the social welfare benefit trap. Some respondents in my study endure what they describe as an 'awful job' in order to meet their financial needs.

Contrary to labour market reports of migrants progressing on to paid employment, the real stories of the reasons and conditions under which these gains occur are silenced. In as much as the Eastern and Western Europeans record higher success rates in lower socio-economic sectors than their African counterparts, the initial employment opportunities open to them are mainly in roles with adverse working conditions that are unattractive to Irish-born citizens – racialised language jobs for which the natives cannot compete or awkward nightshift hours such as 2:30am–9:00am, while the majority of their Irish counterparts are observed working morning shifts, which are usually calmer, easier on the body clock and with a safer public transport commute. Others face adverse working conditions in the form of sporadic working hours.[9] In this regard, the notion of interest convergence demonstrates how the need for an income converges with an employer's need for staff who can work zero-hour contracts.[10] The 'decent work deficits' associated with these types of employment thrive in situations where people feel they have very limited choices or opportunities (Lynch, 2014: 2). Others end up in roles which lack career progression and mental stimulation, resulting in highly skilled workers feeling stuck. Some migrant workers report their agreed wage has sometimes changed, with the employer claiming the worker didn't understand the employment terms because English is not their first language. Despite the adverse work environment and employment conditions, the convergence of the needs expressed by members of migrant groups fuels their gravitation to low-skilled and low-paid work with minimal work incentives within the society.

Migrants start their careers in Ireland underemployed, undervalued and underpaid (see chapter 7), while Ireland, the host community, has a choice of highly qualified staff over-performing in roles with minimal rewards. There are cases of shop assistants who are university graduates, and cleaners with Master's degrees. While corroborating the statistical landscape of migrants' labour market outcomes in Ireland, these accounts from my study also uncover how migrants attain individual mobility, the challenges they encounter in the process and how certain groups become over-represented in unskilled work. Although underemployment was more common among Black workers in the study, it is widespread among all migrant groups. The quiet voice of a Spanish migrant saying, 'Every day I had to repeat to myself, it is because of your English, you want to improve your English' is insightful into the impact of underemployment on a person's mental health.

There are a number of problems with interest convergence as a vehicle of mobility in Ireland. First, workers of migrant background will experience immense challenges in accessing roles that reflect their skills and their highest academic level, or with the same working conditions as members of the host community, or roles the host community finds attractive and do not consider it a gain to have migrants in those roles. Secondly, there is a temporary and dispensable attitude towards migrants, especially when a new cohort of workers willing to accept employment with even more minimal rewards becomes available, which can present migrants as 'economic commodities' rather than as social beings (Lentin, 2004). It is for reasons such as these that CRT theorists insist that advancements such as the civil rights gains are superfluous, and can easily be rolled back.

For migrants of African descent, there is an even greater intensity in the resistance to their progressing into paid employment outside the human health and social work sectors. English language, which is the native language for many Nigerians,[11] did not seem to be the main barrier to accessing paid employment. Rather, Black Africans in Ireland are encouraged to ignore their prior education from their home countries and retrain at lower academic levels in order to find paid employment. For example, an IT personnel and psychology degree holder (level 8 qualifications) started their career in Ireland as a care assistant, a post which requires a level 5 qualification. In order to get employed, another Black African female, mother of four young children, drove one and a half hours to reach her workplace. She was told on her first day that she was offered the job because they were certain she would not take it because of the distance. In addition, African males do not benefit from male privilege in Ireland as they do not fare any better than their female counterparts. Many resort to self-employment by engaging in taxi driving as a pragmatic strategy to resist unemployment, through career redirection into sectors with the least resistance.[12] These are primarily low-paid, zero-hours contract jobs and undervalued employment. In these cases, shortage in skilled labour, rather than retraining per se, gives them access to paid employment.

The significance of this is that certain employment opportunities are out of reach for migrants, particularly jobs where the natives do not see gains for themselves in employing migrants but would rather perform those roles themselves. The prevalence of interest convergence as the means of mobility in the labour market shows that the achievement factors of workers such as skills, experience and education are not the primary considerations in progressing into paid employment. This is indeed part of a general problem associated with migrants, according to a Migration Policy Institute report (Papademetrio, Somerville and Sumption, 2009).[13] It showed that many migrants experience significant downward mobility at the point of migration when occupational status or their relative position in the earnings scale is compared with native workers'. It also highlights significant differences in outcome between migrant groups who consistently fare worse in several countries, like the UK, Germany, France, Sweden and the Netherlands, all of which have migrant groups from one or more source countries, or whose outcomes do not improve fast enough to bring them level with even low-skilled native workers (Papademetrio, Somerville and Sumption, 2009: 22). These groups, according to the report, 'all experience high initial unemployment rates and low employment probabilities, that make it difficult to attain parity with natives during their lifetimes' (Papademetrio, Somerville and Sumption, 2009: 7). Highly skilled professionals required for essential services such as medical doctors also progress based on the need for doctors by the majority population. This is evident from the Medical Practitioners Act 2007 that allows the employment of foreign-trained doctors as non-consultant hospital doctors in non-training posts, where they are deemed ineligible for the trainee specialist division despite the shortage of consultants in Ireland (see Irish Times, 2015). The Papademetrio, Somerville and Sumption (2009) report attributes migrants' initial downward mobility to language barriers, differences in educational attainment, difficulties obtaining recognition for credentials and experience gained abroad, and problems accessing opportunities through social networks and other recruitment channels – and these factors all proved true in relation to migrants' mobility in Ireland. In addition to these, however, the country of descent of migrant workers influences to a very large extent the differential outcome among groups even when jobs are available in Ireland. This is in the sense that migrants from Eastern and Western Europe, though they experience difficulties progressing into paid employment, fare better than their African counterparts. The consequence of interest convergence is that it conceals the expendable nature of unwelcome groups in the labour market. This is indeed indicated in the 2011 Census statistics, where between 2002 and 2011 the number of 'Polish nationals' in Ireland increased by 5631.4 per cent from 2,124 persons to 122,585, while the population of Nigerians in Ireland increased by over 81 per cent between 2002 and 2006 and by only 8.2 per cent between 2006 and 2011. These figures would not have been significant, bar the period coinciding with the negative sentiments about migrants of African descent that culminated in the 2004 citizenship referendum; the opening of European borders from EU15 to EU25; and increased access to a large pool of more 'welcome' and 'acceptable' labour stock from within the European Union – a White group. This was not simply an anti-Nigerian or anti-African change but part of a growing worldwide anti-immigrant rhetoric, as evident in the election and tenure of President Donald Trump in the US and the outcome of the 2016 Brexit referendum in the UK and the xenophobic hate that has been unleashed since 2016.

There is a striking pattern in the way Black labour is treated differently from White labour in Ireland. This is characterised by underemployment, while engagement with unpaid employment through volunteering does not yield the anticipated progression into paid employment that people envisage. Rather, the growing fragmentation of the labour market in Ireland has an over-representation of Black migrants disproportionate to their population within the unpaid segment. There has been a noticeable shift from the dual labour market, as propounded by Doeringer and Piore (1971) in the United States, to the emergence of tri-labour or three-tier labour market segmentation.[14] Many migrants start their employment journey in the unrecognised but rapidly growing and exploited unpaid employment segment, which remains unnamed as such. From there, some progress to the secondary segment, which is characterised by low pay, unfavourable working conditions, unskilled work, menial tasks and casual attachment between workers and firms. Such roles have gained more popularity in recent times, being described as '3D' areas of employment, meaning 'dirty, dangerous and demanding' (Connell, 1993).[15] Only one of the thirty-two people in the study started their labour market participation in Ireland in the primary segment, or a high-skilled professional role. This exhibited pattern conforms to the claim that expansion in the economy absorbs the native workforce into the upper and middle segments of the labour market and creates shortages of labour in the lower segment, which offers low-paying and low-status jobs (Piore, 1979).

Mobility through the convergence of interest between members of the majority populations and their foreign-born workforce who are used to fill shortages, creates groups of underpaid, underemployed and over-performing migrants such that we risk creating racial ghettos in the labour market. While there is acknowledgement of ghettoised neighbourhoods based in marginalised housing and areas where people of low status live, the experiences and labour market outcomes of migrants delineate the formation of racialised job ghettos in the labour market. This is characterised by the over-representation of certain nationalities and races; the experience of social, legal and economic pressures and injustices; physical hardship, undervalued or cheap labour for high-quality services, and adverse working conditions which are generally unacceptable to the indigenous population. Standing (2011) described people with insecure, short-term, precarious income or jobs as the Precariat, which he called the emerging class. Their characteristics, which resemble a waiting disaster, depict the experiences of many workers of migrant descent.

Social capital – networking my way up the economic ladder

Another means by which migrants change their place in the labour market is through the use of social networks and 'social capital'. Three key players in the development of the concept of social capital are the French sociologist Pierre Bourdieu (1930–2002), American sociologist James Coleman (1926–1995) and the political economist Robert Putnam (1941–). Bourdieu, who was interested in the ways in which society is reproduced and how dominant classes retain their position, identified three dimensions of capital whose resources become socially effective. He argues that their ownership is legitimised through the mediation of symbolic capital, whether it be economic, cultural or social (Bourdieu, 1986: 13). From the Bourdieuan perspective, social capital is seen as

> the aggregate of the actual or potential resources which are linked to possession of a durable network of more or less institutionalized relationships of mutual acquaintance and recognition – or in other words, to membership of a group – which provides each of its members with the backing of the collectively-owned capital, a 'credential' which entitles them to credit, in the various senses of the word. (Bourdieu, 1986: 248)

Putnam (2004) described social capital as the available resources that people have through their social interactions, referring to social networks and associated norms of reciprocity. Coleman (1988) linked social capital and economics, and highlights it as an important resource for individuals from all kinds of communities. He argues that:

> Because the benefits of actions that bring social capital into being are largely experienced by persons other than the actor, it is often not in his interest to bring it into being. The result is that most forms of social capital are created or destroyed as by-products of other activities. This social capital arises or disappears without anyone willing it into or out of being and is thus even less recognised and taken account of in social action than its already intangible character would warrant. (Coleman, 1988: 118)

Irrespective of the views each of these theorists takes, the main point about social capital is that social networks are a powerful asset, both for individuals and for communities. While individuals with more networks of contacts are believed to have more social capital than those with fewer and less diverse networks, lack of networks might become erroneously blamed for the poorer outcomes of groups with such a deficit. Just as access to economic capital brings certain privileges to a group, individual and cultural capital sets a group or individual apart from their less privileged peers. Social capital supplies the network and connections which allow continued and future access to privilege. In Ireland, it is evident that access to friends who know about vacancies makes a difference to labour market outcomes (see chapter 7). When we think about what counts as a resource, the major challenge, which Bourdieu correctly delineates, is how the convertibility of such social capital to economic capital is recognised. The difficulty lies in the extent to which the economic values of the social and cultural capitals are 'disguised' as mere customs and connections (Bourdieu, 1986: 245). In order to have a level playing field for all groups, we must recognise that social and cultural capital are ontologically forms of currency, in just the same manner as mercantile or economic capital, and it should be possible to 'establish the laws whereby the different types of capital … change into one another' (Bourdieu, 1986: 243).

Considering that having access to social capital is not an offence or criminal act, addressing how it can foster inequality becomes more complex. Though some will argue that Bourdieu's approach to social capital is 'going too far', there is general consensus that social capital can be exclusionary (Gauntlett, 2007: 63–70). In explaining its mechanism for the reproduction of privilege, Gauntlett argues it also provides unique insight into the nature of social exclusion, particularly its relational nature in the sense that it comprises a competitive market in which not all players end up winning. Social capital is one of the vehicles through which movement between the secondary and primary labour market segments is attained by migrants in Ireland. There are important considerations on the types of barriers encountered in these segments, how social capital differs across groups, the properties and social structures that facilitate social capital, and how the racial positioning of actors influences accessibility to it.

One of the significant factors that attracts foreign-born workers to Ireland, in spite of the lower social status they encounter, is their need to study the English language. Migrants are also attracted by better pay compared with their home countries, particularly among those coming from countries with a lower GDP, and the possibility to be part of a global and international network and economy. The hierarchy theory presents the labour market as a social hierarchy where the accumulation of social status, rather than purely income, induces people to work (Piore, 1979). This perspective insists that people engage in the labour market to maintain or advance their positions in the hierarchy. Though it would appear that many migrants are prepared to work in jobs at the bottom of the hierarchy and in dead-end jobs, they definitely desire to progress from such jobs. Many who start out in 3D jobs progress to other jobs, while some are unsuccessful despite investing considerable effort.

Unlike the primary segment, where work is typically stable and well paid with prospects of upward mobility, the secondary segment is often characterised by sporadic work, low pay and poor working conditions, with little or no prospect for promotion or career progression. One of the hypotheses advanced by the dual labour market model and workers in the secondary segment is that economic mobility between the two segments is sharply limited; hence workers in the secondary segment find themselves trapped there (Wachter, 1974).[16] While both secondary and primary segments are functionally interdependent, their boundaries are said to be rigid, presenting increased difficulty for workers intending to switch from one segment to the other, particularly from the secondary to the primary segment. Peck (1996) argues that what keeps the boundaries rigid are the differing rules guiding labour market engagement. More recently, Standing (2011: 12) has argued that the precariat 'lack a work-based identity'. Though there are many reasons for the restriction in the admission of migrants into the primary segment in Ireland, there was also a remarkable difference in terms of race and nationality. White[17] Western and Eastern European migrants who experience restriction or who seek work in the secondary labour market do so mainly due to limited levels of spoken English – the language of the host community. Black workers from outside the EU explicitly name skin colour and race as the main restrictor to the primary segment of the labour market.

Some migrant groups are able to negotiate their way through the labour market, either from unemployment or lower-paid employment, into better pay with better conditions and stability through the use of social capital. For example, the more rapid progression of migrants of Spanish descent into roles with better conditions in Ireland is facilitated by their social networks (see chapter 7 and Joseph, 2019). This comes in the form of introduction to managers by friends/employers, by previous colleagues in new roles and interview tips from friends who are employed in similar roles. Some organisations operate a system of rewarding their staff for recommending friends. While this is helpful for jobseekers who find employment in that way, it is extremely problematic for groups with fewer members in such organisations. This is because the more represented the group is in such workplaces, the better the chances of connecting with someone to make a recommendation.

While this makes the recruiters' job easier, these processes have a high propensity to homogenise the workplace and inadvertently perpetuate inequality (this might be the aim of such processes – to recruit personnel similar to the 'good' staff in the hope that the current staff will only recommend people like themselves). In these cases, connection with others from within their own community in paid employment unreservedly provides advantage over others, particularly in progressing into paid employment.

White males from the EU also experienced the same advantage from having social networks. They experience favour in the labour market due to sameness based on nationality and having a common EU language. For one interviewee, singing in Spanish under his breath initiated conversation with a female colleague who connected him thereafter to his first paid role in Ireland. Even with limited language skills for those who self-report the need to learn English, social networking with peers from the same country initiated social capital for their progression into paid employment. The use of social capital did not, however, mean that the migrants were guaranteed jobs; in fact, they were often overqualified, over-performing, underemployed and underpaid for these jobs. Nonetheless, compared with other groups, the progression of White Europeans into paid employment is facilitated by their social network, which is a form of social capital. These social networks are not simply restricted to friends providing information, links and contacts to possible job opportunities; they also include access to family support at short notice without visa restrictions. For example, European workers often benefit from social networks in the form of support from parents or siblings being able to arrive without visa restrictions to support their childcare needs, enabling them to return to employment.

Concerning upward mobility within the workplace, access to social networks is also a determinant of progression in Ireland. For example, a male kitchen porter of Polish descent who self-reported a lack of aspiration to be a chef, found he progressed in the sector from low-skilled menial work to a highly skilled role with less precarity, better wages and higher social status due to social networking with the head chef. Mobility up the hierarchy of the labour market should be initiated by line managers, but when you have no social capital with that manager, many find themselves stuck, while some advance because they are liked. Though the experiences and characteristics of foreign-born White workers are in some ways similar to those of the developing precariat, they also exhibit some form of connectedness based on their shared similarities, such as language and nationality, which provides potential for a 'solidaristic labour community' (Standing, 2011: 12). Human connections such as these, which typically go unreckoned by society as an actual resource, can in the Bourdieuan notion of capital, particularly social capital, have currency, thereby increasing the ability of the actors to advance their interests.

Due to the abysmal labour market outcome for migrants of Black African descent in Ireland, many of them recourse to unpaid work based on a pragmatic decision to change their position in the labour market by generating this form of capital. Although White migrants are able to draw on their readily available and accessible social capital, Black migrants are mainly able to cultivate that form of capital through unpaid work. Some Nigerian respondents in Ireland who took the 'foot in the door' approach to unpaid work insist volunteering was the only way they were going to get a chance to demonstrate their capability to perform those roles and work in those organisations. Moreover, the racial positioning of actors in the labour market means that those positioned lower on the strata will have less access to the networks than is available to those at the top, consequently limiting their access to social capital. This sheds light on how, on a micro level, access to social capital or lack of access thereto exacerbates inequality and serves as a mechanism through which racial orders are maintained. One scholar who agrees with this view is DiTomaso (2013: 6), who insists that Whites show each other favouritism 'through the hoarding and exchange of social capital'. Indeed, Bonilla-Silva and Baiocchi (2008: 146) insist that explaining differential outcomes without taking into cognisance the social context and structural inequalities which operate along racial lines, is to 'seriously minimise the impact of racism'. They further argue that there is a 'missing link in the social capital theory' because in a racialised society, social networks and norms of social behaviour are often mobilised to defend racial exclusion.[18]

The higher unemployment rate of Africans in Ireland cannot be accounted for using a migrant deficit approach because, in reality, their lack of access to this unacknowledged resource makes the field of play unequal by advantaging and disadvantaging groups against each other. Groups with a higher representation in paid employment in the labour market are more likely to benefit those who share similar attributes with them. This is evident in the outcomes of the research population in the labour market, where those having the European Union, nationality, language and skin colour in common have a bigger stake in paid employment. Despite the economic value and currency of social capital, developing this form of capital proves immensely difficult for many migrants, particularly those of African descent. Conversely, for Whites, possessing social capital occurs seamlessly. For the migrants of Black African descent, personal effort, resilience, and ability to quickly overcome rejection and personal anxiety are mandatory attributes. Some difficulties they encounter during attempts to socialise with members of the host community, particularly in the workplace, include age difference with work colleagues, cultural difference in ways of socialising, time – particularly for those with young families – and emotional energy spent navigating workplace microaggressions (intended or unintended), financial constraints and the requirement for common interests for effective socialising. The most challenging for many is being the only Black or visibly different person on the team and navigating non-inclusive work environments or conversations that exclude the other.

In spite of this, some migrants of Black African descent, on the other hand, make conscious effort to generate social capital particularly with the management team because they see it as a way to avoid the bottom of the societal ladder. There is, however, mixed feeling about this among the migrant community. While some are keen to develop social capital, many others express apathy towards building relationships with their work colleagues and management teams due to some form of race-motivated exclusion which they have previously encountered in the workplace. In Ireland, the valuable asset of social capital is unavailable or lost to many migrants generally and Black Africans in particular. Though they appreciate the benefits of developing this form of capital, previous unsuccessful attempts are a major deterrent to its further pursuit. In the study, many interviewees recounted unsuccessful attempts to build relationships with their colleagues at the beginning of their employment journey. They mentioned observing bonds easily being formed between their White colleagues who would socialise together – before they gave up trying to build relationships with them. Without being prescriptive of what each individual should do because self-care is important in how people manage their work spaces, isolation in the workplace can worsen the field of play by making it more unequal between people with the same academic attributes. The onus should, however, not be on the one Black person in the organisation or the only visible minority to integrate; it should be on the organisation to be inclusive and welcoming of 'difference'.

In an egalitarian-oriented meritocratic society, the general idea is that a person's effort and human capital will ultimately influence their socio-economic outcomes in the society. However, the movement of migrant groups from unemployment to secondary or primary segments in the society is not simply dependent on personal effort but on a combination of different forms of capital which are influenced by their positioning on the labour market strata. The White EU migrants who are stratified higher on the economic and racial ladder enjoy more access to this desired resource, and have more similar attributes, which increases their access to social capital. The migrants from outside the EU, as demonstrated by the accounts of the Black workers of Nigerian descent in the study, have limited access to social networks and subsequently limited social capital, and thus limited labour market mobility opportunities.

Equality of opportunity: the twenty-first-century myth

Equal opportunity is a stipulation that everyone should be treated in the same way, unhampered by barriers, prejudices or preferences. How, then, can we account for someone in an economic terrain wherein the unemployment rate as at June 2019 is 4.5 per cent, with two undergraduate degrees, two Master's degrees, three level 5 qualifications and ten years' work experience (mainly in a volunteering capacity and precarious part-time work), who has not been able to find employment in the last two years?[19] Equality of opportunity is not very prominent as a means of labour market mobility in its real form for all groups in Ireland. Migrants in Ireland expect equality of opportunity, but they do not expect to have it for themselves. Despite the ways various barriers hamper their progress in the labour market, ambiguity about the meaning and effectiveness of equal opportunities is ongoing. The result is that many migrants who experience multiple disadvantages due to their intersecting stratifiers such as visible difference, gender, classed race and age, in reality do not expect equal opportunity to aid their progress into paid employment because of discrimination in recruitment and the arbitrary nature of feedback given to unsuccessful applicants. Similarly, the use of social networks to get jobs which gives beneficiaries advantage over others, even when it might seem unfair, is not prohibited by law. In Ireland, the onus is on workers to prove that they have been discriminated against rather than the employers proving they did not discriminate against the applicant. This is a very difficult process. It can exhaust one's time and deplete one's resources, and is one which demands resilience, confidence and persistence.

Movement (upward) in the labour market for many migrants, particularly the darker-skinned Africans, is not often governed by the fair principles of equality of opportunity. Considering the prevalence of interest convergence and social capital as vehicles for mobility, it is not surprising that migrants do not explicitly enter the labour market on meritocratic grounds alone. This does not mean that migrants do not have the credentials for the role, but rather that they are mainly considered for roles only after groups that demonstrate similarities with the host community.

This is a discriminatory practice which raises fundamental questions about the fairness of the rules of labour market engagement which exclude migrant workers from the primary and secondary segments. The experience of exclusion is not restricted to Ireland as, for example in the Canadian context, studies show that migrants are also excluded from primary segment occupations by institutionalised cultural practices of credential non-recognition (Girard and Bauder, 2007). OCED reports (2014, 2018) also show that qualification and experience are two means by which migrants are restricted from labour market participation. Although race has been widely acknowledged as an illusion that is socially constructed, skin colour and nationality of descent continue to influence socio-economic outcomes. Various studies across Europe that measure the experience of discrimination indicate that the highest levels of discrimination based on ethnic or immigrant background are in the area of employment, and are higher towards non-White minorities (EU MIDIS 11, 2016; Zschirnt and Ruedin, 2016; McGinnity et al., 2017; Joseph, 2019). These studies show that skin colour, foreign-sounding first or second names, accent and nationality of origin were the main reasons cited by respondents for their experience of discrimination. In the Irish context, where a migrant deficit is more prevalent, skin colour is not a prominent feature in the everyday discourse; neither is race a central theme. Migrant deficit theories attribute differentials in outcome to some form of deficit among marginalised groups; they are counterproductive and should be discouraged as they perpetuate racial stereotypes and create a 'shut up' experience for migrants trying to tell their stories of marginalisation. In practical terms, they help to camouflage the exponential increases in levels of inequality of opportunity experienced by migrants the darker they are in our economic terrain.

Racial ghettoes in the labour market

The complexity of classed race, gender positioning and visible characteristics of different migrant groups influences the layering of actors on the racial strata even among groups of the same race. The stratification of Black and White actors in the labour market through the interaction between race, gender and class becomes visible not by focusing on human differences but on the responses to exhibited and perceived differences. Though the complexity of race is undeniable, and it is a key determinant of outcomes in the labour market as I have argued in these chapters, it is important to reiterate that race per se is not the main problem. Rather, the problem is human response to visible racial difference. This does not equate to saying that race is not relevant; to the contrary, as I argue in relation to migrants being assigned a default position on the racial strata, race is instrumental in their positionality at the top or bottom of the economic strata. Although these positions are not fixed but are changeable, the claim by Bonilla-Silva (2003) that societies will have to first operate a racialised system to continuously maintain actors in such positions becomes even more relevant. These racialised systems are experienced through a segmented labour market comprising three segments: the secondary and primary sectors and an unpaid segment (an emerging segment which has an over-representation of more marginalised groups, and particularly Black workers).

Changing one's place in the labour market as a migrant in Ireland is more likely to happen from interest convergence between migrants' needs and society's needs due to shortages in the host community, rather than from individual merit or equal opportunity. Also, having access to social capital plays a key role in labour market mobility by conferring advantage on White European migrants through the conflating of race and nationality. This exacerbates the inequality among migrant groups by creating advantage for some while conversely disadvantaging others. Migrants accessing the labour market in Ireland typically commence with underemployment in the unpaid or secondary segment of the labour market. This has a propensity to create racialised ghettos – clusters of migrants who are underemployed, underpaid, over-performing and overqualified – if their progression is adversely restricted for prolonged periods. This is significant for policy makers as Ireland risks creating racial ghettos with adverse working conditions in the labour market.

Notes

1 Though female Spanish migrants in the study have higher third-level education than their male counterparts, they did not do as well as their male counterparts, with fewer progressing to paid employment. Females: males taking care of the home as their primary role are in a ratio of 11:1.

2 Joint research by the Department for Business, Innovation and Skills (BIS) and the Equality and Human Rights Commission (EHRC) investigated the prevalence of pregnancy discrimination in the workplace. The survey shows that 11 per cent of pregnant women reported they were either dismissed, made compulsorily redundant where others in their workplace were not; or treated so poorly they felt they had to leave their job. One in five mothers had experienced harassment or negative comments related to pregnancy or flexible working hours from their employer and/or their colleagues (EHRC/BIS, 2015).

3 See arguments relating to the gendered ideologies concerning the division of labour in the household, and the marginalisation of women's place within it, in Hochschild (1990) and Leonard (2001).

4 Women of Colour are situated within at least two subordinated groups that frequently pursue conflicting political agendas. This need to split one's political energies into two is a dimension of intersectional disempowerment that Men of Colour and White women seldom confront (Crenshaw, 1991).

5 A study on the experiences of Black African men in their transition into the Irish workforce suggests that they experienced the workplace as a threatening environment to their identity and self-concept because of the stereotypes held by the dominant population about them (Akpoveta, 2010: 34).

6 The Employment Equality Act 1998 outlaws discrimination in employment on grounds of Gender, Family status, Marital status, Age, Disability, Sexual orientation, Religion, Race and Membership of the Traveller community. Its scope covers discrimination in relation to access to employment, advertising, conditions of employment, equal pay for work of equal value, promotion, collective agreements, training and work experience. These kinds of discrimination are outlawed whether by an employer, an employment agency, a trade union, a professional body, a vocational training body or a newspaper advertising jobs.

7 Delgado and Stefancic, 2012.

8 Delgado and Stefancic, 2012. See McGinnity et al. (2009) on employment-based discrimination based on name change on résumé.

9 Sporadic working hours and low-paying jobs require people who are not on welfare benefit payments as those in the social welfare system are only paid for the days they are unemployed. A one-hour shift of part-time work means the loss of a day's pay for someone on social welfare benefits, making it unattractive for low-paid Irish earners.

10 Esther Lynch, the Legislative Officer at the Irish Congress of Trade Unions, has said it is difficult to see how zero-hours contract practices are compatible with human dignity and decent work. It takes workers back to a time when they stood at a designated corner and waited for an employer to come by in the hope of being selected to work that day. Today, instead of a corner, the modern zero-hour worker waits at home for a text. Others have their shifts cancelled or are sent home at a moment's notice. They receive payment only in respect of hours worked. Their working hours can be subject to variation on a daily or weekly basis, they receive very short notice of work and this can be by text message. Workers can be sent home from work at very short notice; for example, if it rains or business is quiet (Lynch, 2014).

11 The official language of communication in Nigeria is English, and, as such, it is used in the education system.

12 Taxi driving in Ireland reflects an over-representation of Black African workers, particularly males of Nigerian descent. It has been riddled with clashes between the indigenous population of drivers and those from Nigeria (McGuire, 2019).

13 Papademetrio, Somerville and Sumption (2009), who discuss the social mobility of immigrants and their second generation, argue that many immigrants become more likely to work in low-skilled occupations, and that they often have lower employment rates and experience higher unemployment than natives. They show that many immigrants become more likely to work in low-skilled

occupations, and they often have lower employment rates and experience higher unemployment than natives. They also document how Black and Canadian workers' wages did not increase, and may in fact decrease over a period; and how the earnings of visible minority migrant men in a Canadian study do not converge. These experiences are common in European countries, where migrants from non-OECD countries integrate less easily than migrants from OECD and particularly EU source countries. They highlight the Turks in Germany, Middle Eastern and African migrants in Sweden, North Africans in France, and Turks and Moroccans in the Netherlands.

14 The primary and secondary segments and a growing 'unpaid segment'. Volunteering in Ireland is employed as a holding place, particularly for Black workers where they encounter economic exploitation.

15 Some use 'demeaning' instead of 'demanding'.

16 See the summary of the work of Doeringer and Piore in Wachter (1974). The dual approach to the secondary sector revolves around four interrelated hypotheses: First, there is a dichotomy between the primary and secondary sectors. Secondly, the wage and employment mechanisms in the secondary sector are distinct from those in the primary sector. Thirdly, there is limited mobility between the two sectors. Finally, the secondary sector is marked by pervasive underemployment because workers who could be trained for skilled jobs at no more than the usual cost are confined to unskilled jobs.

17 It is important to make this distinction between White Europeans and 'other' Europeans, as some are Europeans by naturalisation with different skin colour (Black and brown) and experience from Caucasians of European descent.

18 The missing link in the social capital theory, according to Bonilla-Silva and Baiocchi (2008: 146), is that societies which partly distribute resources along racial lines will have their social networks and capital racialised; that the individuals in racialised societies do not have equal access to networks which will themselves be racialised and, finally, the assumption that social capital leads to certain virtuous norms of behaviour is both untenable and confusing of causes and effect.

19 Just one of many stories with which I was inundated after publication of my article on labour discrimination in Ireland (Joseph, 2019), which led to the launch of the #Notobrainwaste campaign.

7

Minority agency, experiences and reconstructed identities: how migrants negotiate racially stratifying systems

As anti-immigrant sentiment increases across the Western world, its goal is to attain racial homogeneity which is among one of the most effective means of social control (Goldberg, 2001). Inequality, economic dominance and racial stratification have indeed been argued to produce behavioural changes (Massey, 2007; Verdugo, 2008; Haney López, 2010). Whereas a stratification approach 'attributes continuing stratification to a broad range of behavioural and systemic practices, from volitional to unconscious, individual to institutional' (Haney López, 2010: 1028), 'the real issue is the way the society responds to an individual's racial identification' (Zuberi and Bonilla-Silva, 2008: 7). In his extensive and sometimes controversial work on Blacks' and Whites' performance gap in education, Ogbu (1994, 1999) insists inequality persists because change has only looked at the barriers in opportunity structure and Whites' treatment of Blacks, without targeting Blacks' responses to racial stratification. Key to his arguments is the notion that minorities develop some survival strategies which facilitate academic success and others which hinder it (see also Foley, 2004). While the notion of minority agency is plausible, the hierarchical proclivity of racial stratification systems lends credence to the argument that a measure of compulsion is required for the sustenance of racial stratification as 'none voluntarily submit to debasement and oppression' (Haney López, 2010: 1052).

To gain insight into how race affects those who live under it, members of society cannot be studied as if their race is an individual characteristic that explains individual outcomes (Zuberi and Bashi, 1997). However, authors drawing on the melting pot ideology still tend to credit the outcome of minorities to their purported in-assimilability (Myrdal, 1962), again making the migrant the problem that needs to be fixed. The theory of immigration and racial stratification criticises this over-reliance on ethnic and behavioural changes, citing the case of the US insisting immigrants on arrival receive a racial tag and are reconstructed into racial identities which affects their outcome (Zuberi and Bashi, 1997). In Ireland, social distance and colour hierarchy reify the racial order, with melanated (dark) skin being a predictor of more pernicious experience, limiting access to paid labour compared with white skin. In this chapter, I discuss the extent to which systemic racial inequity permeates the socio-economic environment. The racial stratification framework shifts attention from individual to collective outcomes to reveal how migrants negotiate, occupy and make meaning of the racial hierarchy in the labour market. The combination of credentials and European citizenship predicts acceptance for White migrants but not their Black counterparts. The focus of this chapter is to present a framework for interrogating the migration to labour market participation process within the following four strands: expectation, experience, negotiation and identity reconstruction. In addition, the typologies in the interviewees' trajectories reveal five characteristic labour market experiences of migrants that become solidified into corresponding reconstructed identities. Based on this framework, I argue that the labour market participation process should be understood as a race phenomenon where a colour-coded migrant penalty is endemic in the proliferation of racial inequality. Racial stratification is not however deterministic because individual migrants can and do express minority agency which influences labour mobility and intra-group hierarchy.

Migration from the individual to the collective

When migrants come into the labour market in racial states, they not only contend with a racialising system which affects their positioning but also the (mis)allocation of resources (Massey, 2007). The ways they make meaning of those experiences are usually different from how racial states, economics, statisticians, academics and sociologists describe them. Despite overwhelming evidence that whiteness and its hierarchical positioning affect the labour market outcomes of migrants (Joseph, 2018, 2019), across OECD member countries, educational attainment, language, credentials and modes of entry have become much more important in explaining these income differentials, even more so than race and gender. Many individuals at the top tiers of the labour market also tend to locate the cause of economic inequality within the victims themselves, as individualistic attributions are said to trump structuralist attributions as the main cause of poverty (Feagin, 1972). The scholarship of immigration and racial stratification in the US insists that, from arrival, changes occur where 'Immigrants lose their ethnic identifiers as they are reconstructed into races' (Zuberi and Bashi, 1997: 679–680). This raises two key areas for consideration about the Irish context. The first is the process migrants go through to access the labour market: are there individualistic paths or are there typologies; what determines any disparities? The second concerns the reconstruction of migrants and the kinds of changes they undergo when accessing the labour market. Do they lose their ethnic identifiers or any other parts of themselves?

In the course of many years of working with people of migrant descent in Ireland, and being one myself, I realised that not only do migrants have a way of making meaning of their experience, but, more importantly, they can also articulate their trajectory. Rather than tell the stories of others, I have adopted CRT's counterstorytelling which gives marginalised groups the opportunity to share their stories in their own words. When they tell their own stories, the view(s) expressed are usually different from the dominant discourse. To achieve this goal, I asked thirty-two workers of migrant descent two questions: (i) I gave them an open invitation to recount their trajectory in the Irish labour market from arrival up to their present roles. This was supported with three sub-questions, relative to changes in their career goal/s, influencers and any attempts they had made to change their jobs. (ii) I asked them about their trajectory into Ireland in order to establish how status and racial identities are ascribed and presented for new migrants to fit into, and the changes and conflict that arise for migrants as a result of differing status between their previous places of residency and Ireland, their new country.

The migration to labour participation process

When migrants journey from their home countries and access the labour market, they go through four stages: expectation, experience, negotiation and reconstructed identity. This is presented here as a framework for interrogating the migration to labour market participation processes (Figure 7.1). In the first strand, which is expectation, migration commences with an expectation of a better quality of life and typically culminates in the pursuit of economic independence. The second strand consists of five characteristic labour market experiences that range from hostile to lenient; accepting to excluding; depending on a person's nationality of descent and race. In the third strand, negotiation

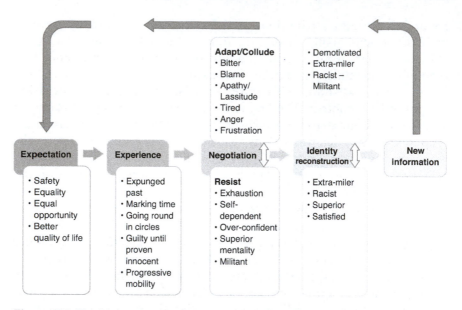

Figure 7.1 The labour participation process of migrants in the labour market

strategies become evident where migrants respond in one of three ways to racial stratification: they resist, adapt or collude with the stratifying systems in the host country. Last is the reconstructed identity. Here, migrants' strategies to navigate their labour market experiences necessitate behavioural changes which become solidified into corresponding reconstructed identities.

Although for ease of explanation, this process has been presented as linear, it is neither simplistic nor linear, for a number of reasons. First, the strands can occur simultaneously, with some migrants staying longer in some phases than others. Secondly, the presence of other intersecting vulnerabilities such as age and family responsibilities hampers some migrants in the process. Moreover, since Ireland is hierarchical (Joseph, 2018), all migrants, due to racial stratification, do not start from the same position. While White Europeans enjoy a head start where whiteness has the functionality of an affirmative action, Black workers start with a deficit in esteem, acceptance and trust of their credentials (Joseph, 2019). Similarly, the circular process as presented in the framework can actually oscillate back and forth depending on individual experiences. Finally, when migrants obtain new information through education, personal motivation or intervention, often through employment programmes like EP, their expectation is renewed and this restarts/can restart the process, making it circular.

Expectation

The first strand of the migration to the labour participation process in this framework is expectation. On arriving in Ireland, the host country, migrants all have a basic expectation for a better quality of life. Irrespective of the reason/s and migration routes, which can range from displacement by war, persecution or natural disaster, thus seeking asylum, to those seeking personal improvement through education or learning the English language, labour migration or family reunification, they all, without exception, arrive ambitious, with high expectation and belief in meritocracy, and in many cases, a good level of (in) formal qualifications and skills. The process of migration, particularly the first generation, self-selects very strong people by the very nature of the difficulties associated with the process. This is even more so for non-European migrants seeking to cross the ever-tightening borders of both fortress Europe and the United States. Because of the difficulties associated with the process, first-generation migration typically selects those with academic excellence, the industrious and risk takers with a desire to build a better quality of life. Migrants' expectations culminate in the pursuit of paid employment in the labour market to enable them to access resources. While this is not always achieved by many migrants, as depicted by their high(er) unemployment rate across the EU, economic independence continues to be their desired end.

Experience

The experiences of migrants negotiating the Irish labour market are presented as the second strand of the labour participation process framework. Despite variations in the demographics of the participants in the study, it was race, nationality of descent and skin colour that presented marked differences in their labour market experience. Most White migrants on entering the Irish labour market commence with a lateral at best, but often downward, mobility into precarious jobs such as cleaning, bar tending, accommodation assistants and childminding, while some are able to progress to language-related roles in call centres. Black migrants who, on the other hand, find it difficult to access such precarious and menial jobs typically commence their career journeys with volunteering and down-skilling by retraining in order to access low-skilled roles (see Figure 7.2). The stories presented in this framework challenge the meritocratic myth of equal opportunity as the vehicle of labour market mobility, while at the same time exposing the salient ways a group's racial category affects their by-products – meaning their

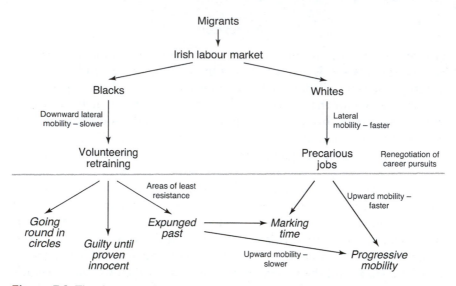

Figure 7.2 The characteristic experiences of migrants in the Irish labour market

credentials (education, skills and experience). The pathways migrants encounter when accessing employment in Ireland – presented as the five characteristic labour market experiences of migrants include *going round in circles, expunged past, guilty until proven innocent, marking time and progressive mobility*. While these experiences have been presented as linear for ease of representation, please note that some pathways are interlinked as shown in Figure 7.2.

Also note the following about how these data are presented. The storytelling technique of CRT's counterstory (discussed in chapter 4) helps weave the narratives of the participants into dialogues between composite characters based on information from the semi-structured interviews to give readers a sense of the participants' experiences. To this end, you will encounter two characters, John and Phil, in this section. They are representative composite characters developed to portray the political ideologies of members of the dominant group in management roles in the labour market in Ireland. These two fictional characters and their dialogue created from the dominant discourse in Ireland are based on information from interviewees when recounting their experiences across the labour market in Ireland. The characters of John and Phil are portrayed in conversation with migrants to draw out the context presented in the narratives of the interviewees in the study. Please note that all comments from the migrants in the dialogue are real, not fictitious, and are direct quotes derived from my research interviews. Although the typologies presented in this study are not new, together they are a contribution to scholarship on the theory of immigration and racial stratification as it relates to Europe. They shed light on the socio-economic terrain migrants are navigating, their labour market experiences and how migrants make meaning of these experiences. With the current discourse on knowledge epistemicide, it is important for researchers to find opportunities to include the voice of their research subjects particularly in collaborative studies, where research is for and not on the research subject. It allows silenced groups to interpret their marginalisation. The migrant voices in this study have articulated their experiences with words different from the usual discourse on migration and labour market outcomes, and in the process they highlight the unchallenged, oppressive social arrangements in the labour market.

Five characteristic labour market experiences of migrants

Going round in circles

Let us start with the most pejorative of the five experiences unveiled in this study – the *going round in circles* experience, which becomes evident from Rita's stories. Rita is a Black African woman.

> *Setting*: *John, an HR Manager, and Phil, his colleague, overhear two women conversing about their labour market experience as migrants.*
> *Priya*: I am Spanish. I completed my Master's in Spain before coming to Ireland as a child-minder, but it was bad, with no opportunity to learn English with my host family. So I left the job. I was very desperate as I was spending [all] my savings to stay here [Ireland] and I wanted to immediately apply for jobs. Because of my English, I decided to go for a factory job and some voluntary work. My manager was very good. She was my referee. It took two years, but I am working in my specialty now and I'm satisfied. What about you Rita?
> *Rita*: Er, I am a qualified solicitor from Nigeria with eighteen years' practice. My career goal when I got here was to get a job and rise through the ranks. At that time, I was eager and looking at middle-level positions. I applied for a public service job and completed all the interviews from the written, oral, … medical, everything. I was told at the end that I couldn't get it because I hadn't lived here [Ireland] for up to five years, which was not stated in the advertisement at the time. So I realised that my career goal had to be different and I needed to do a rethink. So chatting to someone, I was advised to start small. … But the small is still not leading me anywhere as I am just *going in circles*. [*Long pause*] … After completing a master's degree at level 9, I was told I needed a level 5 course to get a job. I did it, then applied again for jobs, but I was told I don't have enough experience. Then I spent two years volunteering. I see other volunteers come and become paid

staff. … But two years on, I am still on their books as a volunteer. I left them and completed another Master's … thinking it will increase my chances. Ten years in Ireland and I'm stuck … worried of not being a good role model for my daughters. There is still no opening for paid work, but I have started another level 5 course as a care assistant. Many of my African friends seem to find employment as carers.

John: Do you think her experience is because she is Black?' [*John asked as they left the coffee shop.*]

Phil: I would hate to think so.

Rita's experience is what I have framed as *going round in circles*. It is migrants' experience of becoming stuck transitioning between various unpaid employment, (re)training and education, usually at levels lower than their prior education, with limited success accessing paid work. It is characterised by unemployment, underemployment and unpaid employment which usually culminates in their exclusion and marginalisation. This experience is an impasse where migrants' credentials (foreign academic qualifications, skills and work experience) are ascribed inferior status and deployed in ways which actively hinder their access to paid employment. As highlighted through Rita's story, first, their work experience is reckoned as insufficient for their desired employment pursuits and, when that criterion is met mainly through years of unpaid work, their educational qualifications are evaluated as inadequate, and vice versa. While this experience confirms that migrants encounter the age-old segmented labour markets where 'occupational gatekeepers' control the access and allocation of resources (Vidich and Bensman, 1968), it also highlights institutional discrimination and the ascription of incompetence on possessors of non-European credentials and European credentials in Black African bodies. Here, credentials are employed as barriers that are fluid and constantly (re)defined to favour groups with more perceived similarities to the host community, while simultaneously disfavouring and excluding those categorised as different. In this way, the 'going round in circles' experience can resemble and produce downward or lateral mobility, particularly for highly skilled and educated migrants. Immigrant-sending countries suffer a brain drain and receiving countries a brain waste as foreign-trained workers have been reported to become stuck in low-skilled work (Ożden and Schiff, 2006; Sumption, 2013).

The effect of this experience is often described as becoming 'professional students' and as 'career suicide'. My continued push for change is motivated when I remember the words of a tearful migrant on narrating her experience that 'I'm just stuck. … You remember you are not looked at as okay to be paid for the job. … I am sorry I am getting emotional right now but I am upset because it just shows me that I have not gone beyond where I was when I first came [to Ireland].' This going round in circles, which was the most pernicious experience identified by participants, was only reported by migrants of Nigerian descent – the only group in the study with black skin. Although the sample size might suggest these are idiosyncratic experiences, their prevalence among this group suggests otherwise and implicates nationality, race and skin colour in this migrant penalty. The Nigerian males who encountered similar experiences in my study did not seem to benefit from a gender advantage as they did not fare much better than their female counterparts. This raises questions about meritocracy in the in(up)ward mobility of migrants as Irish citizenship and achievement factors did not advantage all groups equally. This is not to say that the native-born or Irish 'others' (Irish Travellers) do not experience disadvantage; neither does it mean that lack of recognition of qualifications does not affect other migrants. What I argue is that the level of disadvantage experienced by the Nigerian migrants, and by inference Black workers, is particularly acute. It is important to note here that those with this experience do not only have foreign qualifications, as they typically retrain to acquire qualifications in Ireland as part of the process of going round in circles. All the interviewees of Nigerian descent in this study had retrained in Ireland to Master's degree level at the time of these interviews.

Expunged past

The second experience is the *expunged past* which occurs when migrants' prior learning and skills are unrecognised in ways which erase their prior achievements. It is characterised by the inferiorisation, disempowerment, non-recognition and the over-performance of actors whose foreign credentials, particularly those from outside the European Union and the United States, are undervalued in ways which undermine their access to paid employment. The main difference between this and the going round in circles experience is that their targeted retraining (into areas of skills shortage) in their new country gives them access to paid employment, albeit at the lower end of the economic ladder. This is common with migrants who arrive in their host country educated to university and postgraduate degree level, often combined with years of work experience, but are unable to access paid work at levels matching their qualifications and skills. In this experience, non-European credentials are automatically assigned inferior status, while those obtained in the EU are ascribed superiority. Such constructed hierarchy of European superiority is problematic for non-Europeans and for people with non-European qualifications as Europe is set up as the measuring standard for people (Zuberi, 2011) and their credentials. The 'expunged past' experience is predicated on Eurocentrism that metes out a migrant penalty which selectively victimises possessors of non-European credentials. While this apparent preference is usually attributed to lack of trust in foreign qualifications (OECD, 2014), the racial bias in the socio-economic environment in which these credentials compete is undeniable. This composite dialogue from the participants' narratives illustrates the expunged past:

> *Setting: John was mulling over the conversation between the women in the café when a call came through from his Nigerian tenants, Abayomi and his wife Seun. After the pleasantries, John decided to gather more information.*
> John: You and your wife are both working. How was it finding employment in Ireland?
> Abayomi: [*Self-conscious laugh*] Um …, to be quite honest, it was as if all the work I had done in the past was irrelevant because it wasn't from Ireland. That really disturbed me.
> Seun: I quickly came to the realisation that recognition of what I have is non-existent, never mind accepting that I even have it. … I don't think that is fair because that is akin to *expunging* a lived life. (Emphasis added)

The experiencing of an expunged past, though not gendered as it affects males and females, is raced as it was also only reported by migrants of Nigerian descent. Regarding Polish and Spanish migrants, their access to a European language gave them an advantage over their Nigerian counterparts while proficiency in English language was deployed as a gatekeeper restricting their labour mobility to racialised, low-skilled, low-paid or language-related jobs. Nigerians with English-language proficiency were less advantaged in the labour market than White European migrants with English as a second or other language. The purported 'hierarchy of English superiority' (Kohli, 2016) seem dependent on race. Eighty per cent of Nigerian migrants in Ireland, according to the 2016 Census, were reported to have a higher level of English language than Polish (at 39 per cent) and Spanish (68 per cent) migrants, yet the level of spoken English of the Nigerian population does not advantage them in accessing paid employment. Regarding highly skilled roles, however, all the groups experience an expunged past as their credentials are deemed inadequate for professional roles, except in sectors such as healthcare, where demand for skilled labour far exceeds supply. This is one channel through which highly skilled migrants become polarised into low-skilled jobs.

Guilty until proven innocent

Let us now consider the next experience, which is the *guilty until proven innocent* experience, as depicted through the narrative of Gbemisola, a female Community Development worker of Nigerian descent who at the time of the interview was a naturalised Irish citizen and had lived in Ireland for almost ten years. Her conversation with her friend Chidi, gives us insight as to why a simple question was upsetting and a microaggression.

> *Chidi* [*Observes Gbemisola's frown*]: Are you okay?
> *Gbemisola*: Oh I had one of those upsetting experiences today. After facilitating a workshop for primary school students, one of the teachers said to me, 'Your English is so good. How long have you lived here [Ireland]?' … Ten years I answered innocently, ready for a long conversation about Ireland. 'No wonder, your English is so good,' she replied. Can you imagine that! I am really tired of this low expectation people have of us just because of our skin colour. They expect me to be an asylum seeker whom they teach English. … They expect me to be incompetent, despite the level of education I have acquired back home and in Ireland. It is so disheartening …

Encounters like Gbemisola's, which are riddled with microaggressions, are the *guilty until proven innocent* experience. They highlight the preconceived views about a person's abilities based on their name, nationality of descent, and how they look and sound. In the 'guilty until proven innocent' experience, recognition, respect, trust and expectation of competency in the language of the host community and ability have currency as they advantage workers in gaining paid employment and career advancement (Joseph, 2019). The symbolic and cultural capital in this experience presents as a hidden resource. While it is automatically made available to White workers, Black workers have to prove themselves against racialised, bipartite prejudgement based on their perceived race to be considered eligible to receive it. In this regard, White Europeans mainly encounter positive prejudgement which advantages them in progressing into paid employment, compared with their Black counterparts who encounter mistrust, low expectation of their competency and of their commitment to work. For example, Polish candidates can benefit from being seen as hard working. Considering the high levels of reported discrimination during job searches by migrants, this is not surprising. Rather, during recruitment such practices influence outcomes, as illustrated in this composite story where the positive stereotype advantaged Slavomir and the negative one disadvantaged Tunde:

The hotel manager considered both candidates with university degrees. Tunde from Nigeria had better spoken English than Slavomir of Polish descent ... but Nigerians can be loud and rude sometimes she thought. ... Considering that most of the other staff are very hardworking Eastern Europeans who never give problems ... Aisling selected Slavomir for the role.

Although labour market theories are loaded with reports of migrant deficit, a disposition towards black deficiency – that is, the belief that Blacks have a deficit that is from their internal characteristics – is common in this experience. The negative prejudgements encountered by White migrants like Polish and Spanish migrants primarily relates to their communication in the English language. In that sense, the negative bias does not present structural barriers to their career pursuits. They are still advantaged by whiteness and their nationality against their Black Nigerian counterparts. Although I emphasise access to resources both in the form of economic and cultural capital through paid employment by the Polish and Spanish migrants in these instances, it is important to note that these progressions are predominantly into precarious jobs that are significantly lower than their highest academic qualifications.

Marking time – nowhere to grow

Now consider the following story to help you understand and give context to the fourth experience in this framework, which is the *Marking time* experience.

> **Setting**: *John was at the back of a taxi with a Black African driver and he immediately picked up his conversation about migrant workers.*
>
> *John*: You don't have to answer, but I am curious about how you chose taxi driving.
>
> *African taxi driver*: Oh it's simple. It was either that or be on social welfare. I am Nigerian. I used to be a solicitor in Nigeria. When I got here [Ireland], I got a job as a mortgage administrator in 2007 ... before taxi driving happened to me. ... Don't look so shocked. [*He laughs as he catches John's eyes in the rear view mirror while smoothly navigating the Dublin City centre traffic.*] ... That story is not unique to me. Many of my male, African friends are in exactly the same boat or worse ... or worse. [*He repeats while emphatically nodding his head*] In 2008, when the recession hit, I was made redundant. I kept applying for other jobs and after a series of unsuccessful interviews, I decided to try self-employment as a taxi driver.
>
> *John*: Really?
>
> *African taxi driver*: Yes. I mean, the whole idea was that maybe I can upgrade and become a solicitor here, but I saw it involved two years'

retraining without earnings and a financial requirement which I did
not have ...

John: You were able to get a job in 2007 though.

African taxi driver: It wasn't all good in the job too. Everyone knew my
law background, it wasn't hidden. One year, they were looking for an
assistant to the in-house solicitor. They didn't ask me. They gave the
role to a girl who only did it for two weeks and asked to be transferred
back to her previous department. They then gave it to another man. ...
But I felt that ordinarily, my background was well known and that
offer was not extended to me.

John: [*Feeling an unusual defensiveness rising as if the driver was
criticising him*] Did you ask?

African taxi driver: Oh I did indicate an interest. There wasn't an open
application process, they only selected people for the job.

John: And you think your race influenced your work opportunities?

African taxi driver: Don't you think so?

John: How?

African taxi driver: In the financial sector, new staff will come in,
I will train them and after a while, I will find they've been given a
portfolio. ... Like being given some brokers to manage while I'm
still there doing general administration. ... Six ... seven years later, I
have regressed. Here I am driving a taxi. It is not great ... it is not the
best, it is not fulfilling because you know that is not what you are
trained for. You are just doing it because you don't want to be sitting
at home doing nothing or be stuck receiving social welfare. You don't
get any satisfaction, you are just there *marking time* hoping for
change but if that will happen, it remains to be seen. (Emphasis
added)

This 'marking time' experience uncovered by the African taxi driver's
narrative is common among participants who encounter prolonged
delays and difficulty accessing paid employment. They respond to the
numerous unexpected occurrences first by renegotiating their career
objectives to settle for small increments, typically in roles below their
highest academic attainment. The intense opposition encountered and
the effort expended in attaining these roles combined with disillu-
sionment about meritocracy curtail further career pursuits. Similar
to the Linguist trajectories (Knight, 2014), the White highly qualified
participants in these cases attain career advancement, particularly from
precarious jobs, to opportunities with better conditions (see Figure 7.2).
Those with basic levels of education also progress more than they envis-
aged before migrating. While the participants were all not fully satisfied
with their progress, these roles appeared to be the ceiling of their
employment progress, as evidenced by Priya's reports.

I went from a bad childminding job to factory work, now a marketing assistant. To be honest, I felt when I got this marketing job, it was the best job I could get in Ireland. ... They opened some internal positions and my manager asked me to apply but I didn't because in the end, I am going to leave the country. ... Some of my colleagues complain because you are given more responsibilities but not much financial return and there is not much level to grow. For me it is enough as I can live on it [income] and save a little. I am not looking for any other job now. (Priya, Spanish, Female, Masters in Marketing)

The absence of significant difference when controlling for gender, race, nationality and educational qualification among participants who reported this experience points to a general ceiling with stricter restrictions into primary sectors. It means there is a much broader migrant penalty with barriers to upward mobility operational against all migrant groups in Ireland.

Progressive mobility

Despite the limiting experiences I have discussed, migrants can be seen to occupy professional and management roles in Ireland, albeit in low proportions. This composite dialogue from the participants' narratives illustrates *progressive mobility*. It is a composite of four different narratives brought together through the inquisitive mind of John, our fictional character, and the real stories shared with me during the semi-structured interviews.

> *Setting*: *John is meeting with four middle-level managers of migrant descent in Ireland.*
> *John*: Thanks for meeting me.
> *Efe*: [*A very determined-looking banker of Nigerian descent*] I'll kick this off by saying that my working in a multinational was not accidental.
> *Lucja*: [*Polish female programme officer in the not-for-profit sector*] It took me a few years to get to my present role. ... My education and working hard definitely helped ... but more of luck.
> *Dayo*: [*Male, Nigerian doctor*] My plan was to sit for an exam with the Royal College of Physicians, after which we had to attend interviews.
> *Santiago*: [*Spanish, male, transaction specialist*] I can say I am satisfied with my evolution in work in this country, because before I came here, I wanted to work in this kind of company in a similar position. [*Throws back his head slightly, lost in thought*]. You know ... I remember how it started. I was singing softly in Spanish as I cleaned the canal in Dublin when I was volunteering. 'It seems you are Spanish,' a lady working beside me said and we got talking. I speak

three languages and I am looking for a job, I told her quickly. 'You're in luck. There is a job opening where I work. Send me your CV, she replied. ... That was it really. ... That was my entrance to employment in Ireland. [*Gentle sigh*]

Efe: I left the shores of Nigeria to compete on a global scene to be able to improve myself. I hadn't even completed my Master's by the time I applied for the job ...] in the heat of the recession when it was really hitting everybody hard. I knew that to get anything, I will have to give it my best. ... It was difficult but I got the job and after a few years of performing well, I was promoted. They finally listened to me ... I actually created my current role and it is not too different from back home. My first degree in Economics already made a way in the financial service. It was great that I didn't have to deviate.

Lucja: Actually, it took a good few years between my first job and the one I have now, but I am satisfied with my *progress*. ... Making friends here and the networks helped. ... I made a few mistakes along the line and studied a Master's I didn't need. ... So I did two Master's here with student loans. [*Grimace*] ... but I am happy.

Dayo: I started as a house physician outside Dublin. I also did a Master's in Public Health and I presently work as a registrar, so I'm good.

Santiago: I got an interview and worked in the company the lady recommended me for. In the meantime, I had attended another interview in a multinational company and got hired. After fourteen months, I got my promotion letter just before coming here today. So I can say I am quite satisfied.

'Progressive mobility' involves migrants who are able to advance in the labour market. It consists of: (i) those progressing in line with their career goals, who are either achieving levels higher than they had in their home countries or had retrained and were achieving upward mobility; and (ii) migrants at entry-level roles who either had lower levels of education on arrival and advanced in their careers after upskilling, or the cohort of young graduates and school leavers at the beginning of their careers. This experience is characterised by upward mobility, social capital, and similarity/assimilation by adopting their host's culture and traits.

The White migrants with this experience enjoyed labour market credit from their group membership, not just as European citizens as the Nigerian-Irish participants who were all Europeans through naturalisation at the time of the interviews did not enjoy similar credit, but as White Europeans. Having similarities with the host or the ability to attain similarity, for example in physical appearance, name, language, credentials, culture and behaviours, influences this outcome. The Nigerian workers with this experience attained it mainly by targeting areas of skills shortage such as healthcare, social work or roles where it was necessary to have migrant expertise, particularly in community-based roles working with specific migrant groups.

This experience was identified predominantly among the White European migrants, who were of a younger age group with similar representation between males and females. Only one in four of the Nigerians in the study reported this experience. This occurred after they had encountered some of the other experiences like the expunged past experience, then retrained to areas of least resistance before they went on to progressive mobility. Many spent an average of 2–10 years before they attained the progressive mobility while their White counterparts often attained that mobility within 2–4 years.

Negotiation

With labour markets in Europe being increasingly unequal arenas rife with the marginalisation and exploitation of migrant workers, this strand frames the strategies migrants use in negotiating their way up the paid labour supply chain. There is evidence that the mobility of foreign-born workers is hindered by what is in practice a segmented labour market system (Reich, Gordon and Edwards, 1973), and migrants' belief that a combination of hard work and meritocracy will ease their access to paid labour is severely challenged by prolonged encounters with systemic barriers. This does not mean migrants are passive victims of racially stratifying systems, but rather that they exercise agency by negotiating the adverse labour market conditions through dialectical interactions with these stratifying systems. Analysis of the narrative of the interviewees shows three strategies migrants employ which create an intra-group behavioural hierarchy in the labour market. These are: (i) resist, (ii) adopt/adapt and (iii) collude with the system. Although racial stratification is a recruitment of actors into a ranked racial group by birth and descent, Ogbu (1994), in his highly contested essay mentioned above, argues that one of the reasons inequality persists is that minorities' (Blacks') responses to racial stratification have not been targeted for change. My study shows that migrants who are able to resist the racially stratifying systems have a better individual outcome and are stratified at the top of the labour market among migrant groups, in what I call a behavioural hierarchy (see Figure 7.3).

The strategies migrants use to attain mobility typically commence with renegotiating their employment pursuits. This can be in the form

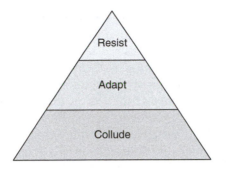

Figure 7.3 Minority agency and intra-group behavioural hierarchy

of a downward renegotiation of their initial employment expectations in order to find open points of entry which are the areas of least resistance into paid labour. The extent of the downward renegotiation varies depending on the intensity of the barriers encountered. Others – mainly the Black cohort – retrain to attain a more 'accepted' education from the European education system while being simultaneously involved in unpaid work to bridge the purported gap in their European work experience. Blacks commence with unpaid work, volunteering or training while Whites typically commence with precarious work. For workers of migrant descent where English is a second language, like those from Spain and Poland, advancing for them means first learning to speak English, while those from Nigeria take on unpaid work, healthcare or self-employment in the Black economy. Rather than migrants simply seeking low-paying or unskilled work or the groups displaying 'non-White inferiority' on which white supremacy is premised (Mills, 1998: 110), the minority agency adopted by various groups are strategies they employ to circumvent the pervasive structural barriers perpetuated through discriminatory practices and the various ways credentials are deployed in maintaining groups in different racial strata.

Resisting racially stratifying systems
Those who resist are typified by unrelenting attempts to access the labour market and subvert the exclusion experienced. Migrants who resist exhibit the most visible mobility. Immediately on arrival, they either retrain or obtain Irish qualifications and seek employment in areas experiencing skilled labour shortage, requiring migrant representation or specialist skills such as an EU language. They also resist by self-assimilating into the Irish system. While one might be tempted to focus on individual motivation as the reason for the disparity in outcome, we cannot ignore the hierarchical nature of the socio-economic environment

which means that migrants initially stratified at the bottom of the racial ladder are faced with harsher conditions, thus requiring more effort to access paid labour at their desired level. In other words, mobility is dependent on where one's group is located on the strata. The system teaches those at the bottom of the economic ladder to assimilate or mimic the attributes of those at the top of the racial ladder in order to access paid labour, or they remain at the bottom. The labour market can often appear like a system where you either assimilate or become marginalised. One noticeable difference in this group is that they upskill when they retrain, unlike some migrants who down-skill. They also adopt more of their hosts' characteristics, ethnicity, behaviours and culture. Even when engaged in unpaid employment, they usually seek unpaid internships/roles in sectors experiencing shortage to gain work experience from Ireland – their host country.

Adapt

Those who adapt to the system often internalise their experience and adjust their employment pursuit to match the sectors offering the least resistance. Some migrants indeed respond to the stratifying systems by reducing their expectations; targeting less financially rewarding roles with less stringent selection criteria and gravitating towards jobs where they encounter the least resistance. This is dependent on the intensity of the barriers encountered. Many down-skill from degree courses ranked at level 8 and 9 on the qualifications framework to courses which are three to sometimes five academic levels lower than their highest educational attainment. Others – mainly the Black cohort – retrain to attain a more accepted education from the European education system while simultaneously being involved in unpaid work to bridge the purported gap in their European work experience. Examples are migrants with Master's degree qualification, many with two undergraduate degrees, retraining to level 5 qualifications to access customer service, retail or care assistant roles. This is the kind of brain waste which many migrants experience in the labour market in Ireland which has triggered the #NoToBrainWaste campaign – resisting the underemployment and lack of opportunities for documented and fully qualified people of migrant descent in Ireland.

Collude

The third group, who collude with the system, are migrants who grow weary from the continuous opposition and difficulty encountered attaining mobility in the labour market; they reduce their attempts to the barest minimum, and end up transitioning between unemployment, un(under)paid and low-skilled work (into areas offering them points of entry to any form of labour participation). The worst outcome is among migrants who retrain to four or five levels below their prior qualifications and are still unable to access paid employment. Many take recourse to unpaid employment to gain individual labour market mobility and work experience from Ireland; (up)re-skilling through training courses and unpaid internships in any available opportunity. Compared with those who resist racial stratification, many in this group often down-skill after they encounter difficulties, which can include discrimination and racism in the labour market. It is important to note that those whom I describe here as colluding with the system of racial stratification are not people who do not want to work. They are people who have come to the Irish system motivated to work but have become discouraged and respond to the negative environment by reducing their labour market activity.

This group, who encounter so much difficulty, can be supported in the following ways. Programmes like EP should support them to be more strategic when retraining; they should be encouraged to upskill rather than down-skill; and employers should be mandated to give this group written feedback on their applications in order to deter covert racism and arbitrary scoring during the shortlisting process. Lastly, employers should be responsible for proving they have not been discriminatory against these applicants if challenged.

Identity reconstruction

The fourth strand of the migration to labour participation process focuses on how migrants' responses to racially structured labour markets influence their identity changes. Consent is not sought from migrants in Ireland or anywhere in the world about what race they want to belong to. Rather, races are ascribed based on how a person looks and race is inscribed on White and Black bodies. The reconstruction of migrants is concomitant with a loss of their ethnic identifiers in the United States (Zuberi and Bashi, 1997). In the Irish context, the five experiences discussed above over time became solidified into corresponding identity changes (Figure 7.4). These changes were observed by paying special attention to the points in the migrants' narrative which signified any form of reconstruction, including changes in identity and characteristics; any observed loss of ethnicity and their triggers; and the behaviours migrants adopt to circumvent the racialised structural barriers they encounter in the labour market.

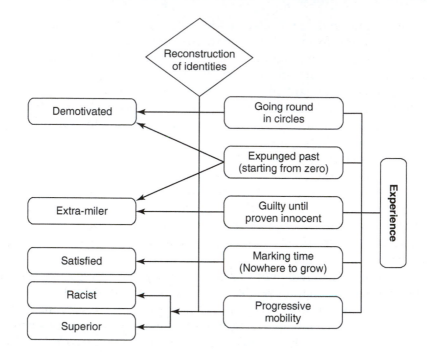

Figure 7.4 The identity reconstruction of migrants

Demotivated migrant – living the marginalised life
The 'demotivated migrant' identity develops in marginalised foreign-born workers who feel stuck from protracted periods spent in the 'going round in circles' and 'expunged past' experiences. They constantly vacillate between decisions, particularly in relation to remaining in their current roles or seeking new employment; relocating from their host country or remaining; re-attempting to access the labour market through new training courses or engaging in additional unpaid work; integrating by maintaining social contact with members of the host community or segregation by separating themselves to their own community; fluctuating between emotional unease and hope; between low self-esteem and feelings of superiority against members of their host community. Similar to the 'precariatisation' of workers, where pressure and experiences may affect the minds of workers resulting in the four A's – anger, anomie, anxiety and alienation (Standing, 2011: 19) – this group also exhibits feelings of frustration and controlled/passive anger.

Attempts to address mental health issues and antisocial behaviours without addressing labour market inequalities, discrimination, racism and lack of access to jobs will be futile. There is no integration of people into society without jobs. Imagine a parent, after twenty years of not being able to obtain paid work. While mental health difficulties will be an issue, this is not the main problem but a consequence of living for prolonged period in unmet expectations. Their coping mechanisms will become solidified to become their reconstructed identity. This is linked with unmet expectations being exacerbated by prolonged underemployment and undervalued and under-utilised skills which are common among migrants who become or end up demotivated. While this might seem like the development of internalised characteristics within migrants, the demotivated identity is a consequence of the selectively discriminatory hostile socio-economic environments in the labour market. The resultant loss of motivation among victims leads to an increased feeling of lassitude which is disguised by an attitude and positioning of 'I don't care'. Funmi, a Nigerian female, expresses this feeling aptly:

> I don't think I need anybody to accept me, because it is a personal choice whether you accept somebody or not. So I don't need the society to accept me. I am here, so live with it. Because I cannot change the colour of my skin. ... I couldn't be bothered if they accept me or not. I cannot help them in their perception, I cannot help them with their acceptance war ..., I don't know if that is the right thing to call it.

Experiencing exclusion in the labour market triggers migrants' segregation from their host. Although some migrants experience a pull towards home, withdrawal from the host community by 'demotivated migrants' is typically in response to inaccessible and hostile labour markets. This is displayed not only by their holding fastidiously to their ethnic and cultural values, but they also tend to reject the host – a process which further emphasises difference. Two migrants who exhibited this identity reconstruction of the demotivated migrant described their state saying: 'Confidence zero, no motivation, because I can't win.' 'At that point, I kind of felt really unmotivated. ... I began to feel maybe it was time for me to move on.' White Europeans in the study did not report this experience and they did not display this identity change. This is because different socio-economic environments are provided for White and Black migrants in Ireland, despite their European citizenship. This does not mean that White Europeans do not become demotivated; what it indicates is that (i) Migrants who experience the 'going round in circles' or an 'expunged past' in the labour market have a higher propensity to become demotivated migrants. (ii) There is a strong connection between migrants' isolation and experiencing exclusion in the labour market. (iii) That migrants with more visible racial markers and attributes perceived as different from the host community are more likely to experience severe forms of exclusion. They also have a higher propensity to become demotivated migrants. It is important to recognise that this group is facing a systemic problem and not simply a case of inner weakness.

Extra miler – proving myself up the ladder

The 'extra-miler' is the identity change in migrants who counter experiencing an expunged past by going the extra mile in their everyday lives in order to gain upward mobility on the labour market. It is characterised by over-achievement, over-performance, self-determination and usually the adoption of the ethnic identifiers of the host community. Going the extra mile for this group in practical terms means having a higher level of education than their peers of native Irish descent, in order to achieve the same goals; punctuality at work including never being late, never leaving earlier than others, abstaining from taking sick leave – even when desperately unwell – and maintaining an unblemished attendance record; learning every aspect of the organisation's work; being proactive to proffer solutions to others, which is like being the 'go to' person in times of difficulty; and learning and adopting the new culture, their way of being, communication and socialising with team mates and denying their initiative by silently following their organisation's rules. Their 'extra miler' performance serves as a strategy to subvert the unequal treatment they encounter, and resist the lower strata to which they are consigned on the economic ladder.

In order to gain upward mobility in the primary segment of the labour market, the extra miler's path is usually characterised by resistance and immense personal effort which they describe with words like 'fight', 'struggle', 'survive' and 'proving'. Let us consider some examples of how extra milers describe their labour market experience:

> For you to be able to compete, you have to be able to offer more than your Irish counterpart has to offer.

> You have to fight every step of the way to get there.

> I seem to answer the questions they are looking to be answered.

> As a foreigner, you have to give it extra, more hard working, you have to be more educated to get up there. Compared to your peers to get the same role you just have to be ....

Migrants who match the extra miler identity also display assimilationist characteristics. They learn early on from their prior contact with their host which performance achieves approval and positive esteem and which ones to avoid in order to avert negative outcomes. Inherent in the process of becoming extra milers is a high propensity to strip away the alienable attributes of migrants which do not resemble attributes of members of the host community. These cultural and ethnic changes are evident, for example, in terms of language where extra milers tend to lose their own language and accent in public spaces and adopt the host community's in the guise of professionalism. It is, however, important that such changes should not be seen as strictly due to a rational choice, but rather as requisite for attaining upward mobility in segmented labour markets and avoidance of the pernicious migrant penalty suffered by visible minorities.

Superior migrant – progressing by personal effort

Migrants who only attribute their access to paid labour to the immense personal effort exerted in overcoming the structural barriers in their labour market trajectory develop the 'superior migrant' identity. This is a complex behavioural pattern that arises from adopting the extra miler characteristics to attain 'progressive mobility'. They differ in that they express superiority towards members of their own community who are not achieving upward mobility in the labour market, and towards members of the host community, particularly workers and line managers they believe have lower credentials than themselves. Unlike the militant migrants (which I discuss in further sections), however, they do not homogenise and categorise whole races as inferior; rather, they judge individuals' perceived action or inaction.

Considering that the progressive mobility experience which triggers this identity reconstruction tends to demand and reward migrants' assimilation, this group also typically adopts the identity of their host community. The assimilation model, where newcomers have been argued to lose their racial identifiers, is evident as superior migrants align to the normative configuration of their host, not only in language, dress, culture and way of socialising, but also in conforming to their credentials. In this way, they experience the Irish labour market as rewarding sameness such that social creativity for mobility is closely related to how migrants can pass as members of the host community. Interestingly, these migrants tend to distance themselves from the stereotypical attributes of their own communities such that not fitting their groups' ascribed stereotypes is reckoned an accomplishment. They typically believe other group members can attain similar achievement if they put in the same effort. People with the superior migrant identity blame other group members for their lack of labour market mobility while showing ambivalence about their own struggles with structural barriers.

This is problematic, particularly as it is premised on an assimilation model of a baseline social type to which individuals and communities must conform.

Racist migrant – becoming militant

Those who develop what I present here as racist or militant behaviours towards others typically homogenise groups based on their national- ity of descent and view them as inferior. Racism is usually expected to be unidirectional, going from the indigenous population to minority groups. Some have even argued that racism cannot be from the powerless to the powerful, while others based on the Irish case caution about being side-tracked by colour as the only possible locus of what race means at a given time and place (Garner, 2009). From my study, migrants who have struggled to achieve progressive mobility tend to develop either of two identities: the 'superior migrant' or the 'racist/militant migrant'. The disaffection of the developing racist migrant identity is linked to the perceived disproportionate effort they feel they must invest to achieve similar labour mobility to their native peers. These experiences act as triggers and are erroneously used as justification for racist actions which they exhibit not only towards groups whom they see as racially inferior to themselves, but also to members of their own community who are stratified lower down the social class strata. In the same vein, some migrants on lower socio-economic strata tend to exhibit some form of racism towards those stratified higher than themselves, particularly natives they believe to have lower qualifications or less expertise.

The racist/militant migrant, who typically make themselves the base- line for others, become defensive of their race and respond in one of two ways. One group take on the shame of their group stereotype by distancing themselves, not only physically but also in the behaviours they exhibit to avoid the lower strata to which their group members are assigned. They at times become extremely critical of their own race and group members. The other describe their group more favour- ably and align very strongly with their racial grouping by identifying with their ascribed stereotypes. They romanticise their group, refusing to critique or see any of their weaknesses. This group also exhibits extreme criticism of other groups, particularly the host community. This experience of developing racist/militant characteristics can also occur to varying degrees among migrants who are most marginalised. The Black migrants who exhibit this quality tend to be more militant and Afrocentric than racist – because of the power dynamic required for racism to be performed, while the White migrants tend to be more racist than militant.

Satisfied migrant – making the most of the glass ceiling

Migrants whose pursuits of career advancement become curtailed, and who attribute their experience of marking time in the labour market to barriers of an almost insurmountable nature due to racial difference and discrimination, develop the 'satisfied migrant' identity. For Black workers, these barriers are linked to race or skin colour, while for the White workers the main barrier is linked to proficiency in the English language. This identity change is characterised by prolonged underemployment, lassitude and gratitude for their accomplishments despite encountering racialised structural barriers. The pernicious nature of the obstacles in their trajectory from their initial roles (which is usually from precarious work) depletes their drive to pursue further career advancement. Though they express satisfaction with their career progress, it is usually ambiguous and of a precarious nature as it acts as a buffer against their disappointment and underlying feeling of lassitude.

Assimilate or be marginalised

Unlike in the United States, where migrants are reconstructed into racial identities, labour market experiences in Ireland, which is a racially stratified society, influence the identity reconstruction of its newcomers. Race and the response to perceived racial difference are at the core of migrants' labour market experiences in Ireland. This operates in ways which guarantee disparity in outcome among different migrant groups where Black workers are automatically disadvantaged vis-à-vis White workers, despite similarity in their credentials. Although foreign-born workers in Ireland and their credentials are ascribed lower status based on nationality of descent rather than citizenship and race, which in turn affects their access to allocated resources, it operates through a stratification system where the closer to a White European a worker is, the higher they and their credentials are esteemed. The anti-discrimination laws in Europe are an indication of its interest in inclusion and integration. The system is, however, inherently hierarchical in ways in which the positioning of foreign-born workers and their credentials compel people of migrant descent into adopting behaviours which produce associated identity changes if (in)upward mobility is to be attained. This is an assimilating process which seeks to homogenise the workforce by whitening migrants seeking acceptance into the labour market in white supremacist economies.

With the exception of migrants in sectors experiencing acute labour shortage, migrants in Ireland typically start their labour market trajectory in precarious employment. It is a system where whiteness advantages

Eastern and Western European workers, who spend from three months and up to two years in precarious roles. Many then progress to racialised language-related roles such as multilingual customer service or call centre roles, while many Eastern Europeans move to physically exerting roles characterised by long, unpleasant working hours in the service industry. In the case of Black workers, despite having equivalent education from their country of descent, many can spend long periods of up to five years first being assimilated into Eurocentric norms through years retraining to attain European qualifications. While exchanging labour for free proves sufficient for White Europeans through unpaid work to reduce the gap and progress to paid employment, it proves insufficient for Black workers for whom mobility is mainly possible through adopting the 'extra miler' identity. The dearth of opportunities for qualified Black workers in Ireland means they suffer a double dilemma of being a brain drain for their sending country and a brain waste in their receiving country.

Injustices in labour practices are disguised as non-recognition of non-European credentials. This is in fact linked to the racial stratification of groups, and taken as the norm while producing dire consequences particularly for Black workers. It maintains the racial order of Whites at the top and Blacks at the bottom of the economic ladder. This should not be taken to confirm the dominant discourse that Black workers are more likely to be unemployed, as the inference in such statements can be misleading. Rather, Black workers with non-European credentials or European credentials in Black bodies suffer a harsher migrant penalty and selection criterion in the labour market than their White counterparts. While both views indicate similar outcomes for the workers, the former is easily interpreted to blame the workers for their marginalisation while the latter focuses on the institutionalised systems.

Conclusion

By recounting the narratives of migrants at the top and bottom of the Irish labour market, the stories of marginalised groups in this chapter give voice to previously silenced experiences. Labour market marginalisation of migrants is often legitimised through research that centralises the mode of entry while obscuring race and the heterogeneity in their experiences. We are all affected by our experiences. Labelling someone a migrant, Black or non-White does not preclude them from being affected by how they are treated. We have seen in this chapter how the five characteristic experiences of migrants reconstruct their identity, with the bipartite nature of the labour market producing more adverse conditions for darker, non-Western workers than White workers. While all the interviewees experienced varying degrees of difficulty progressing in the labour market, most of the White Europeans were able to progress from precarious employment to jobs with better working conditions. The Black workers, on the contrary, were mainly characterised by downward/lateral mobility. I also illustrated how the main structural barrier which served as gatekeeper against White workers was the English language, and non-recognition of non-European credentials for Black workers. There is a connection between racial stratification and the country of origin/descent of a person and their credentials. The assignment of inferior status to qualifications obtained outside Europe is deployed to exclude newcomers, while European credentials are esteemed. The framework of the migration to labour participation process of migrants in racially stratified societies reveals micro-level processes which make the disparity in outcomes among groups inevitable. While the analysis was based on empirical data generated from Ireland, it suggests that the marginalisation of Black workers in racially stratified societies which are predominantly white is endemic rather than atypical. There is also a high propensity to create racialised ghettos in the labour market, with certain migrant groups segregated into sectors with poorer working conditions. For these reasons, I propose that the labour market participation process should be understood as a race phenomenon which acts to integrate migrants into the racial order in their new countries such that racial inequality is endemic and its proliferation inevitable.

8

Policing the racial order through the group favouritism continuum

The pervasiveness of economic and racial inequalities is undeniable. It is evident from the whiteness of the top tiers of the labour market, to the escalating overt anti-migrant sentiments of right-wing nationalists, not overlooking the higher unemployment rate of Black workers compared with their White counterparts – in Ireland and across Europe. Despite the growing population of Europeans of Black African descent with credentials acquired in European institutions, many labour forces in the Western world are still able to retain homogeneity like a well-frothed cappuccino with chocolate sprinklings. This is a world racial order where Blacks are at the bottom and Whites at the top, not because of a class of 'lazy' workers as some claim, but due to systemic organisation of people which influences their starting point, and thus their outcome – enabling the racial preference of white supremacy.

By examining the Irish context, the central task of this chapter is to present the favouritism–disfavour continuum (hereafter favouritism continuum) as the system through which these inequalities, injustices and economic exploitations are proliferated in modern states. The system operates through four interrelated structures, including group favouritism – which ensures some groups are favoured over others – and social acceptance – which determines where groups are placed on what I describe as the favouritism continuum. The third structure is the psychological implicit bias – which operates in racially stratified labour markets in conjunction with the favouritism continuum. Here I discuss how implicit bias produces explicit discrimination and how groups on lower racial strata try to circumvent its negative effect. The last structure comprises human contact – the connectors through which the racial stratification system operates.

The chapter concludes by making three key arguments. First, that the favouritism continuum determines the outcome of actors by the position they occupy on the continuum. Secondly, that although racial stratification is restrictive, the outcome is fluid and changeable due to minority agency and individual mobility. And thirdly, the continuum is the machinery which maintains homogeneity in a heterogeneous labour market, thus producing racial inequality.

Group favouritism: simply looking after our own

The response to difference and sameness along racial lines is one of the main mechanisms through which the racial stratification of Black and White actors is maintained on the labour market. When sameness is treated more favourably than difference, it exacerbates the disparities in outcome among migrant groups. By sameness, I mean the possession of characteristics similar to members of the host community. These similarities are judged more favourably, resulting in the positive outcome of its beneficiaries, while difference is judged more harshly, resulting in negative outcomes. Sameness does not only include visible physical difference such as skin colour, hair texture or lip size, but also ethnic and cultural leanings including nationality of descent, accent, names and credentials (education, skills and experience). The unfair favouring of group members with similar attributes over members of other groups is group favouritism.

Group favouritism is highly accepted and utilised as the de facto mode of operation by its beneficiaries. It is typically portrayed as harmless and is scarcely acknowledged as a resource. Many modern states today are heavily invested in generating new avenues to favour and protect their citizens from outsiders and real/perceived hostile conditions. The 'America First' anti-immigrant rhetoric from Donald Trump including building a wall to keep 'unwelcome' migrant groups out, the Brexiters, Irexiters, the increasing nationalist, far right and white supremacist groups across Europe all claim to be driven by a need to take care of citizens first. Group favouritism is systemic, farreaching, and able to simultaneously produce positive and negative effects. Those who experience its negative effects and are penalised by it describe it as a discriminatory practice. Those who benefit from it and experience its positive effects often display ambivalence about its existence yet they actively draw on it (Joseph, forthcoming). Group favouritism operates through rewarding sameness in ways in which the more people have in common with members of the host community, the more they experience its benefits. Conversely, the more they differ from the host community the less favour they experience. In fact, the further away groups are in characteristics and features from the host community, so favouritism changes to disfavour, producing disadvantage and dire outcomes. Interestingly, the criteria which make group favouritism accessible to individuals and groups are not actively acknowledged by its beneficiaries, and neither do those who practice it formally acknowledge the parameters for selecting beneficiaries. These factors are, however, linked to Eurocentric norms, particularly culture, ethnicity, skin colour, names, language and geographical location in terms of being of European or non-European descent. Among groups who suffer high levels of disfavour in Ireland, when controlling for educational attainment and other achievement factors, workers of Black African descent fare worse. To get an accurate picture, it is imperative that we compare like with like by comparing the outcome of group members with third-level education, further education or primary education among themselves. To compare group outcomes without the particular characteristics will skew the data.

Group favouritism is beyond liking, familiarity or being more comfortable with possessors of the same attributes. It actually determines how people are treated, their mobility, access to social capital and share of resources. White Europeans can experience group favouritism as leniency or patience for actions which in others are evaluated negatively and harshly. For example, speaking in a direct manner, or challenging or questioning employers is often received as being assertive, proactive and confident while in others, particularly people categorised as Black, such actions are viewed negatively as rude, aggressive and loud. Whites who claim to be unaware of their advantage readily discount how nationality and race influence the responses of employers and managers at work. It gives them access to trust, positive regard and ascription of proficiency, all of which are resources which advantage group members.

Race, which is one of the most pervasive and pejorative markers of visible difference, is a key trigger for some of the most hostile experiences. While Blacks in Ireland find it five times harder to find employment (CSO, 2016), a White European with a lower level of communication skills in the English language has a higher chance of securing a customer-facing role compared with their Black counterpart with good communication in the English language. This is evident from the state's Census statistics, where there are more Eastern Europeans in the retail sector. The situation of White European migrants in Ireland is not perfect. It is, however, better than that of Black workers who do not experience any of these types of automatic positive responses or regard. The racial categorisation of Black workers subsumes their European identity and most of the automatic privileges which it bestows on their

White counterparts. Similarly, European citizenship advantages its possessors differentially and its potency comes to the fore when it is mixed with phenotypic whiteness. This means that sameness is a determinant of a person's acceptability. It is also able to reduce the differential in labour market outcomes between the Irish natives and workers of migrant descent who exhibit similar attributes to their host. Cultural similarity also influences workplace relationships. This includes being made to feel comfortable and welcome in the office. It facilitates after-work socialising and collegiality, which in turn promote cooperation among members. Blacks typically experience the negative spectrum of group favouritism, which is at the disfavour end of the continuum.

In egalitarian societies, merit and personal effort are expected to be the primary determinants of progression in the labour market. This is, however, undermined by the after-effect of group favouritism as it advantages favoured groups, giving them a head start similar to affirmative action. For example, in Ireland and across Europe, nationality of descent is employed to determine the beneficiaries of group favouritism. Though it can be seen as simply favouring people of European descent, its presence as a means of assessing who to employ reifies racial inequality. It advantages the Irish born over non-Irish, European over non-European and White over Black. Such policies on a micro level operate as part of the othering[1] process of marginalising racial minorities. In as much as these types of policies operate through selection criteria that affect non-possessors of these attributes/elements, it is not framed as discrimination or racism, but as working for the 'national good' of citizens.

Group favouritism in the labour market is often invoked by similarity in race, culture, ethnicity, nationality, language, physical location and physical features. In its operation, the parameters through which various groups are favoured are treated as de facto in society and protected by state policies. The practice itself is discriminatory by nature due to the disadvantage which automatically accrues to groups who do not possess similar attributes to the host. White Europeans, who are the main beneficiaries of group favouritism, are not unaware of its potency. Rather, they actively seek, draw from and utilise these advantages when possible while maintaining a culture of silence about it. For example, the unquestioning expectation and acceptance that being a White EU citizen confers rights of movement, similarity in culture, trust of education, skills and rights to be advantaged over Black bodies gives a picture of the automatic use of whiteness to garner group favouritism. Rather than group favouritism being a device used by a few, it is an unregulated top-down machinery in the Western world which (re)produces and maintains the racial order. DiTomaso (2013: 6), in her award-winning book, *The American Non-Dilemma: Racial Inequality without Racism*, insists 'the act of favouritism that whites show to each other (through the hoarding and exchange of social capital) is what contributes most to the continued racial inequality'. It raises key questions for consideration which are not being addressed. Notwithstanding if groups are performing explicit acts of racism or discrimination per se, favouring people from groups simply because they have similar characteristics or are from similar groupings is group favouritism, which is inherently discriminatory. The practice of, or engagement in, group favouritism is a performance of discrimination and racism.

Social acceptance

Everyone wants to be accepted, what I do not yet understand is why we are not talking about it. Acceptance is a common need, yet a search only throws up the passive forms of 'accepting of one's fate' or 'providence'. Think about it: one of the first demands made by marginalised people is to be accepted. In a study I conducted in Ireland with a small cohort of information-rich European citizens, despite having good jobs, good homes, the language of the host community and access to medical care, not feeling accepted was the main reason they reported for not feeling integrated in Ireland (Akpoveta, 2011). The focus has, however, mainly been on concepts like the 'aversion to being rejected' (Leary, 2001: 3), and exclusion and its propensity to disrupt society (DeWall and Bushman, 2011). Seeing that rejection is undesirable, why are we not researching acceptance, what it is and how it can help in managing human difference?

The struggle for social acceptance

The problem we have today is not one of belonging but one of acceptance. The acceptance of human differences, or lack thereof, influences the labour market outcomes of migrants in Irish society. Considering the progress made by people with black phenotype all over the world, many people will be appalled at the idea that Blacks feel they are still not being accepted as human beings, as this would seem to be more in line with the pre-1900s racist states. In Europe in general, and Ireland in particular, race is often framed within individual acts of discrimination and racism. However, race theorists like Du Bois (1908: 1), who insisted 'the problem of the Twentieth Century is the problem of the colour line', routinely argue that race affects the humanity of Black people because the Black person is not seen or treated as human. In my conversations with people of Black African descent, they overwhelmingly refer to experiences which impinge on their personhood. If we deconstruct race, the identity of Blacks in the Western world is intricately linked to two key problematics: first, to be automatically recognised as human beings, and secondly to be treated as equals.

Migrants and people of migrant descent occupy an outsider positioning relative to the host community. This places the host community in the position of receiving or having to 'accept' others, thus making them the in-group or insiders. Though this is not new, it is worth highlighting the two-way dynamic involved. On the one hand, the migrants come into the new community, negotiate their way to find where they fit and belong, and the host community is to 'welcome' (Baker et al., 2009), 'recognise' (Taylor, 1994) or accept them. This is, however, not always the case: as based on a group's racial identifiers, the insiders (host community) either accept them – in which case migrants experience inclusion, or they reject them – where the migrant experiences exclusion. This leads to experiencing an 'excluding inclusivity' (Reay et al., 2007: 1054), which Bryan (2010) argues 'fails to disrupt, yet brilliantly disguises, power relationships between majoritised and minoritised groups in society'. The request to be accepted (with their difference) and treated equally is typically framed in the social sciences as a belonging need which is a psychological need (Erikson, 1968; Maslow, 1970; Kune, 2011). In the politics of recognition, denying people recognition as human beings can cause harm and misrecognition. We have supporters of President Donald Trump shouting 'send her back' at Democrat House of Representatives member, Ilhan Omar. Meanwhile, Ireland is working on laws to make it possible to revoke the citizenship of migrants who obtained it by naturalisation (Department of Justice, Equality and Law).

Acceptance is, however, necessary for newcomers to be integrated in their host society. The positioning of the host as insiders places the responsibility for recognition and acceptance with them. Though this in itself is not unproblematic, mainly because it suggests a power dynamic where the host community are more powerful and stratified higher, it offers newcomers better prospects than rejection and exclusion. The level of acceptance experienced by migrants in the labour market continues to be very specious, particularly depending on their race. This is evident from the superficial acceptance of migrants during the economic boom period when labour was needed and the quick turnaround resisting migration. Bryan (2010) also problematises the notion of 'accepting' and highlights the power relationship implicit in the relations between those who do the embracing and those who are embraced, and insists interculturalism in Ireland is utilitarian and is based on what people can offer the economy. It is not rooted in a human rights approach; rather, it is 'dependent on the self-perceived altruism or generosity of the "host"' (Bryan, 2010).

Characteristics of acceptance

Acceptance is dependent on human contact. It is fluid, as it changes from person to person and from group to group. People often become more accepting or more open to accepting others with increased positive contact, knowledge about people's credentials or getting to know people as individuals. Some can, however, look at positive contact/interactions with others as exceptionalism and thus not be influenced. Acceptance is triggered by either actual or virtual contact and then undergoes internal evaluation.

This brings me to a very important point, which is human judgement. Acceptance is hinged on judging others, things or situations. Though judgement or perception is part of the way human beings make meaning of their lifeworld (see Hovland and Sherif, 1980, on social judgment; Mezirow, 1995, on transformative learning and frame of reference),[2] the type of judgement Blacks experience in racially stratified labour markets is problematic. This is because they are based on group's stereotypes – the negative perceptions people hold about them – and these stereotypes act in ways which can limit the expectations and capabilities of their victims.

This is where human responses become tricky. For us to judge something, we have to weigh it against a set of standards and rules. Judgement is fundamental to social categorisation (Kerbo, 2000), where we begin to classify groups as good, bad, better or best. When these measuring standards are Eurocentric, then all that do not conform to European norms will be judged negatively or more harshly and then rejected, while those that do conform will be judged positively and recognised and then accepted. These are variants of acceptance because acceptance is receiving something/someone as valid and true. There is, however, a power dynamic in the way acceptance is positioned. Since the host community are already occupying the spaces newcomers are coming into or seek to enter as the in-group, they are positioned in a way to accept migrants: rather than the outsiders simply choosing to belong to the in-group, the responsibility of accepting the other is on the host. Acceptance in an economic milieu which is racially stratified is not a passive relationship. Rather, it involves a two-way process which requires active participation from the host and those stratified higher. It is a visible phenomenon that is observable from a person's body language, tone of voice and actions. For example, a friendly disposition and open communication are important parts of acceptance, as well as public recognition of a person's effort and contributions, and accepting all aspects of a person such as their religion, nationality of descent, race or skin colour.

Authentic acceptance

From my work with people of migrant descent in Ireland, I define acceptance as the state or act of receiving someone during un-harmful social interactions as true and valid without imputing judgement. Just as we have superficial forms of acceptance, we also have its authentic form. Have you ever entered a room, started a new job or attended a meeting where you don't know anyone and you wonder how you will be received; if you will be accepted or welcomed; if you will have to hide parts of yourself to fit in or if you will be accepted just as you are? You can almost notice when people decide you 'are' your group's stereotype or when they decide otherwise. Well, most minority groups, particularly those with visible difference, experience that regularly. Acceptance is visible to marginalised groups and outsiders. Both the authentic and superficial forms of acceptance are visible.

When marginalised groups ask for acceptance, they are not asking us to receive their harmful actions; rather, there are three key requests. First, is to be fairly judged, such that a person and their attributes should be received free of predetermined negative judgement. The second is to have a sense of being a part of the system as insiders and not on the fringes. The third request is to be unhampered in the process of fulfilling one's humanity. Similar to our understanding of integration, authentic acceptance is a two-way process. Acceptance from the host community is usually the problematic end of the process, as they have to deal with the difference which they encounter in the newcomers. The main point of contestation is really how difference is treated and not the difference per se.

Let's consider one interviewee who mentioned feeling blocked and unable to communicate at meetings and with colleagues, but spoke with me without expressing any self-consciousness. When I asked her why she was able to talk clearly with me, she said 'You are not judging me'. The role of acceptance is to provide a space where people are not judged based on something which has nothing to do with them – their group's stereotypes. Accepting relationships do not judge individuals based on their group's stereotypes but on the actual conflictual actions. People want their difference accepted, and not to be used as a reason for which they are judged and assigned a lower stratum on the racial ladder.

It is important not to confuse this form of acceptance with lack of self-acceptance; a view commonly held about Blacks that their feeling of not belonging is related to internalised feelings of inferiority. This is typically advanced based on the discourse of managing group difference from the perspective of need for belonging, a deficit model which blames out-group members for their marginality. Due to the positioning of the in-group members in the two-way process of acceptance, they receive automatic acceptance which makes them best placed in the mutual process to extend a reciprocal acceptance to newcomers. Although belonging needs and acceptance are closely linked, they should not be used interchangeably. The absence of acceptance for an individual or group of people can create belonging needs because it means their difference is not being recognised, and it can result in experiencing exclusion. The presence of acceptance can also satisfy belonging needs and build group or individual esteem. Whites enjoy this group esteem already by being automatically accepted into the human race, not by reason of their individual action but by their collective as Whites.

Psychological implicit bias – contact, fears and triggers

While 'unconscious bias' has been widely hailed as a new diversity paradigm – one that recognises the role that bias plays in the day-to-day functioning of all human beings (Hassouneh, 2013: 183), I am cautious about the 'unconscious' aspect which tends to absolve us of our responsibility. The focus here will be on implicit bias, particularly with the increasing awareness of 'unconscious biases'. The increase in worldwide migration translates into an increase in social contact between migrants and host countries' populations in many spheres of life. The nature of this contact in the economic sphere and the implicit bias held about each group on the basis of race and ascribed attributes has proved problematic. Recent racially motivated incidences and fatal shootings in the United States have impacted on the proliferation of the science of implicit bias in the public discourse.[3] Meanwhile, in the employment scene, not only does implicit racial bias exist, but there is also empirical evidence across Europe and Ireland that it is a thriving practice. The discourse is, however, not often framed in terms of psychological implicit bias. For example, a study of responses to CVs with similar information showed a differential response from recruiters based on the names of the applicants which indicates a racial bias (McGinnity et al., 2009). In a mapping of rich countries and the minority groups they discriminate against, a similar 2014 OECD EU-wide study showed that, compared with the majority population, Sweden, Switzerland and Ireland ranked highest on the résumé to call-back ratio. That is, the average number of résumés someone with a recognisably minority name submits before they get a call-back for a job interview, compared with résumés with the exact same skills but from candidates whose names identify them with the majority population group in that country. A ratio of 2 means someone would need to make twice as many applications for a job to get a call-back, compared with an applicant with a name associated with the country's majority population.

Among the scholarly disciplines, law and psychology are in the forefront in developing the idea of implicit bias and how it influences people's outcomes. The recent *Implicit Bias Review* (Staats, 2014) by the Kirwan Institute at The Ohio State University gives a comprehensive report of the prevalence of implicit bias in all spheres of life.[4] Though social behaviour has ordinarily been treated as being under human conscious control, some studies support the view that social behaviour often operates in an unconscious manner (see EEOC report, 2013). Considering that a group's racial markers determine their access to resources, status, racial positioning and how they are treated, we can safely say that the stereotypical views held about a group bias human actions and how they treat others. Consider a real example reported by one of my interviewees, where a manager asked his design team not to include Black faces on billboards in a professional area. How does this demonstrate implicit bias? If we consider what his actions are saying about Blacks, then we can imagine what he thinks about the group. The overt view, first of all, is that Blacks are unemployable, do not live in certain areas or that an advert about working people should not reflect people with Black physiognomy because Blacks are not working. In other words, the advert is not targeting Blacks and the product is not for them. Note how in this example, this supposed 'unconscious' belief would have remained hidden but it came to the fore when triggered by the need to portray his idea of working people or his interpretation of his employer's target group. Analysing and understanding implicit bias is not simply looking at the actions or what happened; it is examining what the action is based on, the belief and underlying stereotype.

Implicit bias is rooted in unquestioned beliefs held about others. They are not often considered as biases, but usually lie dormant in people until triggered into effect by contact which can be either physical or virtual. These biased views can be held about nationalities, racial groups, level of education, language, and in the myriad of opportunities where we experience difference. The continent a person hails from can be held in low esteem and judged negatively. Similarly, racial markers such as physical appearance, including skin colour, serve as triggers of implicit bias which is usually dormant until individuals come in contact with difference – their trigger. Though one would assume that contact occurs only when groups meet physically, it nonetheless also occurs in nonphysical forms. For example, contact through CVs, foreign-sounding names, public opinions, media reports and even the conversations of others all serve as channels of contact which can trigger our psychological implicit biases. Think about it: the level of bias against immigrants was not very obvious until the Syrian crisis forced responses across Europe and the US. Today, many nations are content to let human beings die at sea based on their categorisation – asylum seekers and illegal immigrants. We have also enacted laws that criminalise compassion by making it illegal to rescue drowning immigrants.

A common trigger in the labour market in Ireland is language or accent. The belief in this case might be that people who speak with such accents do not understand English; and that customers will not understand them. The natural automatic thought (NAT) is that they cannot be proficient in the task/job/role. The action might then be, do not employ them. Let's take another example. Say the trigger is skin colour or foreign-sounding names, where Black skin colour or names that sound like they come from the African continent trigger bias of black deficiency and white supremacy. While people might never openly admit having a bias against others, contact often triggers and exposes implicit bias. White employers, managers and recruitment personnel particularly do not openly own up to their biases against Blacks. However, the level of discrimination reported by Blacks in the labour market (EU MIDIS 11, 2016) and their higher unemployment rate say otherwise. These examples are usually classed as unconscious biases, but they are not. I will define unconscious biases as thoughts and beliefs we have about others that we are too embarrassed to openly admit we hold, yet we base our actions on them and allow them to control our actions/responses.

A question to one of the 2018 presidential candidates in Ireland, Peter Casey, revealed not only his bias against Irish Travellers but also that of almost a quarter of the voting population, as his anti-Traveller sentiments saw support for him rise steeply from 1 per cent to almost 23 per cent within one week.[5] Implicit bias is intricately linked to the operation of group favouritism in that difference similarly triggers harsh responses, negative evaluation and disfavour, while sameness or similarity to the host or the familiar is employed as the standard to measure others who exhibit difference. Implicit bias is used as the justification for our actions and how we treat others and their groups, whether with favouritism or disfavour.

Fear of triggering implicit bias

The invidious consequence of being treated unfairly results in some minorities becoming mindful of triggering the implicit bias, particularly in those stratified higher than themselves on the racial ladder. Thus, in a bid to avoid negative treatment which can influence their labour market outcomes, many end up adjusting their behaviour in ways which can potentially alter their identity. Groups stratified at the bottom of the racial ladder additionally are burdened with the extra task of monitoring and modifying their behaviours to disprove the negative views held about their group. Minority groups are at a higher risk of developing a fear of incurring negative judgement which is not simply an opinion but a determinant of outcome. This fear itself can serve different purposes. On the one hand, it can lead to an identity change in the victims of such implicit bias where they adopt the behaviours of the host community – for example, malleable attributes such as culture, socialising style, language, food and taste are easily exchanged for those of the host community. On the other hand, it can reify the belief underpinning the implicit bias as the victims in their fear tend to become self-limiting – for example, the fear of not being understood because of accent can hinder minorities from participating and everyday socialising which is a key part of workplace culture in many Irish workplaces. In my study, interviewees reported this as feeling blocked and holding back from expressing themselves due to uncertainty. Whereas in places where they felt comfortable, confident, trusted and known, they were able to express themselves without the fear of being judged negatively and communication was not a problem.

The fear of triggering the implicit bias in others and incurring negative treatment can act as a self-inflicted, self-limiting policing system. Similar to how racial stratification is maintained, migrants or those subjected to psychological implicit bias can sometimes respond to systemic pressures in ways that reify the biased belief held about their group. In the case of Black Africans, the triggers and fears are typically linked with their racial markers. For example, there is an ongoing aversion among Blacks in Ireland to the question, 'where are you from?' People of Black African descent consider it an open invitation for Whites to introduce stereotypical beliefs about Blacks, Africa and Africans. The conversation usually goes on from there to be about asylum seekers, aid to Africa, debt, bad governance, fraud, or one sickness or the other, and rarely about the positive impact of Africa, Africans or Blacks. Those who respond with silence or by closing off the conversation are seen as lacking in communication/socialising abilities, while those who respond defensively are seen as confrontational. Interestingly, the fear of triggering the implicit bias in others means you have to stereotype others as well. This is because in a similar manner, minorities here would, even before direct contact, have to pre-empt the other and adjust their actions in ways that will stop the implicit bias from being activated.

Eradicating psychological implicit bias

The malleability of implicit biases is an indication that they can be unlearned and changed. Researchers have given considerable attention to studying various ways of eradicating bias under the notion of debiasing, which views biases as malleable and able to be unlearned through various debiasing techniques (Staats, 2014). A study of the labour market outcomes of migrants during the recession in Ireland suggests that missing information on CVs being filled from stereotypes by employers exacerbates the problem. The authors recommend that employers gain more information about migrant groups as a way of addressing it (Kingston, McGinnity and O'Connell, 2015). This is the approach which is routinely taken in Ireland and which has resulted in ineffective integration strategies, involving learning about the dress, dance and diet of the 'other'. It also assumes that the issue of psychological implicit bias and its prevalence against certain groups is individual rather than systemic.

   This approach is problematic because the negative attributes ascribed to our human differences have both a historical and contemporary origin, operating along racial lines. This cannot be resolved simply by providing missing information to individuals, as that would suggest that individual ignorance is the reason for racial inequality rather than the racialised socio-political and economic systems. To the contrary, psychological implicit bias operates within individuals and can remain dormant until triggered by contact with difference or sameness. While it triggers positive responses to those who exhibit sameness, it triggers a negative response to difference in a way that serves to maintain the racial order, by advantaging and rewarding homogeneity in a heterogeneous community. Thus, monitoring how human decisions are made, how people respond to difference, how we judge the difference we encounter, what we see as difference and how we categorise difference are vital to debiasing the human mind. Do you, your organisation or team see things and groups using the bad, good, better, or best lenses or do you accept people as true and valid representations of themselves? I return to this conversation at a later stage on how to manage difference and what we should teach.

The favouritism continuum – policing the racial order

With the continuing struggle for world domination, the European Union has enacted policies[6] to protect its citizens against increasing hostility and volatility, particularly in the markets. It has also promulgated laws on the sharing of resources, access to markets, free trade, movement and workers. Similar policies have also been established by nation states to protect themselves and their citizens.[7] The result is that these processes operate by favouring citizens or those who exhibit sameness with citizens. In such cases, sameness is openly and legally rewarded along racial lines based on a person's nationality, mode of entry to the state and residency status while simultaneously (re)producing disadvantage to the non-possessors of the selected in-group attributes. Managing sameness, though problematic, is, however, not the main challenge in the labour market but how we manage difference in society.

I now want to present how the socio-political and economic systems operate and the mechanisms through which they reproduce and maintain the racial order in individual lives. What I do from hereon is to view group favouritism as operating on a continuum of favour to disfavour, with a broad spectrum comprising a positive and negative end (see Figure 8.1). The positive end, which favours sameness, is the favouritism end of the continuum, while the negative end features persons with little similarity with the host nation, who are thus recipients not of group favouritism but of disfavour. While the response to sameness is favour, the response to difference from my study is disfavour, and these only change when disrupted by individual acts. In the latter case the group's outcome remains unchanged, and it only changes for the individual/s concerned, who then have a different outcome from their group outcome. These individual acts include migrants who exercise their minority agency and resist the system or become 'extra milers' (see the discussion in chapter 7). It is this end of the spectrum which I call the disfavour end (Figure 8.1). The second thing I do is view in-group favouritism and out-group disfavour not as distinct elements, but as a whole, fully functioning system encompassing both the in-group and out-group experience at the same time as occurs in real-world interactions.

Note that it is the 'disfavour' end of the continuum which is problematic, because beneficiaries of group favouritism do not reject being esteemed positively or being favoured. Rather, it is those in-between and at the further end who demand a change in the system. This favouritism continuum, which I present here, is a politico-economic system that maintains the racial stratification of a group or person by either facilitating or impeding their agency depending on their positioning

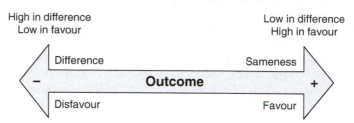

Figure 8.1 The favouritism continuum

on the continuum. The positioning of a group on the favouritism continuum determines how group members will be treated when navigating the labour market, the share of resources they can access and the level of difficulty or ease with which they access any and all forms of capital. Due to the central role racial difference plays in how people are distributed on this favouritism continuum, addressing the ways in which race is employed to influence the position of groups on the spectrum is vital. The component parts of the system include: (i) group favouritism – which decides which groups to advantage over the other; (ii) acceptance – which determines how to respond to groups and group members; (iii) psychological implicit bias – which provides the justification and sustenance of the continuum; and (iv) human contact – considering systems are inert without drivers, humans operate the system. Legal systems are put in place to protect this system in our government, policies, institutions and services.

Let us take a practical look at this system. First, there is a correlation between the positioning of different groups on the racial strata in Ireland and their positioning on the labour market based on the analysis of their outcomes (CSO, 2011, 2016). This also correlates with where groups are positioned on the favouritism continuum, as can be gleaned from the characteristic labour market experiences presented in this book. The Irish born experience more group favouritism than migrants of Western European descent, who in turn experience more group favouritism than the Eastern European migrants, and they in turn more than the Nigerian migrants of Black African descent. A simulation of the complexity of what a scale of favouritism might look like does not mean putting differences on a scale; rather, it is the response to the difference that is on the scale. The main human characteristics through which human subjects appear assigned to the continuum include skin colour, where whiteness, white culture and its by-products generate responses located towards the right, producing favour, while the black phenotype, its culture and its by-products are located to the left, receiving disfavour. Again, we can see that Black workers, Black culture and workers who have become 'blackened' by their deviation from the standard (White and whiteness) generate responses located more towards the negative, disfavour end. In other words, the further human subjects and their attributes move away from the host or the person in contact with the difference, the more disfavour they will incur. Blackness here is not only in skin colour, it encompasses cultures and ethnicities that are seen as deviant because they are different from Eurocentric norms. Other characteristics which function in the same way (though it is not an exhaustive list) include a person's name – whether it is foreign sounding or Irish; nationality of descent not naturalisation; and perceived rather than actual culture and ethnicity.

Race is a major determinant of the outcome of migrants in the labour market, where the 'Blacker' a person is, the more negative the outcome, and the Whiter you are, the more positive the outcome. While this may sound simplistic, studies have shown that darker skin colour is a significant factor and is implicated in the probability of men gaining employment in the US.[8] Gomez Cervantes and Kim (2015) also showed that Asian and Black women were disadvantaged against White migrant women. In Ireland, the unemployment rate of Black Africans is 43–63 per cent while for White Europeans it is 13–17 per cent, and 3–8 per cent for the Western European population. This means that physically 'Blacker' people are at least five times more likely to be unemployed in Ireland. While we do not like to agree that Whites in 2019 still engage in a wholesale discrimination against Blacks, statistical evidence shows the stark reality.[9]

Fostering inequality through racialised responses to difference

How we respond to racial difference is central to racial inequality. In the labour market in Ireland, group favouritism, acceptance and implicit bias are component parts that influence responses to the difference and sameness exhibited by various groups and their members. They do not, however, operate separately, but form an interconnected system that maintains the racial order by influencing the position of groups on the favouritism continuum. These structures are racialised gatekeepers that decide where different actors will be positioned, and consequently how they are treated. Group favouritism, acceptance and implicit bias are grounded in maintaining and rewarding homogeneity in a rapidly advancing heterogeneous environment. Thus, human contact in the labour market is not value free; it (re)produces and maintains the racial order, particularly through its selection and reward of people who are similar, thus creating homogeneity in the midst of a heterogeneous population. All modern nation states are complicit in reifying racial inequality. They exclude in order to 'construct homogeneity' and this is predicated on their capacities to restrict heterogeneity in the interest of securing political, cultural and racial homogeneity (Goldberg, 2001: 23).

Consequently, groups that exhibit difference are disadvantaged and consigned to the disfavour end of the continuum, in a way in which difference is racialised. The implication is that migrants from groups with attributes characterised as more acceptable will fare better than migrants with less acceptable attributes. The experience of acceptance in the labour market in Ireland is colour coded and racially determined – in other words, the more attributes actors have similar to the Irish born, the more towards the favour end of the continuum they are positioned, and vice versa. The persistent experience and restriction to the disfavour end of the spectrum results in exclusion, which becomes visible as marginalisation. When race determines how groups and their members are located on the favouritism continuum, it leads to the marginalisation of the group(s) that is darker or perceived as darker. One of the main challenges in the way this mechanism is able to function and foster the proliferation of inequality is that it marginalises others covertly, while being left unacknowledged and unchallenged as the de facto mode of operation in the labour market. While we focus only on policy and laws, these policies and laws are, however, organised based on this favouritism continuum system. We need to tackle that system – name it, acknowledge it and make it visible in order to change it.

Although the modern state has always conceived of itself as racially configured, thus absolving itself of being an active determinant of differential outcomes among groups (Goldberg, 2001), the favouritism continuum fosters covert racial projects which aim for homogeneity in heterogeneous societies. There is extant evidence of the involvement of the Irish state in various racial projects like the restriction of movement through the visa system, and the promulgation of policies at organisational, local and EU levels which favours and rewards sameness, which in itself reifies racial inequality. While many feign ignorance about why disparity occurs in the labour market between groups that exhibit more racial difference in Ireland and those who are similar to the host, these kinds of practices favour the host and similar communities by guaranteeing their automatic positioning over newcomers while undermining the achievement factors of those it others. They confirm the meritocratic myth and raise questions about equality of opportunity as a vehicle of labour market mobility. These nationalist practices which are framed in terms of 'working for the common good' as opposed to explicit forms of discrimination or racism, must out of necessity operate through racialised systems. They not only have the tendency to exacerbate racial inequality, but they also guarantee the permanence of racism (Mills, 1997) as they make the playing field permanently uneven, favouring Whites, white culture and possessors of whiteness who have characteristics similar to the Irish born.

In addition, the prevalence of a psychological implicit bias operated through this favouritism continuum justifies how difference is treated. Despite the advancement of people of different races, the historical view that Blacks are at the bottom and Whites at the top of the labour market still prevails. These internalised views continue to influence group outcomes such that Black bodies and credentials have a higher risk of being located at the negative end of the favouritism continuum, in contrast to White bodies that are more likely to be at the positive end. These standards, which shape White over Black relations in the labour market, mean the greater a person's ability to adopt the characteristics of the members of the host community, and share the practices, behaviours and patterns of that community, the more readily their incorporation into the labour market is achieved. Successful Black workers from outside the EU are compelled to 'pass' in relation to their mutable characteristics such as hair, clothes, language and education to be able to access higher strata and avoid or reduce the risk of negative treatment when navigating the labour market. In essence, groups that exhibit attributes closer to the host community are more likely to be spared and enjoy easier access up the economic ladder while those from outside the EU or European credentials in Black bodies are inferiorised and thus receive disfavour.

Managing difference: tolerance versus recognition

The best way to express equal respect to everyone continues to be problematic, particularly when it comes to managing difference in the social, political and economic terrain. This issue has driven a range of theoretical perspectives proffered to manage difference. The 'politics of recognition' suggests respecting difference and treating group differences in one of two ways. First, as 'pre-existing, benign, cultural variations that an unjust interpretive scheme has maliciously transformed into a value hierarchy' (Fraser, 1996: 9). In this case, it seeks to celebrate, not eliminate, group differences. On another level, it insists that 'group differences do not preexist their hierarchical transvaluation but are created contemporaneously with it through a discursive framework of binary oppositions'. Here, it aims to deconstruct the very terms on which such differences are currently elaborated (Fraser, 1996: 9–10). The 'politics of difference', which also demands recognition for people's differences, rejects the uniformity it takes to be implicit in universalism. What requires recognition in this case 'is the unique identity of this individual or group, and their distinctness from everyone else' (Taylor, 1994: 38). This is not what the society feels needs to be recognised but 'everything depends on precisely what currently misrecognised people need in order to be able to participate as peers in social life' (Fraser, 1996: 35). This argument is still true today and we cannot impose on groups without taking cognisance of their context.

In the early part of the 2000s, when the notion of interculturalism was the trend in Ireland, the discourse among many scholars and politicians alike was tolerance, which was peddled as the solution for managing difference. Embedded in the intercultural approach at that time was the idea of recognition and celebrating difference which became more prominent from about 2007, just before the economic crash. These two responses to difference are problematic and open to contestation. Supporters of the equality of condition, who tend to talk about the appreciation or celebration of diversity, say that 'differences from the norm are to be welcomed and learned from rather than simply permitted' (Baker et al., 2009: 34). The difficulty is having a blanket attitude of welcoming and celebrating all differences because not every group is prepared to celebrate or even to tolerate others.

Tolerance, which is one of the oldest methods recommended by political and religious powers in managing difference, is presented as the idea of extending acceptance to others. In orthodox usage, however, to 'tolerate' means one is enduring or permitting what they find objectionable (Jones, 2010: 39). In other words, tolerating occurs when we disapprove of or dislike. What makes toleration distinctive and interesting is its combining negative appraisal with a refusal to disallow what it appraises negatively (Jones, 2010). This paradoxical characteristic of toleration means that it is perfectly possible to tolerate someone while maintaining a sense of one's own superiority. The two conditions necessary for toleration, disapproval or dislike and an ability to prevent the thing that is disliked, raise serious questions about how egalitarian or just the notion of toleration really is. The idea that toleration is 'extended' to the other locates the source and power imbalance in favour of the dominant group. Contrary to the claim that toleration can be mutual (Jones, 2010: 49), Baker et al. (2009: 34) insist that 'dominant cultures can tolerate subordinate ones and not vice versa'. Many CRTs on the issue of race are of a similar view that the minority race, particularly Blacks, cannot effectively be racist against the majority group because of the power dynamics. In other words, the hegemonic positioning of the dominant view is seen as the norm and the tolerated view deviant. If toleration can be 'extended', it implies it can be withheld. Even as we think it better to be tolerant than intolerant and better to extend recognition than to withhold it, the understanding of toleration as an expression of inequality and condescension serves as its main source of criticism.

Social acceptance: the missing link in managing difference

Tolerance should really only be a passing attitude: it should lead to appreciation. To tolerate is to offend. Goethe (1998: 116)

Historically, tolerance has been routinely suggested and practised as a means of managing difference. Although toleration was obviously not the goal but a temporary measure, many have stopped at toleration as a way of living with others in our world that is increasingly becoming more diverse than ever. Acceptance is a social phenomenon which has the capacity to manage difference while also fulfilling the belonging needs in marginalised groups. From here on in, I will refer to acceptance as 'social acceptance' in order to differentiate it from the acceptance associated with general psychology where a person has to come to terms with a negative situation. Social acceptance is different from tolerance – which is unidirectional from the powerful to the other – in that it is two-way. It also does not evaluate others negatively. Wherever or whenever social acceptance is present, it indicates the inclusion of its beneficiaries into personhood and as equals. Though recognition and tolerance are routinely employed in managing difference, real inclusion depends on what marginalised people need in order to feel integrated and participate equally in everyday life. Thus, rather than ignore human difference as suggested by race sceptics, who encourage colour blindness yet treat difference with negative evaluation, 'what we are asked to recognise is the unique identity of this individual or group, their distinctness from everyone else' (Taylor, 1994: 38).

Social acceptance is the state or act of receiving someone during un-harmful, social interactions as true and valid without imputing judgement. Its two main components suggest that the aspect of taking a person as 'true' and 'valid' signifies other people's views and beliefs can be respected without necessarily agreeing with them. The introduction of 'un-harmful' in this definition protects people against interactions which cannot be socially acceptable; for example torture, abuse or any act that violates a person's human rights. This definition is not unproblematic considering that human beings and societies function by judging others, and this is often based on societal views or prior contact with members of the group in question. The presence of judgement has proved extremely problematic, particularly in how people respond to and manage difference such that expressing equal respect has been riddled with contestation. One question which still appears unanswered is how to actually treat others as equals in practical terms.

In thinking through social acceptance as a means of managing difference, I draw on the politics of recognition which encompasses the kind of general respect that is associated with personhood. While respect, as used in 'respect for persons', invokes an idea of status rather than merit, people can recognise only if they can ascribe positive value to one another's differences (Jones, 2010). Toleration, on the other hand, is called to the fore when a negative value is ascribed to difference. Figure 8.2 shows these two positions for managing difference as two extremes, with recognition to the right, judging and ascribing positive value to the difference, and tolerance is to the left, evaluating the difference negatively. This presents us a horizontal view where, rather than viewing tolerance and recognition as two separate, opposing and conflicting positions, we see them as a continuum (this is not a new continuum but how acceptance maps onto the favouritism continuum). In essence, when human subjects are in contact with difference (human, idea, behaviour, anything at all), if that difference is evaluated positively, it will receive recognition and respect; if it is evaluated negatively, it will require toleration to be able to live with it and this will be to the left of the continuum (Figure 8.2). In this equation, 'social acceptance' from the definition above is when a difference is received as simply 'different' and neither a negative or positive judgement is imputed. When that difference is received and perceived as a valid and true representation of the person/thing/idea, then acceptance of that person and their difference can be said to have taken place. In other words, social acceptance is the middle ground and tipping point when contact is established with

Figure 8.2 The recognition–tolerance continuum

people from different communities. This needn't be only through direct contact but can also be through CVs or other media.

This is significant, as I have argued exhaustively that the imputing of negative evaluation to the attributes of marginalised actors is the problematic aspect of race relations which also fuels inequality and exacerbates the experiencing of misrecognition. Let's remember that demands for recognition are commonly protests against forms of misrecognition in which the standing of the misrecognised group is diminished in the eyes of others because of its particular identity (Jones, 2010). From my conversations with a mixed group of migrant workers in Ireland, their demand is not that others should positively applaud their identity, behaviours and beliefs, but rather that others' stereotypical views of their identity should not be used to deprive them and their members of access to equal status and treatment. This is the demand made by migrants stratified at the bottom of the racial ladder in the labour market. In Ireland, this group are mainly the Black African persons, males, females, young and old. The nature of the judgement imputed to difference is not simply a matter of categorisation, as evidenced by the empirical data I have presented in this book. It influences the access of its victims to social capital, state resources, status and the place they occupy on the favouritism continuum. The potential of social acceptance to address the pervasive and pejorative imputing of judgement during race relations indeed presents a cogent argument for advancing this notion. In spite of the negative nature of tolerance 'toleration will cease to be necessary only when we cease to disagree' or 'when we become comprehensively unable to impose our views on one another' Jones (2010: 41). Mills (1997) made a similar argument in relation to the permanence of racism in world systems when he also suggested the unseating of white supremacy. The notion of social acceptance is invaluable because basic disagreements hinge on the positive or negative judgement placed on others, their features, attributes, culture, beliefs and credentials.

The notion of acceptance is not however free of contradictions, one of which concerns who is doing the acceptance. This makes the practice of acceptance seem dependent on the other. Similarly, acceptance has a degree of being indifferent to another's difference and the question arises whether it is dissimilar from tolerance, which I have interrogated in this book. To this I say, though acceptance is not the ultimate solution, it is well away from tolerance and on the path to respect and recognition, which is the desired goal. I asked a group of attendees at a seminar if any one of them left their homes that morning with a desire to find someone who would tolerate them or their difference. There was not a single hand raised. When we listen to marginalised groups, on the other hand, their first request is not for handouts or undue advantage, or even affirmative action; they all unequivocally ask for acceptance, not even recognition or respect. So, to the question: what should we teach – tolerance, acceptance or recognition? I will say we need to begin to teach from a very tender age and up to those in the top tiers of the labour market social acceptance and how to be accepting of each other's difference without imputing negative judgement. At our 'unconscious bias' workshops, we need to teach management at every decision point to ask themselves if their recruitment/promotion decisions were from imputing judgement based on reality or were from ascribed stereotypes. Then we will be well on our way to seeing real social change through racial equality in the labour market.

Notes

1 Sociologist Ronit Lentin (2007) insists Ireland has evolved from a 'racial state' to a racist state, where governmental 'biopolitics' and technologies of racialising indigenous groups and regulating immigration and asylum dictate the discursive and practical construction of Irishness otherness.

2 Hovland and Sherif (1980), in social judgement theory, see attitude change or persuasion as mediated by judgemental processes and effects. In other words, a person's position on an issue is dependent on their most preferred position; judgement of the various alternatives, which is spread across what Hovland and Sherif describe as their latitudes of acceptance, rejection and non-commitment; and the person's level of ego-involvement with the issue. Jack Mezirow (1995) described the frames of reference through which adults learn and make meaning of their lives.

3 The public outcry, particularly in the US, over the acquittal of George Zimmerman in the second degree murder trial for the death of seventeen-year-old Trayvon Martin, the Ferguson protests over the police shooting of teenager Michael Brown, and the Baltimore riots over twenty-five-year-old Freddie Gray, who died of a broken spine while in police custody, sparked talks on how implicit racial bias may have influenced the response, the trial proceedings and even the verdict.

4 A March 2013 report released by the US Equal Employment Opportunity Commission listed unconscious bias and perceptions about African-Americans as one of the seven major obstacles hindering equal opportunities for African-Americans in the federal work force. They declared that the more subtle discrimination that exists in the current society can often be directly attributable to unconscious bias (EEOC, 2013).

5 Presidential hopeful, Peter Casey, among other questions was asked if Irish Traveller ethnicity should be recognised. His extremely racist comments sparked public outcry amidst calls for him to step down from the race, the same time when he got 1 in 5 of the total votes (see Downing, 2018; Doyle, 2018).

6 EU citizenship forms the basis of the right of persons to move and reside freely within the territory of the Member States. The Lisbon Treaty, which confirmed this right, also includes the general provisions on the Area of Freedom, Security and Justice.

Similarly, various projects outlined at EU level to support the migration and working conditions of EU migrants are written into treaties and laws. For example, with Articles 45 and 46 TFEU, Regulation (EU) No 492/2011 lays down provisions intended to achieve freedom of movement for workers on a nondiscriminatory basis by ensuring the close cooperation of the central employment services of Member States with one another and with the Commission.

7 The Irish 2004 Citizenship Referendum removed the birthright citizenship from children born in Ireland who do not have at least one parent who is an Irish citizen or entitled to Irish citizenship. Laws concerning parents of Irish-born children from outside the EEA granted conditional stamp 4 in 2005 after the referendum, as they were not entitled to free third-level education, nor were they entitled to education grants (for stamp 4 see www.inis.gov.ie/en/INIS/Pages/registration-stamps).

8 Andrea Gomez Cervantes and Chang Hwan Kim (2015) found that, among men, darker skin colour negatively influenced the likelihood of employment, even after accounting for the effects of race and other demographic and education-related variables. See also Devaraj, Quigley and Patel (2018), New Immigrant Survey (2006) and Hersch (2008).

9 On the issue of being 'blackened', see my discussion in chapter 2 on Irish Whiteness and racism. The book *How the Irish became White* by Ignatiev (1995) implies not only that Whites can be 'blackened', but also that Blackness is used symbolically to signify negative attributes. Tsri (2016) also writes exhaustively about symbolic 'blackness' in his book, *Are Africans Black*.

Conclusion: towards a critical race theory of the labour market

Racial stratification is not an unproblematic concept. It is widely acknowledged by many race proponents as a key determinant of socio-economic outcomes among groups based on their racial categorisation. In chapter 5 of this book, I described racial stratification as a homogenising system of structured inequality, where an assigned default starting position determines access to scarce and desired resources based on racial group membership. While it is clear that the equal positioning of human subjects on the racial strata will have a significant impact on labour market outcomes of migrants, the oxymoronic nature of such a pursuit is equally evident. By this I mean that the mere existence of a hierarchy – in this case racial strata which are predicated on racial inequality, cannot be fully addressed simply by repositioning actors on the strata unless the racial structures that sustain them are dismantled. We need racial emancipation that is reflected in the labour market, not only in Ireland but in all of Europe and the Western world. This is because people who are categorised as Black or are 'blackened' by their intersectional stratifiers do not have the same experience in the labour market as their White counterparts.

Racial emancipation can, however, only occur when the overarching system of racial inequality is eliminated. This means the elimination of white supremacy from the way society organises its people on a daily basis. It will entail removing Whites and whiteness from the centre and promoting a deracialised way of organising and analysing society – in this case, the labour market. We will need a race consciousness, the centring of race and awareness of racial stratification in any analysis and understanding of society. In Ireland, Blacks are problematised and only centred when Whites want to 'fix' them – a system which recreates the colonial imaging of Blacks and hegemonic white spaces which reify

Whites and whiteness in the centre and Blacks on the margins. W. E. B. Du Bois and many other critical race theorists insist Blacks or difference is not the problem. The origin of race and its use today continues to be for the racist separation of White Europeans from others. I have presented racial stratification from the perspective of a critical race theorist of Black African descent. I further contend that for a deracialised, anti-racist analysis and understanding of the labour market, three core elements of CRT become vital: the centrality of race, race consciousness and the voice of colour through counterstorytelling.

Why we should centre race in the discourse on the labour market

Despite the ongoing arguments on the relevance of race today, every European country and institution still structures access to its resources and residency rights around race and nationality. Whether a person is categorised as EU or non-EU, from the Third World, developing or developed world, it impacts on their labour market outcome. It affects the status, privileges and judgements attached to each category and the challenges they present to the categorised person when exercising their agency. Considering the various ways race impacts on labour market outcomes, it is imperative that race is central to the discourse, interventions and interpretations of data and outcomes. When race is centred in an inquiry, a societal deficit is implicated; when individualistic attributions are centred, a migrant/Black deficit is implicated. This is significant both to CRT that insists on centring race and labour market theories as it suggests the central element in a study influences the findings. While race is a socially constructed phenomenon, skin colour is used as an identifier for non-Whites with real social consequences. It is therefore important to understand what the possession of whiteness does to the possessors and non-possessors of whiteness and the ways it structures their lives.

Centralising race in problematising labour market outcomes among groups that are categorised as racially different from a racial stratification framework is beneficial as it can reach and uncover those silenced and difficult to reach experiences. The black–white binary in this book is a paradigm that suggests that Blacks 'constitute the prototypical minority group' (Delgado and Stefancic, 2012: 75). Despite the undeniably contentious and even divisive nature of such thinking, based on the lived experience of Black workers and on statistical evidence, the impact of race needs to be made plain. Anything less will fuel the ambivalence by Whites about the impact of race on labour market outcomes which often silences victims and demonstrates a lack of commitment to addressing the consequences of racial inequality. It is also a way of denying White advantage and the implication of race. Whites, however, rarely openly acknowledge that possession of white skin colour advantages and often-times protects them in society. While centring race in mainstream, First World political philosophy is challenging, it should not and cannot be ignored. Unless we centre race and name it in its entirety, it will continue to provide an unfair advantage for Whites while remaining unacknowledged yet powerful in destabilising any effort towards levelling the playing field.

Race consciousness

While we have all come to the modern way/s of studying race in the post-colonial society, the forerunners and scholars of CRT strongly advocated for explicit race consciousness in understanding the interactions between race and outcomes in society. If you could only share your experience of racism, discrimination or microaggression in the workplace with a White or Black friend, who would you choose? If you are Black, you would most likely choose a Black friend because they will hear your story from a place of cultural sensitivity. They are more likely to understand your inner dialogue and self-questioning; the psychological impact and the reassurance you seek that the experience was not imagined but real. Scholars like W. E. B. DuBois, Frantz Fanon and Carter G. Woodson discussed race differently from Emile Durkheim, Max Weber and Karl Marx. They displayed an explicit race consciousness that influenced their writings. Race consciousness among Blacks is real. When you look around and the majority at the bottom of the racial and economic ladder despite their levels of academic qualifications are people of Black African descent, you will have to begin to think that race or, at the very least, skin colour is playing a part in the outcome and experience. The experience of being at the bottom because of your race not only changes you, but it also teaches you to become conscious of race.

Race consciousness is found among those at the bottom, but we can learn from them what it means and what it entails. In the face of growing knowledge epistemicide, we must be aware that 'the imagination of the academic philosopher cannot recreate the experience of life on the bottom' (Matsuda, 1987: 325); rather, we should look 'to the bottom', because one's position in the social structure of race relations influences how we see and experience the world. Thus, with the understanding that CRT is a way of thinking about and analysing race and its impact,

I recommend four overarching themes with which a race theorist has to be conversant to carry out an anti-racist analysis of the labour market. Without this, researchers and research will be a variant of distilled stock stories that at best provides a descriptive representation of the experiences of Blacks and non-Whites without disrupting the ambivalence and inaction of race scepticists. The themes are the changing meaning of race, hierarchical stratification and dominance, managing racial difference and, lastly, inclusive spaces.

The changing meaning of race

First, we require an understanding that race is not fixed. Because race is socially constructed, its meaning changes with time and across space. In a country like Nigeria, where Blacks are the predominant population, a person of Black African descent will experience race differently from another Black person in, for example, South Africa. The experience of race will be different on some levels in white spaces, for example Blacks in the UK, while experiencing race in the same way particularly when it comes to racial stratification, will experience slight differences in terms of the intensity of opposition they encounter when accessing the labour market. This is because the UK has its second-, third- and fourth-generation migrants in various roles who are more visible because of their higher numbers and the historical context of Blacks in the UK. They all, however, still experience race to a level that makes race problematic in both old and new migration states. Winant (2000: 182–183) insists the central task facing racial theory today 'is to focus attention on the continuing significance and changing meaning of race'. This prompts the following questions which will help prepare the race researcher for hidden aspects and a critical race consciousness that we advocate for as Black scholars with a lived experience of racial stratification.

1 What is the present understanding of race in the country [in this case Ireland], and how does it shape migrants' lives as minorities?
2 How is a person's race recognised and categorised and how do migrants respond to their racial category?
3 How do migrants experience their possession or lack of whiteness and that of others?
4 How is race experienced in predominantly white modern states, and how does it privilege or disadvantage groups and individuals in their economic pursuit?
5 Despite race being widely acknowledged as a social construct, what political machinery keeps it a lived reality?

Despite the overarching experience which I maintain is influenced by individuals' or groups' racial stratification, these are some key considerations that will influence how race is nuanced in different countries, institutions and organisations.

Hierarchical stratification and domination

Second is the notion of hierarchical racial stratification and domination. This is because racial inequality is not simply a matter of not having the same as others with similar abilities. Rather, it is a hierarchical positioning which is linked to dominance of one group over the other. The idea that migrants of various national origins are 'forced' to assimilate as members of different racial groups because of racial stratification (Zuberi and Bashi, 1997: 672–673) provides lenses to critically examine the issue of race. Key questions which will heighten a race consciousness and help prepare researchers for a non-Eurocentric standpoint include:

1 Understanding racial stratification and the racial order that exists in the country of the study. How it operates, is maintained and reproduced in the labour market.
2 Considering human/minority agency, how do people of migrant heritage respond to their racial positioning; is it static or fluid, and how do they change their place on the labour supply chain?
3 Since racial stratification is a site of otherness for Blacks, how do migrants experience, manage or use it as sites of action, production and/or resistance?
4 In the process where new arrivals are 'forced' to assimilate or fit in with the racial understanding of themselves in their new country, how does a person's racial positioning reflect on their labour market outcomes and identity change?

Managing racial difference

The third race consciousness for a non-Eurocentric study involves understanding how racial difference is managed in the country, society or organisation being studied. As I have argued and echo the voice of W. E. B. Du Bois, the 'Negro' is not the problem; neither is their difference. Rather, it is how we (society) respond to their real/perceived difference. An extant demand in all societies is the demand by groups for a more inclusive concept of citizenship which recognises (rather than excludes) their differences (Kymlicka, 2002). Minorities and marginalised people want their differences normalised and not to be the basis of their evaluation. Key questions for consideration to help ground an anti-racist and non-Eurocentric understanding include:

1 How does the country/organisation/institution being studied manage racial difference in the labour market?
2 Considering everyone is not treated the same way, how is racial difference and sameness treated in the country under investigation?
3 In what ways do or can that society transition those experiencing exclusion to inclusion?
4 What counts as difference in terms of having an impact on labour market outcome?
5 How does the group being investigated understand/recognise and manage their difference?
6 Seeing that human difference is not the problem, how does the society respond to the difference under study?

Inclusive spaces

Lastly, everywhere in the world, irrespective of the difference exhibited, people want to be accepted in ways that do not require having to hide or mask their difference. People who have experienced differential treatment because they exhibit some form of difference typically ask for their difference to be accepted not tolerated. Whether it's a person who has more weight in a group than others; or someone who exhibits a different sexuality, religious belief, gender, race or skin colour from the majority population; everyone wants that difference to be accepted. In this regard, some required basic understanding and grounding for an anti-racist, non-Eurocentric research/er includes:

1 What is the relationship between acceptance and the economic outcome of migrants in the labour market?
2 How do migrants in that country define and recognise acceptance? What difference does it make to their progression in the place of study?
3 What are the precursors of acceptance for your target group or subjects?
4 What is the locus of acceptance in your space? Is it a sociological concept – meaning it is located within the society and therefore the responsibility of the society; or is it a psychological concept and therefore a belonging need in the individual or group?

Race consciousness means developing an understanding of what life looks and feels like for those at the bottom. If you would truly search for and open your eyes to gain a comprehensive understanding in these elements listed above; while you might not fully have the same relationship with race from having lived or been categorised at the bottom of the racial order, it is a piece of knowledge that changes how you see race and raced people. It transcends head knowledge to become embodied knowledge. A CRT standpoint like this takes away your blinkers, it does not allow you to hide; neither can you feign ignorance when you truly engage with CRT with a race consciousness.

CRT of the labour market: a plea for composite counterstorytelling

Counterstorytelling, and more specifically, composite counterstories (CCS) has been one of the most invaluable tenets of CRT in my studies. We all tell stories. Politicians, academics, historians, journalists, economists, archaeologists – we all use different tools to paint a picture of society with our data. The composite characters John and Phil in chapter 7 of this book allowed me to bring all the nuances in the interviewees' narratives in short synopsis which captured the views of both the dominant group and the marginalised groups. CCS is a powerful call to action which allows readers to make their judgement and enter the lived world of research subjects (Joseph, forthcoming). Storytelling has been argued to be a political act which can defend or contest social arrangements through how we portray the past, ourselves and our fellows (Roy, 1999: 9). It has been a way through which the unseen stories and depth of marginalisation of the other have been uncovered. Blacks and Whites have, however, historically told different stories about race and racism. Although Black experiences are rarely theorised, Delgado (1989) insists there are benefits in out-groups telling stories and others listening when they do. Mari Matsuda (1987: 324) insists that 'those who have experienced discrimination speak with a special voice to which we should listen'.

CCS 'represent[s] an accumulation, a gathering together, and a synthesis of numerous individual stories' (Hunn, Guy and Manglitz, 2006: 245). It is not just a narrativised writing style but a research method which has gained credibility among CRT scholars in Education. It 'critically examines theoretical concepts and humanises empirical data while also deriving material for counterstory's discourse, setting, and characters from sources' such as 'statistical data, existing literature, social commentary, and authors' professional/personal experiences concerning the topics addressed' (Martinez, 2014: 69). Like all counterstories, it speaks against the master narrative – a narrative that is based on the social and cultural history of the dominant race. CCS aids in demonstrating the way in which People of Colour have a shared history with racism, discrimination and white supremacy. Delgado's (1995: xix) work in the Rodrigo Chronicles demonstrates how CCS differs from other counterstories in that the various characters do not have a one-to-one correspondence to any one individual; rather, they are representative of various political ideologies and are written as composites of many individuals. This composite character, which is the defining characteristic of CCS, allows the dialogue to speak to research findings and 'creatively challenge racism and other forms of subordination' (Yosso, 2006: 11). CCS has been deployed successfully in Education research to highlight the discriminatory employment experiences of Black minority ethnic scholars and students, and would have a similar fit in labour market research.

Storytelling aids talking about race

When Black and Brown people tell stories, what can we learn from them? Strong arguments alone are often ineffective when talking about race to race scepticist, White audiences or people who are generally ambivalent about race. Employing statistical evidence coupled with authentic counterstories can be powerful when talking about race and its impact. Many CRT scholars have advocated for the use of storytelling as both research method and analytical tool. The use of counterstorytelling has many advantages and benefits for CRT theorists. Although stories told have been the privilege of those historically influential in knowledge generation, Blacks, migrants and minorities are clearly able to explain their labour market experiences. While they articulate these occurrences differently from academic discourse, they provides powerful windows into the transition points in their career travels.

When migrants talk about race, they interpret their experience in terms of the opposition(s) they encounter when accessing the labour market. They typically highlight the differential treatment of workers, where labour markets operate different rules for different groups. For example, between migrants/natives; citizens/non-citizens; documented/ undocumented; Whites/Blacks. Their stories usually focus on how race, nationality of descent and skin colour influence labour market outcomes and dynamics.

When interpreting labour market experiences, Black workers are more likely to centre race while Whites who 'are taught … to see themselves as individuals rather than as part of a racially socialised group' (DiAngelo, 2011: 59) will more likely centre any other concept but race, in this case, individualistic attributions.

Benefits of storytelling to researchers' education

When research generates a large data set with many interweaving elements on how race is nuanced in the labour market, two issues that can ensue include how to present opposing views generated from the same research and data set; and how to write about the multifaceted nature of race without losing the human elements uncovered in interviewees' narratives. Creating composite characters allows authors to honour both the informants and their information from qualitative research. You will notice in my stories in chapter 7 that I was able to preserve the words of my informants within the contexts they described in my writing while highlighting the impact of race on Black lives in the labour market. The storytelling method immediately challenges narrow, discriminatory views espoused through stock stories Whites tell which Delgado (1989) insists enables them to remain comfortable about racial inequality. It creatively unveils different roles and gatekeepers in the labour market without over-explaining. Some roles that I have exposed using the storytelling technique include the marginalised, defenders of white supremacy, white allies, tellers, hearers and defenders of stock stories (Joseph, 2019).

Blacks and Whites benefit from storytelling

The effect of in-group stories on marginalised groups benefits both Blacks and Whites. Rather than taking extracts from informants to buttress different arguments, creating composite portraits humanises interviewees' experiences, distress and emotions while also portraying their thoughts and thought processes. While Whites who have come to expect to be favourably treated, respected and at the top of the racial hierarchy as of right, find it hard to tell stories of racial marginalisation, a well-told counterstory not only emboldens Black storytellers to tell their stories but also their White counterparts are encouraged to tell others' stories. While storytelling emboldens members of the same group (Delgado, 1989), members of the dominant groups are also emboldened by well-told, authentic counterstories to share stories of others they know or have seen who are marginalised. Lastly, a well-told counterstory reveals and helps shatter complacency and ambivalence demonstrated by groups and individuals who say race is not an issue. Bringing others to an understanding that race matters through a well-told counterstory can be transformative for marginalised groups. It helps debunk the idea that one is being over-sensitive or imagining things as Blacks have been accused of doing whenever they mention issues of race or microaggression.

Whiteness as a hidden resource and affirmative action for Whites

In a racial stratification framework, the White-over-Black ascendancy in Ireland serves two interrelated purposes; first, it means Whites in Ireland who are now used to being at the top of the racial and economic ladder have also come to expect to always be at the top in any sphere. For Whites to always be at the top in Ireland, we had to have practised what Bell (1992) described as the permanence of racism. This means labour market mobility is no longer strictly based on achievement factors only, but as a right to be at the top. Policies, the law and human contact rigidly police this positioning of Whites at the top and Blacks at the bottom by every means possible, including covert discrimination.

The second purpose which is linked to this is the unspoken use of whiteness as a resource that provides affirmative action for Whites. While whiteness today is not seen as a resource, it continues to advantage Whites against their non-White peers in the world of work. The unequal access to symbolic, cultural and social capital in the labour market exacerbates discriminatory practices and inequality because they are unreckoned resources which advantage Whites, providing them with affirmative action in their economic pursuits. This is evident from the ways some groups are given positive regard and ascribed positive attributes. For example, the expectation that White Europeans will be hard working, punctual, trustworthy and competent, while people of Black African descent, even as Europeans, experience disregard, disrespect, ascription of incompetency, mistrust, and an expectation to have poor-quality education and communication. These attributes automatically ascribed, oftentimes before the actors perform in the workplace or during recruitment, influence outcomes by disadvantaging Black workers against their White counterparts through a taste-based discrimination similar to the operation of the Bourdieuan concept of cultural capital.

This rekindles questions on what counts as resources in equal opportunity societies where human capital is expected to be the main determinant of outcomes. Group membership according to Bourdieu (1986) provides members with the backing of their collectively owned capital, a 'credential' which entitles them to credit in the various senses of the word. However, similarities in credentials, race, ethnicity and skin colour which are potential opportunities for a 'solidaristic labour community' (Standing, 2011: 12), as we have between White Europeans and the native Irish population, typically go unreckoned as actual resources. We, however, see that these attributes have currency in ways which increase the ability of actors to advance their interests. Racism, and particularly White racism of the worst kind, exists in Ireland because despite its salience in the economic, social and political domains, there is continuous denial, ambivalence and sometimes outright shock when confronted with statistical evidence of racial inequality. This is not saying that Ireland is the most racist country, because it is not. Rather, that the prevalence of white denial about racism in Ireland makes it difficult to address. In 2019, we are still debating if Ireland is racist or not; if Ireland benefited from slavery or not; if we are white supremacist or not.

Critical race theory of the labour market

At what point are we 'allowed' to decide what best speaks to our experience as Blacks? As attractive as CRT is to race scholars, there is resistance and scepticism/fear from the academic world in Europe. When I commenced researching the disparity in outcomes among migrants in Ireland, I was encouraged to look for other, more 'acceptable' theoretical frameworks. As a race scholar of Black African descent I have experienced race and racism in society, the workplace, and higher education institutions both as a scholar and student; I have seen it in sports, restaurants and stores, and this is one piece of advice I am glad I did not take. CRT is not just a methodological and analytical framework; its social justice arm means it is also a call to action. You cannot truly learn and practise CRT and not be transformed. It sharpens the lenses with which you view and understand society, events and organisations. It stirs the activist in you. While we know that to remain silent about the benefits of whiteness is to deny the significance of race, which can cause harm to others, CRT reveals the privileging attributes of whiteness in ways that make it undeniable. When Whites accept the benefits of whiteness and do not acknowledge its advantaging properties for possessors of whiteness and the disadvantaging of non-possessors of whiteness, they too become defenders of whiteness; and thus defenders of white supremacy. I recommend CRT and a racial stratification framework for examining the labour market because it explicitly centres race.

The theory of immigration and racial stratification of the US is in many ways applicable to the racial order in Ireland and its operations. Though, as we know by now, race is a theoretical construct and stratifier, racial groupings are also living realities with economic, social and psychological consequences. Race unequivocally influences the labour market outcomes of people of migrant descent in Ireland because it influences where people start in the racial order. Racial stratification involves an interplay between a person's ascribed race, the belief held by the more powerful about their difference, and the maintaining of a covert white supremacy world racial order of Whites and white culture at the top, and Blacks and black culture at the bottom. The impact of racial stratification is more common and has become the de facto way society is organised. Notwithstanding Europe's claim of commitment to integration and equality, many of its actions and policies function in ways which guarantee stratification and maintain this present racial order. State laws enacted to protect citizens conversely produce structural barriers against those categorised as 'other' or who stray from its homogeneity agenda. Let us, however, remember that racial stratification means all groups do not start from the same racial positioning in the Irish labour market. The power of racial stratification is not about where you end up but where you start. When people start so low down, where they end up becomes inevitable wherever they are in the world. This is what we need to know, this is what we need to change, the default starting positioning ascribed to people based on race and nationality of descent.

Bibliography

Akpoveta, E. (2010), 'An exploration of the experiences of Black African men in their transition onto the Irish workforce', unpublished postgraduate thesis, National University of Ireland, Maynooth.

Akpoveta, E. (2011), 'Beyond integration', unpublished PhD thesis, National University of Ireland, Maynooth.

Ansley, F. L. (1997), 'White supremacy (and what we should do about it)', in R. Delgado and J. Stefancic, eds, *Critical White Studies: Looking behind the Mirror*, Philadelphia, PA: Temple University Press.

Aranda, E. M., and Rebollo-Gil, G. (2004), 'Ethnoracism and the "sand-wiched" minorities', *American Behavioral Scientist*, 47(7): 910–927, doi: 10.1177/0002764203261071.

Arnold, S., Quinn, E., Groarke, S., McGinnity, F., and Durst, C. (2019), 'Policy and practice targeting the labour market integration of non-EU Nationals in Ireland', ESRI Research Series Number 89, June, https://doi.org/10.26504/rs89.

Asante, M. K. (1990), *Afrocentricity and Knowledge*, Trenton: Africa World Press.

Back, L., and Solomos, J. (eds) (2000), *Theories of Race and Racism: A Reader*, London: Routledge.

Baker, J., Lynch, K., Cantillon, S., and Walsh, J. (2009), *Equality: From Theory to Action*, Basingstoke: Palgrave Macmillan.

Bashi, V. (1998), 'Racial categories matter because racial hierarchies matter: a commentary', *Ethnic and Racial Studies*, 21(5): 959–968, doi: 10.1080/014198798329748.

Beckles, H. Mc. D. (1990), 'A "riotous and unruly lot": Irish indentured servants and freemen in the English West Indies, 1644–1713', *William and Mary Quarterly*, 47(4): 503–522.

Bell, D. A. (1980), 'Brown v. Board of Education and the interest convergence dilemma', *Harvard Law Review*, 93: 518–533.

Bell, D. A. (1992), *Faces at the Bottom of the Well: The Permanence of Racism*, New York: Basic Books.

Bell, D. A. (1996), 'Racial realism', in K. Crenshaw et al., eds, *Critical Race Theory: The Key Writings that Formed the Movement*, New York: The New Press.

Bernal, D. D. (1998), 'Using a Chicana feminist epistemology in educational research', *Harvard Educational Review*, 68(4): 555–579.

Bhattacharyya, G., Gabriel, J., and Small, S. (2002), *Race and Power: Global Racism in the Twenty-first Century*, London: Routledge.

Blinder, S. (2011), Migration Observatory, University of Oxford, 'UK public opinion toward migration: determinants of attitudes', www.migrationob servatory.ox.ac.uk/sites/files/migobs/Briefing%20-%20Public%20Opinion-Determinants%20of%20Attitudes.pdf (accessed 28 January 2020).

Blinder, S. (2014), Migration Observatory, University of Oxford, 'UK public opinion toward immigration: overall attitudes and level of concern', http://migrationobservatory.ox.ac.uk/briefings/uk-public-opinion-towardimmigra tion-overall-attitudes-and-level-concern (accessed 1 May 2015).

Bonilla-Silva, E. (1997), 'Rethinking racism: toward a structural interpretation', *American Sociological Review*, 62(3): 465–480.

Bonilla-Silva, E. (2001), *White Supremacy and Racism in the Post-Civil Rights Era*, Boulder, CO: Lynne Rienner.

Bonilla-Silva, E. (2003), '"New racism", color-blind racism, and the future of whiteness in America', in A. W. Doane and E. Bonilla-Silva, eds, *White Out: The Continuing Significance of Racism*, New York: Routledge.

Bonilla-Silva, E. (2013), *Racism without Racists: Color-Blind Racism and the Persistence of Racial Inequality in America*, 4th edn, Lanham, MD: Rowman and Littlefield.

Bonilla-Silva, E., and Baiocchi, G. (2008), 'Anything but racism: how sociologists limit the significance of racism', in T. Zuberi and E. Bonilla-Silva, eds, *White Logic, White Methods, Racism and Methodology*, Lanham, MD: Rowman and Littlefield.

Bourdieu, P. (1984), *Distinction: A Social Critique of the Judgement of Taste*, Cambridge, MA: Harvard University Press.

Bourdieu, P. (1986), 'The forms of capital', in J. G. Richardson, ed., *Handbook of Theory and Research for the Sociology of Education*, New York: Greenwood Press.

Brettell, B. C. (2011), 'Experiencing everyday discrimination: a comparison across five immigrant populations', *Race and Social Problems*, 3(4): 266–279.

Brubaker, R. (2001), 'The return of assimilation?', *Ethnic and Racial Studies*, 24(4): 531–548.

Brubaker, R. (2004), *Ethnicity Without Groups*, Cambridge, MA: Harvard University Press.

Bryan, A. (2010), 'Corporate multiculturalism, diversity management, and positive interculturalism in Irish schools and society', *Irish Educational Studies*, 29(3): 253–269, doi: 10.1080/03323315.2010.498566.

Butler, R. (1969), 'Ageism: another form of bigotry', *The Gerontologist*, 9(4): 243–246.

Byrne, M. (2016), 'Shades of White: Irish professionals' response to immigrants', in A. Dada and S. Kushal, eds, *Whiteness Interrogated*, Oxford: Oxford University Press.

Caldwell, P. M. (1991), 'A hair piece: perspectives on the intersection of race and gender', *Duke Law Journal*, 365–396, http://scholarship.law.duke.edu/dlj/vol40/iss2/5 (accessed 12 December 2013).

Central Statistics Office (CSO) (2011, 2016), http://www.cso.ie.

Cantillon, S., and Vasquez del Aguila, E. (2011), 'Older people and age discrimination in the Irish labour market' University College Dublin. *Social Justice Series*, 11(4): 28–48, http://hdl.handle.net/10197/4495 (accessed 15 June 2015).

Charles, T. (1994), 'The politics of recognition', in A. Gutmann, ed., *Multiculturalism and the Politics of Recognition*, Princeton, NJ: Princeton University Press.

Chávez, A. F., and Guido-DiBrito, F. (1999), 'Racial and ethnic identity and development', in C. Clark and R. Caffarella, eds, *An Update on Adult Development Theory: New Ways of Thinking about the Life Course*, New Directions for Adult and Continuing Education, 84, San Francisco: Jossey-Bass, 39–48.

Chávez, A. F., Guido-DiBrito, F., and Mallory, S. (2003; 1996) 'Learning to value the "other": a model of diversity development', *Journal of College Student Development*, 44(4): 1–17.

Chiswick, B., Lee, Y., and Miller, P. (2005), 'A longitudinal analysis of immigrant occupational mobility: a test of the immigrant assimilation hypothesis', *International Migration Review*, 39(2): 332–353.

Clough, P. (2002), *Narrative and Fictions in Educational Research*, Milton Keynes: Open University Press.

Coakley, J. (2012), *Nationalism, Ethnicity and the State: Making and Breaking Nations*, London: Sage.

Coakley, L., and Mac Einri, P. (2007), 'The integration experience of African families in Ireland', Integrating Ireland, http://emn.ie/files/p_2012111610 52282007_The-Integration-Experiences-of-African-Families-in-Ireland.pdf (accessed 23 May 2015).

Cole, M. (2009), 'Critical race theory comes to the UK: a Marxist response', *Ethnicities*, 9(2): 246–269.

Coleman, J. S. (1988), 'Social capital in the creation of human capital', *American Journal of Sociology*, 94: S95–S120.

Collins, P. H. (1990), *Black Feminist Thought*, Boston: Unwin Hyman.

Collins, P. H. (2000). 'Black Feminist thought', in L. Back and J. Solomos, eds, *Theories of Race and Racism: A Reader*, London: Routledge.

Connell, J. (1993), *Kitanai, Kitsui and Kiken: The Rise of Labour Migration to Japan*, Sydney: Economic & Regional Restructuring Research Unit, University of Sydney.

Considine, M., and Dukelow, F. (2009), *Irish Social Policy: A Critical Introduction*, Dublin: Gill & Macmillan.

Cook, A. E. (1995), 'Beyond critical legal studies: the reconstructive theology of Dr. Martin Luther King', in K. Crenshaw, N. Gotanda, G. Peller and K. Thomas, eds, *Critical Race Theory: The Key Writings that Formed the Movement*, New York: The New Press.

Corbally, J. (2015), 'The Othered Irish: shades of difference in post-war Britain, 1948–71', *Contemporary European History*, 24: 105–125, doi:10.1017/S0960777314000447.

Cornell, S., and Hartmann, D. (1998), *Ethnicity and Race: Making Identities in a Changing World*, Thousand Oaks, CA: Pine Forge Press.

Crenshaw, K. W. (1989), 'Demarginalizing the intersection of race and sex: a black feminist critique of antidiscrimination doctrine, feminist theory and antiracist politics', *University of Chicago Legal Forum*, 8(1): 139–167.

Crenshaw, K. (1991), 'Mapping the margins: intersectionality, identity politics and violence against women of color', *Stanford Law Review*, 43: 1241–1299.

Crenshaw, K. (1995), 'The intersection of race and gender', in K. Crenshaw, N. Gotanda, G. Peller, and K. Thomas, eds, *Critical Race Theory: The Key Writings that Informed the Movement*, New York: The New Press.

Crenshaw, K. (2000), 'Race, reform and retrenchment', in L. Back and J. Solomos eds, *Theories of Race and Racism: A Reader*, London: Routledge.

Creswell, J. W., Shope, R., Plano Clark, V. L., and Green, D. O. (2006), 'How interpretive qualitative research extends mixed methods research', *Researching in the Schools*, 13(1): 1–11.

Crouch, S. (1996), 'Race is over: black, white, red, yellow—same difference', *New York Times Magazine*, 29 September.

Crowley, U., Gilmartin, M., and Kitchin, R. (2006), '"Vote yes for common sense citizenship": immigration and the paradoxes at the heart of Ireland's "Céad Míle Fáilte"', NIRSA Working Paper 30.

Curtis, L. P. (1997), *Apes and Angels: The Irishman in Victorian Caricature*, Washington, DC: Smithsonian Institute Press.

Dalal, F. (2002), *Race, Colour and the Process of Racialization: New Perspectives from Group Analysis, Psychoanalysis, and Sociology*, East Sussex: Brunner-Routledge.

Davis, K. (2008), 'Intersectionality as a buzzword: sociology of science perspective on what makes a feminist theory successful', *Feminist Theory*, 9(1): 67–85.

DeCuir, J., and Dixson, A. (2004), '"So when it comes out, they aren't that surprised that it is there": using critical race theory as a tool of analysis of race and racism in education', *Educational Researcher*, 33(5): 26–31.

Delgado, R. (1984), 'The imperial scholar: reflections on a review of civil rights literature', *University of Pennsylvania Law Review*, 132(3): 561–578, doi: 10.2307/3311882.

Delgado, R. (1989), 'Storytelling for oppositionists and others: a plea for narrative', *Michigan Law Review*, 87(8): 2411–2441. doi: 10.2307/1289308.

Delgado, R. (1995), *Critical Race Theory: The Cutting Edge*, Philadelphia, PA: Temple University Press.

Delgado, R., and Stefancic, J. (1997), *Critical White Studies: Looking Behind the Mirror*, Philadelphia, PA: Temple University Press.

Delgado, R., and Stefancic, J. (1999), *Critical Race Theory: The Cutting Edge*, 2nd edn, Philadelphia, PA: Temple University Press.

Delgado, R., and Stefancic, J. (2001), *Critical Race Theory: An Introduction*. New York: New York University Press.

Delgado, R., and Stefancic, J. (2004), *Understanding Words that Wound*, Boulder, CO: Westview Press.

Delgado, R., and Stefancic, J. (2012), *Critical Race Theory: An Introduction*. New York: New York University Press.

Devaraj, S., Quigley, R. N., and Patel, P. C. (2018), 'The effects of skin tone, height, and gender on earnings', https://doi.org/10.1371/journal.pone.0190640.

DeWall, C. N., and Bushman, B. J. (2011), 'Social acceptance and rejection: the sweet and the bitter', *Current Directions in Psychological Science*, 20(4): 256–260.

DiAngelo, R. (2011), 'White fragility', *International Journal of Critical Pedagogy*, 3(3): 54–70.

DiTomaso, N. (2013), *The American Non-dilemma: Racial Inequality without Racism*, New York: Russell Sage Publications.

Doeringer, P. B., and Piore, M. J. (1971), *Internal Labor Markets and Manpower Analysis*, Lexington, MA: D. C. Heath and Company.

Downing, J. (2018), 'John Downing: one-in-five vote for Peter Casey is a major alarm call for all national authorities', Independent.ie, 17 October 2018, www.independent.ie/irish-news/presidential-election/john-downing-one-in-five-vote-for-peter-casey-is-a-major-alarm-call-for-all-national-authorities-37463815.html (accessed 2 March 2020).

Doyle, K. (2018), 'LISTEN: Presidential candidate Peter Casey sparks outrage with his "racist" remarks on Travellers', Independent.ie, 17 October 2018, www.independent.ie/irish-news/presidential-election/article37428508.ece (accessed 2 March 2020).

Du Bois, W. E. B. (1908), 'The souls of Black folk', The Project Gutenberg EBook of The Souls of Black Folk, by W. E. B. Du Bois, www.gutenberg.org/files/408/408-h/408-h.htm (Accessed 1 March 2013).

Du Bois, W. E. B. (1965), *The World and Africa: An Inquiry into the Part Which Africa Has Played in World History*, New York: International Publishers.

Durkheim, E. (1893), *The Division of Labor in Society*, New York: Free Press.

Dyer, R. (1997), *White*, New York: Routledge.

Dyer, R. (2000), 'The matter of whiteness', in L. Back and J. Solomos, eds, *Theories of Race and Racism: A Reader*, London: Routledge.

EEOC (2013), *African American Workgroup Report, 2013*, US Equal Employment Opportunity Commission, www.eeoc.gov/federal/reports/aawg.cfm (accessed 11 March 2015).

EHRC/BIS (2015), 'Pregnancy and maternity-related discrimination and disadvantage first findings: survey of mothers and employers', BIS Research

Paper No. 235. Department for Business, Innovation and Skills (BIS) and the Equality and Human Rights Commission (EHRC), www.equalityhuman rights.com/en/managing-pregnancy-and-maternity-workplace/pregnancy-and-maternity-discrimination-research-findings (accessed 10 March 2020).

Ejorh, T. (2006), 'Citizenship and belonging: the African community and the politics of alienation in Ireland', www.ucd.ie/mcri/african_community_and_irish_politics_of_alienation.pdf (accessed 1 December 2016).

Equal Opportunities Commission (2005), 'Greater expectations: final report of the EOC's investigation into discrimination against new and expectant mothers in the workplace', www.equalityhumanrights.com/en/file/10501/download?token=hq-HrXQq (accessed 10 March 2020).

Erikson, E. H. (1968), *Identity: Youth and Crisis*, London: Faber & Faber.

Erikson, E. (1980), *Identity and the Life Cycle*, New York and London: Norton.

EU MIDIS 11 (2016), Second European Union Minorities and Discrimination Survey – Main results. Available at: http://fra.europa.eu/en/publication/2017/eumidis-ii-main-results (accessed 10 March 2020).

Eurostat (2019), 'Migration and migrant population statistics, Eurostat statistics explained', https://ec.europa.eu/eurostat/statistics-explained/index.php/Migration_and_migrant_population_statistics#Migration_flows:_Immigration_to_the_EU_from_non-member_countries_was_2.4_million_in_2017 (accessed 11 July 2019).

Fanning, B. (2002), *Racism and Social Change in the Republic of Ireland*, Manchester: Manchester University Press.

Fanning, B. (2007), *Immigration and Social Change in the Republic of Ireland*, Manchester: Manchester University Press.

Fanning, B. (2009), *New Guests of the Irish Nation*, Dublin: Irish Academic Press.

Fanning, B., and Mutwarasibo, F. (2007), Nationals/non-nationals: immigration, citizenship and politics in the Republic of Ireland', *Ethnic and Racial Studies*, 30(3): 439–460, doi: 10.1080/01419870701217506.

Fanon, F. (2000), 'The facts of Blackness', in L. Back and J. Solomos, eds, *Theories of Race and Racism: A Reader*, London: Routledge.

Fanon, F. (2008), *Black Skin, White Masks*, New York: Grove Press.

Feagin, J. R. (1972), 'Poverty: We still believe that God helps those that help themselves', *Psychology Today*, 6(6): 101–129.

Feldman, A. (2007), 'Immigrant civic mobilisation', in B. Fanning, ed., *Immigration and Social Change in the Republic of Ireland*, Manchester: Manchester University Press.

Feldman, A. (2020), 'Knowledge justice as global justice: epistemicide, decolonising the university, and the struggle for planetary survival', in B. O'Toole, E. Joseph and D. Nyaluke, eds, *Challenging Perceptions of Africa in Schools: Critical Approaches to Global Justice Education*, Routledge.

Feldman, A., Ndakengerwa, D. L., Nolan, A., and Frese, C. (2005), *Diversity, Civil Society and Social Change in Ireland: A North–South Comparison of the Role of Immigrant/'New' Minority Ethnic-Led Organisations*, Dublin: UCD; Print-well Cooperative.

Feldman, A., Gilmartin, M., Loyal, S., and Migge, B. (2008), *Getting On: From Migration to Integration: Chinese, Indian, Lithuanian, and Nigerian Migrants' Experiences in Ireland*, Technical Report, Dublin: Immigrant Council of Ireland.

Fleischmann, F., and Dronkers, J. (2010), 'Unemployment among immigrants in European labour markets: an analysis of origin and destination effects', *Work, Employment and Society*, 24(2): 337–354.

Foley, D. (2004), 'Ogbu's theory of academic disengagement: its evolution and its critics', *Intercultural Education*, 15(4): 385–397, doi: 10.1080/14675980 42000313412.

Foucault, M. (2003), *Society Must be Defended: Lectures at the College de France*, 1975–76, New York: Picador.

Frankenberg, R. (1993), *White Women, Race Matters: The Social Construction of Whiteness*, Minneapolis, MN: University of Minnesota Press.

Frankenberg, R. (2000), 'White women race matters', in: L. Back and J. Solomos, eds, *Theories of Race and Racism: A Reader*, London: Routledge.

Frankenberg, R. (2001), 'The mirage of an unmarked whiteness', in B. B. Rasmussen, E. Klinenberg, I. J. Nexica and M. Wray, eds, *The Making and Unmaking of Whiteness*, Durham, NC: Duke University Press.

Fraser, N. (1995), 'From redistribution to recognition? Dilemmas of justice in a "postsocialist" age', *New Left Review*, 212: 68–93.

Fraser, N. (1996), 'Social justice in the age of identity politics: redistribution, recognition, and participation', Tanner Lectures on Human Values, Stanford University, http://tannerlectures.utah.edu/_documents/ato-z/f/Fraser98.pdf (accessed 16 October 2013).

Freud, S. (1905), *Three Essays on the Theory of Sexuality*, trans. James Strachey, New York: Basic Books.

Galgóczi, B., and Leschke, J. (2016), *EU Labour Migration in Troubled Times: Skills Mismatch, Return and Policy Responses*, London and New York: Routledge.

Gallagher, C. (1994), 'White reconstruction in the university', *Socialist Review*, 94(1–2): 165–187.

Gallagher, C. A. (2003), 'Color-blind privilege: the social and political functions of erasing the color line in post race America', *Race, Gender & Class*, 10(4): 22–37.

Garner, S. (2000), 'Ireland: from racism without "race" to racism without racists', *Radical History Review*, 104: 41–56.

Garner, S. (2004), *Racism in the Irish Experience*, London: Pluto Press.

Garner, S. (2009), 'Ireland: from racism without "race", to "racism without racists"', *Radical History Review*, 104(104): 1–21, http://eprints.aston. ac.uk/17386/1/Ireland.pdf (accessed 12 November 2015).

Gauntlett, D. (2007), *Creative Explorations: New Approaches to Identities and Audiences*, London: Routledge.

Ghosh, J. (2011), 'Fear of foreigners: recession and racism in Europe', *Race/Ethnicity: Multidisciplinary Global Contexts*, 4(2): 183–190.

Gillborn, D. (2006), 'Rethinking white supremacy: who counts in "White World"', *Ethnicities*, 6(3): 318–340.

Gillborn, D. (2008), *Racism and Education: Coincidence or Conspiracy?*, London: Routledge.

Gillborn, D. (2015), 'Intersectionality, critical race theory, and the primacy of racism: race, class, gender, and disability in education', *Qualitative Inquiry*, 21(3): 277–287.

Gilroy, P. (1993), *The Black Atlantic: Modernity and Double Consciousness*, London: Verso.

Girard, E. R., and Bauder, H. (2007), 'Assimilation and exclusion of foreign trained engineers in Canada: inside a professional regulatory organization', doi.org/10.1111/j.1467-8330.2007.00505.

Glaser, W., and Strauss, A. (2009), *The Discovery of Grounded Theory: Strategies for Qualitative Research*, New Brunswick, NJ and London: Aldine Transactions.

Glynn, I., Kelly, T., and MacÉinrí, P. (2013), *Irish Emigration in an Age of Austerity*, University College Cork. CityPrint.ie, doi: 10.13140/2.1.4766.8484.

Goethe, J. W. von (1998), *Maxims and Reflections*, trans. E. Stopp, London: Penguin Books.

Gold, S. J. (2004), 'From Jim Crow to racial hegemony: evolving explanations of racial hierarchy', *Ethnic and Racial Studies*, 27(6): 951–968.

Goldberg, D. T. (2000), 'Racial knowledge', in L. Back and J. Solomos, eds, *Theories of Race and Racism: A Reader*, London: Routledge.

Goldberg, D. T. (2001), *The Racial State*, Oxford: Blackwell.

Gomez Cervantes, A., and Chang, H. K. (2015), 'The New Immigrant Survey (NIS)', Princeton University, https://nis.princeton.edu/index.html (accessed 10 March 2020).

Gomez Cervantes, A., and Kim, C. (2015), 'Gendered color lines: the effects of skin color on immigrants' employment', paper presented at the annual meeting of the American Sociological Association, Hilton Chicago and Palmer House Hilton, Chicago, http://ipsr.ku.edu/migration/symposium/ppt/Gomez.pdf (accessed 10 February 2018).

Gotanda, N. (1991), 'A critique of "Our Constitution is Color-Blind"', *Stanford Law Review*, 44(1): 1–68.

Grabowska, I. (2003), *Irish Labour Migration of Polish Nationals: Economic, Social and Political Aspects in the Light of the EU Enlargement*, Warsaw: Institute for Social Studies, Warsaz University.

Guglielmo, J., and Salerno, S. (2003), *Are Italians White? How Race is Made in America*, Routledge.

Hall, B. L. and Tandon, R. (2017), 'Decolonization of knowledge, epistemicide, participatory research and higher education', *Research for All*, 1(1): 6–19, doi: 10.18546/RFA.01.1.02.

Haney López, I. F. (2010), 'Post-racial racism: racial stratification and mass incarceration in the age of Obama', *California Law Review*, 98(3): 1023–1074.

Hao, L. (2010), *Color Lines, Country Lines: Race, Immigration, and Wealth Stratification in America*, New York: Russell Sage Foundation.

Harris, C. I. (1993; 1995), 'Whiteness as property', *Harvard Law Review*, 106(8): 1707–1791. UCLA School of Law Research Paper No. 06–35.

Hartog, D., Deanne, N., De Hoogh, A. B., and Keegan, A. E. (2007), 'The interactive effects of belongingness and charisma on helping and compliance', *Journal of Applied Psychology*, 92(4): 1131–1139.

Hassouneh, D. (2013), 'Unconscious racist bias: barrier to a diverse nursing faculty', *Journal of Nursing Education*, 52(4): 183–184.

Hayes, M. (2006), *Irish Travellers: Representations and Realities*, Dublin: Liffey Press.

Heath, A. and Li, Y. (2014), 'Global Exchange on migration and diversity. Global Exchange briefing', www.compas.ox.ac.uk/fileadmin/files/Publications/Briefings/DCLG_global_exchange/Global_Exchange_Briefing_4_Heath-Li_web.pdf (Accessed 1 June 2015).

Helms, J. E. (1994), 'The conceptualization of ethnic identity and other "racial" constructs', in E. J. Thicket, R. J. Watts, and D. Birman, eds, *Human Diversity: Perspectives on People in Context*, San Francisco: Jossey-Bass.

Herrnstein, R. J., and Murray, C. (1994), *The Bell Curve: Intelligence and Class Structure in American Life*, New York: Free Press.

Hersch, J. (2008), 'Profiling the new immigrant worker: the effects of skin color and height', *Journal of Labor Economics*, 26(2): 345–386, https://nis.princeton.edu/downloads/papers/2008_Hersch_Profiling%20the%20New%20Immigrant%20Worker%20JOLE%20Apr08.pdf (accessed 23 June 2017).

Hesse, B. (1999), 'It's your world: discrepant multiculturalism', in P. Cohen, ed, *New Ethnicities, Old Racisms*, London: Zed Books.

Hesse, B. (2001), 'Post-Macpherson: narrating narratives of racism', The politics of race and urban unrest, Workshop paper, University of Salford.

Hickman, M. J. (1998), 'Reconstructing deconstructing "race": British political discourses about the Irish in Britain', *Ethnic and Racial Studies*, 21(2): 288–307.

Hickman, M. (2000), '"Binary opposites" or "unique neighbours"? The Irish in multi-ethnic Britain', *Political Quarterly*, 71: 50–58, doi: 10.1111/1467–923X.00279.

Hickman, M. J. (2002), '"Locating" the Irish diaspora', *Irish Journal of Sociology*, 11(2): 8–26, doi.org/10.1177/079160350201100202.

Hickman, M. J., Morgan, S., Walter, B., and Bradley, J. (2005), 'The limitations of whiteness and the boundaries of Englishness: second-generation Irish identifications and positionings in multi-ethnic Britain', *Ethnicities*, 5(2): 160–182.

Hirsch, A. (2018), *Brit(ish): On Race, Identity and Belonging*, Vintage Publishing.

Hochschild, A. (1990), *The Second Shift*, London: Piatkus.

Hoffman II, M. A. (1993), *They Were White and They Were Slaves: The Untold History of the Enslavement of Ehites in Early America*, Idaho: The Independent History and Research Company.

Hovland, C. I., and Sherif, M. (1980), Social Judgment: Assimilation and Contrast Effects in Communication and Attitude Change. Westport, CT: Greenwood.

Hum, D., and Simpson, W. (2004), 'Economic integration of immigrants to Canada', *Canadian Journal of Urban Research*, 13(1): 46–61.

Hunn, L. R. M., Guy, T C., and Mangliitz, E. (2006), 'Who can speak for whom? Using counter-storytelling to challenge racial hegemony', Adult Education Research Conference, https://newprairiepress.org/aerc/2006/papers/32 (accessed 22 July 2012).

Hylton, K. (2012), 'Talk the talk, walk the walk: defining critical race theory in research', *Race Ethnicity and Education*, 15(1): 23–41.

Ignatiev, N. (1995), *How the Irish became White*, London: Routledge.

Irish Naturalisation and Immigration Service (2018), 'Immigration Statistics', www.inis.gov.ie/en/INIS/Immigration-in-Ireland-Annual-Review-Statistics-2018.pdf/Files/Immigration-in-Ireland-Annual-Review-Statistics-2018.pdf.

Irish Times (2015), 'Training posts closed to many foreign doctors working here. As Ireland culls the number of foreign medical graduates who can train here, doctors seek opportunities elsewhere', 20 January, www.irishtimes.com/life-and-style/health-family/training-posts-closed-to-many-foreign-doctors-working-here-1.2071424 (accessed 20 February 2020).

Jacques, M. (2003), 'The global hierarchy of race', *The Guardian*, 20 September, www.guardian.co.uk/print/0,3858,4757714–103677,00.html (accessed 17 May 2012).

Jones, P. N. (2010), 'Toleration and recognition: what should we teach?', *Educational Philosophy and Theory*, 42: 38–56.

Joseph, E. (2015), 'Racial stratification in the Irish labour market: a comparative study of differential labour market outcomes through the counter-stories of Nigerian, Polish and Spanish migrants in Ireland', unpublished doctoral thesis, School of Social Justice, University College Dublin.

Joseph, E. (2018), 'Whiteness and racism: examining the racial order in Ireland', *Irish Journal of Sociology*, 26(1): 46–70, doi: 10.1177/0791603517737282.

Joseph, E. (2019), 'Discrimination against credentials in Black bodies: counter-stories of the characteristic labour market experiences of migrants in Ireland', *British Journal of Guidance & Counselling*, 47(4): 524–542, doi: 10.1080/03069885.2019.1620916.

Joseph, E. (forthcoming), 'Composite counterstorytelling as a technique for challenging ambivalence about race and racism in the labour market in Ireland'. *Irish Journal of Sociology*.

Kelly, E., McGuinness, S., O'Connell, P., Pandiella, A. G., and Haugh, D. (2016), 'How did immigrants fare in the Irish labour market over the Great Recession?', OECD Working Papers, No. 1284.

Keogh, D. (1999), *Jews in Twentieth Century Ireland*, Cork: Cork University Press.

Kerbo, H. R. (2000), *Social Stratification and Inequality: Class Conflict in Historical, Comparative, and Global Perspective*, 4th edn, New York: McGraw Hill.

King, J. C. (1981), *The Biology of Race*, Berkeley, CA: University of California Press.

King, R. C., and DaCosta, K. M. (1996), 'Changing face, changing race: the remaking of race in the Japanese American and African American communities', in M. P. P. Root, ed., *The Multiracial Experience: Racial Borders as the New Frontier*, London: Sage Publications.

King-O'Riain, R. C. (2007), 'Counting on the Celtic Tiger: adding ethnic census categories in the Republic of Ireland', *Ethnicities*, 7(4): 516–542.

Kingston, G., McGinnity, F. and O'Connell, P. J. (2015), 'Discrimination in the Irish labour market: nationality, ethnicity and the recession', *Work, Employment and Society*, 29(2): 213–232.

Kirby, P. (2002), *Celtic Tiger in Distress: Growth with Inequality in Ireland*, Basingstoke: Palgrave.

Knight, J. (2014), 'The complex employment experiences of Polish migrants in the UK labour market', *Sociological Research Online*, 19(4): 1–12.

Kohlberg, L. (1969), 'Stage and sequence: the cognitive-developmental approach to socialization', in D. A. Goslin, ed., *Handbook of Socialization Theory and Research*, Chicago: Rand McNally.

Kohli, R. (2016), 'Behind school doors: the impact of hostile racial climates on urban teachers of color', *Urban Education*, 1: 1–27.

Kune, N. (2011), *The Need to Belong: Rediscovering Maslow's Hierarchy of Needs*, Paul H. Brookes Publishers.

Kymlicka, W. (2002), *Contemporary Political Philosophy: An Introduction*, 2nd edn, Oxford: Oxford University Press.

Ladson-Billings, G. (1998), 'Just what is critical race theory and what's it doing in a nice field like education?', *International Journal of Qualitative Studies in Education*, 11(1): 7–24.

Ladson-Billings, G. (2005), 'The evolving role of critical race theory in educational scholarship', *Race Ethnicity and Education*, 8(1): 115–119.

Ladson-Billings, G., and Tate, W. (1995), 'Toward a critical race theory of education', *Teachers College Record*, 97(1): 47–68.

Leary, M. R. (2001), 'Toward a conceptualization of interpersonal rejection', in M. R. Leary, ed., *Interpersonal Rejection*, New York: Oxford University Press.

Lentin, R. (2002), 'Anti-racist responses to the racialisation of Irishness: disavowed multiculturalism and its discontents', in R. Lentin and R. McVeigh, eds, *Racism and Anti-racism in Ireland*, Belfast: Beyond the Pale Publications.

Lentin, A. (2004), *Racism and Anti-Racism in Europe*, London: Pluto Press.

Lentin, R. (2006), 'From racial state to racist state: racism and immigration in twenty-first century Ireland', in A. Lentin and R. Lentin, eds, *Race and State*, Cambridge: Cambridge Scholars Press.

Lentin, R. (2007), 'Illegals in Ireland, Irish illegals: diaspora nation as racial state', *Irish Political Studies*, 22(4): 433–453.

Lentin, R., and McVeigh, R. (2002), *Racism and Anti-Racism in Ireland*, Belfast: Beyond the Pale Publications.

Lentin, R., and McVeigh, R. (2006), *After Optimism? Ireland, Racism and Globalisation*, Dublin: Metro Eireann Publications.

Leonard, M. (2001), 'Old wine in new bottles? Women working inside and outside the household', *Women's Studies International Forum*, 24(1): 67–78.

Leonardo, Z. (2004), 'The colour of supremacy: beyond the discourse of "white privilege"', *Educational Philosophy and Theory*, 36(2): 137–152.

Lipset, S. M., and Bendix, R. (1952), 'Social mobility and occupational career patterns II: social mobility', *American Journal of Sociology*, 57(5): 494–504.

Lynch, E. (2014), 'Regulating for decent work: combatting unfair terms in (zero-hour) employment contracts', Irish Congress of Trade Unions, www.ictu.ie/download/pdf/regulating_for_decent_work_final.pdf (accessed 10 March 2020).

MacÉinrí, P. (2003), *Labour Migration into Ireland*, Dublin: Immigrant Council of Ireland.

Malentacchi, M. (2008), 'Precarious work – what needs to be done?', General Secretary, International Metalworkers' Federation (IMF), Global Unions, 3 October, www.global-unions.org/IMG/pdf/Marcello_s_speech.pdf (accessed 16 January 2015).

Martinez, A. (2014), 'A plea for critical race theory: stock story versus counter-story dialogues concerning Alejandra's "fit" in the academy', *Composition Studies*, 42(2): 33–55.

Marx, L. and Engels, F. (1848), *Manifesto of the Communist Party*, www.marxists.org/archive/marx/works/download/pdf/Manifesto.pdf (accessed 1 February 2020).

Maslow, A. (1970), *Motivation and Personality*, New York: Harper and Row.

Massey, D. S. (1988), 'Economic development and international migration in comparative perspective', *Population and Development Review*, 14(3): 383–413.

Massey, D. S. (2007), *Categorically Unequal: The American Stratification System*, New York: Russell Sage Foundation.

Mathews, B., and Ross, L. (2010), *Research Methods: A Practical Guide for the Social Sciences*, UK: Pearson Education Limited.

Matsuda, M. J. (1987), 'Looking to the bottom: critical legal studies and reparations', Harvard Civil Rights–Civil Liberties Law Review, 22(2): 323–400.

Matsuda, M. (1995), 'Looking to the bottom: critical legal studies and reparations', in K. Crenshaw, N. Gotanda, G. Peller G. and K. Thomas, eds, *Critical Race Theory: The Key Writings that Formed the Movement*, New York: The New Press.

Matsuda, M., Lawrence, C., Delgado, R., and Crenshaw, K. (eds) (1993), *Words that Wound: Critical Race Theory, Assaultive Speech, and the First Amendment*, Boulder, CO: Westview Press.

McCall, L. (2005), 'The complexity of intersectionality', *Signs*, 30(3): 1771–1800.

McGinnity, F., Grotti, R., Kenny, O., and Russell, H. (2017), 'Who experiences discrimination in Ireland? Evidence from the QNHS equality modules', The Economic and Social Research Institute and the Irish Human Rights and Equality Commission, https://doi.org/10.26504/bkmnext342 (accessed 1 December 2017).

McGinnity, F., Nelson, J., Lunn, P., and Quinn, E. (2009), *Discrimination in Recruitment: Evidence from a Field Experiment*, Dublin: The Equality Authority and the Economic and Social Research Institute.

McGinnity, F., Quinn, E., Kingston, G., and O'Connell, P. (2011), *Annual Monitoring Report on Integration 2011*, Dublin: Economic and Social Research Institute.

McGinnity, F., Quinn, E., Kingston, G., and O'Connell, P. (2012), *Annual Monitoring Report on Integration 2012*, Dublin: Economic and Social Research Institute.

McGinnity, F., Watson, D., and Kingston, G. (2012), *Analysing the Experience of Discrimination in Ireland: Evidence from the QNHS Equality Module 2010*, Dublin: Brunswick Press Ltd. The Equality Authority and The Economic and Social Research Institute, www.esri.ie/UserFiles/publications/BKMNEXT223.pdf (accessed 15 March 2013).

McGuire, E. (2019), 'Some taxi drivers' bumper stickers target immigrants', www.dublininquirer.com/2019/04/17/some-taxi-drivers-bumper-stickers-target-immigrants (accessed 10 March 2020).

McIntosh, P. (1988), 'White privilege and male privilege: a personal account of coming to see correspondences through work in Women's Studies', Working Paper No. 189, Virginia Women's Studies Association Conference, April, Wellesley, MA, Wellesley College.

McVeigh, R. (1996), *The Racialisation of Irishness: Racism and Antiracism in Ireland*, Belfast: CRD.

McVeigh, R. (2002), 'Is there an Irish anti-racism? Building an anti-racist Ireland', in Ronit Lentin and Robbie McVeigh, eds, *Racism and Antiracism in Ireland*, Belfast: Beyond the Pale.

Mezirow, J. (1995), 'Transformation theory of adult learning', in M. R. Welton, ed., *Defense of Lifeworld: Critical Perspectives on Adult Learning*, New York: State University of New York Press.

Michael, L. (2015), 'Afrophobia in Ireland: racism against people of African descent', https://static.rasset.ie/documents/news/afrophobia-in-ireland.pdf (accessed 3 January 2016).

Miles, R., and Brown, M. (2003), *Racism*, second edition, London: Routledge.

Mills, C. W. (1997), *The Racial Contract*, Ithaca, NY: Cornell University Press.

Mills, C. W. (1998), *Blackness Visible: Essays on Philosophy and Race*. Ithaca, NY: Cornell University Press.

Mills, C. W. (2003), *From Class to Race: Essays in White Marxism and Black Radicalism*, Lanham, MD: Rowman and Littlefield.

Mills, C. W. (2008), 'Racial liberalism', *Modern Language Association of America*, 123(5): 1380–1397.

Mills, C. W. (2009), 'Critical race theory: a reply to Mike Cole', *Ethnicities*, 9(2): 270–281.

Misra, T. (2005), 'Black immigrant women have harder time getting work: age-old stereotypes interact in complex ways when new arrivals look for jobs', *The Atlantic*, 10 September, www.theatlantic.com/politics/archive/2015/09/black-immigrant-women-have-harder-time-getting-work/432768/ (accessed 12 January 2016).

Modood, T., Berthoud, R., Lakey, J., Nazroo, J., Smith, P., Virdee, S., and Beishon, S. (1997), *Ethnic Minorities in Britain: Diversity and Disadvantage*, London: Policy Studies Institute.

Montecinos, C. (1995), 'Culture as an ongoing dialogue: implications for multicultural teacher education', in C. Sleeter and P. McLaren, eds, *Multicultural Education, Critical Pedagogy, and the Politics of Difference*, Albany, NY: State University of New York.

Morgan, D. (1998), 'Practical strategies for combining qualitative and quantitative methods: applications to health research', *Qualitative Health Research*, 8: 362–376.

Morse, J. (1991), 'Approaches to qualitative–quantitative methodological triangulation', *Nursing Research*, 40: 120–123.

Moschel, M. (2011), 'Race in mainland European legal analysis: towards a European critical race theory', *Ethnic and Racial Studies*, 34(10): 1648–1664.

Myrdal, G. (1962), 'An American dilemma', *Race and Class*, 4(1): 3–11, https://doi.org/10.1177/030639686200400101.

Myrdal, G. (1996), *An American Dilemma*, New York: Harper and Brothers.

Myrdal, G. (2000), 'Racial beliefs in America', in L. Back and J. Solomos, eds, *Theories of Race and Racism: A Reader*, London: Routledge.

New Immigrant Survey (NIS) (2006), Princeton University, https://nis.princeton.edu/index.html (accessed 22 June 2018).

NFQ (Irish National Framework of Qualifications), http://www.nfq-qqi.com/index.html.

Ní Shuinéar, S. (1994), 'Irish Travellers, ethnicity and the origins question', in M. McCann, S. O'Siochain and J. Ruane, eds, *Irish Travellers: Culture and Ethnicity*, Belfast: Institute of Irish Studies.

Ní Shuinéar, S. (2002), 'Othering the Irish (Traveller)', in Ronit Lentin and Robbie McVeigh, eds, *Racism and Anti-racism in Ireland*, Belfast: Beyond the Pale Publications.

Nisen, M. and Panofsky, D. (2014), 'Name game: rich countries and the minorities they discriminate against, mapped', in *International Migration Outlook 2014*, Paris: OECD Publishing.

Nozick, R. (1974), *Anarchy, State and Utopia*, New York: Basic Books.

O'Brien, C. (2009), 'Poll shows hardening of attitude towards immigrants', *Irish Times Online*, 24 November 2009. Available at: https://www.irishtimes.

com/news/poll-shows-hardening-of-attitude-towards-immigrants-1.777218 (accessed 15 July 2014).

O'Cionnaith, F. (2013), 'Warning of rise in racism among Irish children', *Irish Examiner*, 30 December, www.irishexaminer.com/ireland/warning-of-rise-in-racism-among-irish-children-253775.html (accessed 30 December 2013).

O'Hearn, C. C. (1998), *Half and Half: Writers Growing Up Biracial and Bicultural*, New York: Pantheon Books.

O'Hearn, D. (2000), 'Globalization: "New Tigers", and the end of the developmental state? The case of the Celtic Tiger', *Politics and Society*, 28(1): 67–92.

O'Keeffe-Vigneron, G. (2003), 'The Irish in Britain: injustices of recognition?', *Revue d'etudes nglophones*, ed. Paradigme, 33–43, hal-00612720.

O'Sullivan, K. (2007), 'Biafra to Lomé: the evolution of Irish government policy on official development assistance, 1969–75', *Irish Studies in International Affairs*, 18: 91–107.

OECD (2014), 'Labour market integration of immigrants and their children: developing, activating and using skills', in *International Migration Outlook 2014*, Paris: OECD Publishing.

OECD (2018), *International Migration Outlook 2018*, Paris: OECD Publishing.

Ogbu, J. U. (1978), *Minority Education and Caste: The American in Cross-Cultural Perspective*, New York: Academic Press.

Ogbu, J. U. (1994), 'Racial stratification and education in the United States: why inequality persists', *Teachers College Record*, 96(2): 264–298.

Ogbu, J. U. (1999), 'Beyond language: ebonics, proper English, and identity in a Black-American speech community', *American Educational Research Journal*, 36(2): 147–184, https://doi.org/10.3102/00028312036002147.

Omi, M., and Winant, H. (1994), *Racial Formation in the United States: From the 1960s to the 1990s*, 2nd edn, New York: Routledge.

Open Society Institute Justice Initiative (2009), *Ethnic Profiling in the European Union: Pervasive, Ineffective, and Discriminatory*, New York: Open Society Institute. www.communitylaw.org.au/flemingtonkensington/cb_pages/images /Full_text__Ethni-2.pdf (accessed 25 March 2011).

Ożden, C. (2006), 'Educated migrants: is there brain waste? International migration, remittances, and the brain drain', in C. Ożden and M. Schiff, eds, *International Migration Remittances and the Brain Drain*, Washington, DC: World Bank and Palgrave Macmillan.

Ożden, C., and Schiff, M. (2006), *International Migration Remittances and the Brain Drain*, Washington, DC: World Bank, http://documents.worldbank.org/ curated/en/426881468127174713/International-migration-remittances-and-the-brain-drain (accessed 10 May 2014).

Papademetrio, D. G., Somerville, W., and Sumption, M. (2009), 'The social mobility of immigrants and their children', Migration Policy Institute, www. migrationpolicy.org/pubs/soialmobility2010.pdf (accessed 13 May 2015).

Pappas, G. (1996), 'Unveiling white privilege', LARASA/REPORT, 3–9

November, http://files.eric.ed.gov/fulltext/ED395085.pdf (accessed 13 June 2014).

Parsons, T. (1940), 'An analytical approach to the theory of social stratification', *American Journal of Sociology*, 45(6): 841–862.

Peck, J. (1996), *Work-Place: The Social Regulation of Labor Markets*, New York: Guilford Press.

Pettigrew, T. F. (1998), 'Reactions towards the new minorities of Western Europe', *Annual Review of Sociology*, 24: 77–103.

Pfeiffer, K. (2003), *Race Passing and American Individualism*, Boston: University of Massachusetts Press.

Piore, M. J. (1979), *Birds of Passage: Migrant Labor and Industrial Societies*, Cambridge: Cambridge University Press.

Putnam, R. D. (2004), 'Bowling together', interviewed by Rory J. Clarke for OECD Observer, OECD Observer No. 242, March 2004, www.oecdob server.org/news/archivestory.php/aid/1215/Bowling_together.html (accessed 18 February 2015).

Reay, D., Hollingworth, S., Williams, K., Crozier, G., Jamieson, F., James, D., and Beedell, P. (2007), 'A darker shade of pale? Whiteness, the middle classes and multi-ethnic inner city schooling', *Sociology*, 41(6): 1041–1060, doi. org/10.1177/0038038507082314.

Reich, M., Gordon, D., and Edwards, R. (1973), 'A Theory of Labor Market Segmentation', *American Economic Review*, 63(2): 359–365, www.jstor.org/ stable/1817097 (accessed 1 March 2019).

Rich, A. (1979), 'Disloyal to civilization: feminism, racism, gynophobia', in: *On Lies, Secrets, And Silence: Selected Prose, 1966–1978*, New York: Norton.

Ritzer, G. (2014), *Introduction to Sociology*, 2nd edn, USA: SAGE Publications.

Rodríguez, C. E. (2000), *Changing Race: Latinos, the Census, and the History of Ethnicity in the United States*, New York: New York University Press.

Roeder, A. (2011), 'Polish migration to Ireland: a literature review', www.tcd. ie/sociology/assets/pdf/Polish%20migration%20to%20Ireland%20-%20 A%20literature%20review.pdf (accessed 28 June 2016).

Roy, B. (1999), *Bitters in the Honey: Tales of Hope and Disappointment across Divides of Race and Time*, Fayetteville, AK: University of Arkansas Press.

Ruhs, M. (2005), *Managing the Immigration and Employment of non-EU Nationals in Ireland*. Dublin: The Policy Institute, Trinity College Dublin.

Sasson-Levy, O. (2013), 'A different kind of whiteness: marking and unmarking of social boundaries in the construction of hegemonic ethnicity', *Sociological Forum*, 28(1): 27–50.

Schuster, L. (2003), 'Common sense or racism? The treatment of asylum seekers in Europe', *Patterns of Prejudice*, 37(3): 233–256.

Sen, A. (1980), 'Equality of what?', in S. McMurrin, ed., *The Tanner Lectures on Human Values*. Salt Lake City, UT: University of Utah Press.

Sidanius, J., and Pratto, F. (1999), *Social Dominance: An Intergroup Theory of Social Hierarchy and Oppression*, New York: Cambridge University Press.

Silverman, D. (2001), *Interpreting Qualitative Data: Methods for Analysing Talk, Text and Interaction*, 2nd edn, London: Sage.

Small, S. (2017), *20 Questions and Answers on Black Europe*, Amrit Consultancy.

Smith, L. T. (2012), *Decolonizing Methodologies: Research and Indigenous Peoples*, London: Zed Books Ltd.

Sollors, W. (1999), *Neither Black nor White, Yet Both: Thematic Explorations of Interracial Literature*, Cambridge, MA: Harvard University Press.

Solórzano, D. G. and Yosso, T. J. (2002), 'Critical race methodology: counterstorytelling as an analytical framework for education research', *Qualitative Inquiry*, 8(1): 23–44.

Song, M. (2004), 'Introduction: who's at the bottom? Examining claims about racial hierarchy', *Ethnic and Racial Studies*, 27(6): 859–877.

Song, M. (2007), 'Racial hierarchy', in G. Ritzer, ed., *The Blackwell Encyclopedia of Sociology*, Oxford: Blackwell Publishing.

Spickard, P. R. (1992), 'The illogic of American racial categories', in M. P. P. Root, ed., *Racially Mixed People in America*, Newbury Park, CA: Sage.

Staats, C. (2014), *State of the Science: Implicit Bias Review 2014*. The Ohio State University. Kirwan Institute for the Study of Race and Ethnicity.

Standing, G. (2011), *The Precariat: The New Dangerous Class*, London: Bloomsbury.

Stephen, C., and Hartman, D. (2007), *Ethnicity and Race: Making Identities in a Changing World*, Thousand Oaks, CA: Pine Forge Press.

Strauss, A., and Corbin, J. (1990), *Basics of Qualitative Research: Grounded Theory Procedures and Techniques*, London: Sage.

Sue, D. W., Capodilupo, C. M., Torino, G. C., Bucceri, J. M., Holder, A. M. B., Nadal, K. L., and Esquilin, M. (2007), 'Racial microaggressions in everyday life', *American Psychologist*, 62(4): 271–286.

Sumption, M. (2013), *Tackling Brain Waste: Strategies to Improve the Recognition of Immigrants' Foreign Qualifications*, Washington, DC: Migration Policy Institute, www.migrationpolicy.org/research/tackling-brain-waste-strategies-improve-recognition-immigrants-foreign-qualifications (accessed: 10 August 2017).

Tajfel, H. (1981), *Human Groups and Social Categories: Studies in Social Psychology*, Cambridge: Cambridge University Press.

Tajfel, H., and Turner, J. C. (1979), 'An integrative theory of inter-group conflict', in W. G. Austin and S. Worchel, eds, *The Social Psychology of Intergroup Relations*, Monterey, CA: Brooks/Cole.

Taylor, C. (1994), 'The politics of recognition', in A. Gutmann, ed., *Multiculturalism: Examining the Politics of Recognition*, Princeton, NJ: Princeton University Press.

Thornton, L. (2014), 'Direct Provision and the rights of the child in Ireland', *Irish Journal of Family Law*, 17(3): 68–76.

Todorov, T. (2000; 2009), 'Race and racism', in L. Back and J. Solomos, eds, *Theories of Race and Racism: A Reader*, London: Routledge.

Touraine, A. (2000), *Can We Live Together? Equality and Difference*, Stanford, CA: Stanford University Press.

Transatlantic Trends Immigration (2010), *Final Report*, http://trends.gmfus.org/files/archived/immigration/doc/TTI2010_English_Key.pdf (accessed 14 June 2013).

Tsri, K. (2016), 'Africans are not black: why the use of the term "black" for Africans should be abandoned', *African Identities*, 14:2, 147–160, doi: 10.1080/14725843.2015.1113120.

Tweed, T. (2006), *Crossing and Dwelling: A Theory of Religion*, Cambridge, MA: Harvard University Press.

Ugba, A. (2004), 'A quantitative profile analysis of African immigrants in 21st century Dublin', Department of Sociology, Trinity College Dublin, www.urbanlab.org/articles/Ugba,%20Abel%20Africans%20in%20Dublin.pdf (accessed 20 May 2017).

Ultee, W. (2007), 'Stratification systems: openness', in G. Ritzer, ed., *The Blackwell Encyclopaedia of Sociology*, Victoria: Blackwell Publishing.

Van den Oord, E. J. C. G., and Rowe, D. C. (2000), 'Racial differences in birth health risk: a quantitative genetic approach', *Demography*, 37(3): 285–298.

Vaus, D. A. de (2001), *Research Design in Social Research*, London: Sage Publications.

Verdugo, R. (2008), 'Racial stratification, social consciousness, and the education of Mexican Americans in Fabens, Texas: a socio-historical case study', *Spaces for Difference: An Interdisciplinary Journal*, 1(2): 69–95.

Vermeulen, H., and Perlmann, J. (2000), *Immigrants, Schooling and Social Mobility: Does Culture Make a Difference?*, Basingstoke: Palgrave Macmillan.

Vertovec, S. (2004), 'Cheap calls: the social glue of migrant transnationalism', *Global Networks*, 4(2): 219–224.

Vidich, A. J., and Bensman, J. (1968), *Small Town in Mass Society*, Princeton, NJ: Princeton University Press.

Wachter, M. (1974), 'Primary and secondary labor markets: a critique of the dual approach,' Brookings Papers on Economic Activity, 3, 637–680.

Ward, C. (1996), 'Acculturation', in D. Landis, and R. Bhagat, eds, *Handbook of Intercultural Training*, Newbury Park, CA: Sage.

Ward, E. (1999), 'Ireland and refugees/asylum seekers: 1922–1966', in R. Lentin, ed., *The Expanding Nation: Towards a Multi-ethnic Ireland*, Dublin: Department of Sociology, Trinity College.

Ward, C., Bochner, S., and Furnham, A. (2001), *The Psychology of Culture Shock*, 2nd edn, Routledge.

Waters, M. C. (1990), *Choosing Identities in America*, Berkeley, CA: University of California Press.

Weber, M. (1922), *Economy and Society: An Outline of Interpretive Sociology*, Berkley, CA: University of California Press.

Wilkinson, R. G. (2005), *The Impact of Inequality: How to Make Sick Societies Healthier*, New York: New Press.

Winant, H. (2000), 'The theoretical status of the concept race', in L. Back and J. Solomos, eds, *Theories of Race and Racism: A Reader*, London: Routledge.

Winant, H. (2001), *The World is a Ghetto: Race and Democracy since World War II*, New York: Basic Books.

Winant, H. (2004), *The New Politics of Race: Globalism, Difference, Justice*, Minneapolis, MN: University of Minnesota Press.

Winant, H. (2014), 'The dark matter: race and racism in the 21st century', *Critical Sociology*, 1–13, https://pdfs.semanticscholar.org/290e/ee0d258b 1c1f20e496abfe53800dfe3420d9.pdf (accessed 10 March 2020).

Yosso, T. J. (2006), *Critical Race Counterstories along the Chicana/Chicano Educational Pipeline*, New York: Routledge.

Yuval-Davis, N. (2006), 'Intersectionality and feminist politics', *European Journal of Women's Studies*, 13(3): 193–209, https://hal.archives-ouvertes.fr/ hal-00571274/document (accessed 10 March 2020).

Zizek, S. (1989), *The Sublime Object of Ideology*, London: Verso.

Zschirnt, E., and Ruedin, D. (2016), 'Ethnic discrimination in hiring decisions: a meta-analysis of correspondence tests 1990–2015', *Journal of Ethnic and Migration Studies*, 42(7): 1115–1134.

Zuberi, T. (2011), 'Critical race theory of society', *Connecticut Law Review*, 43(5): 1573–1591.

Zuberi, T., and Bashi, V. (1997), 'A theory of immigration and racial stratification', *Journal of Black Studies*, 27(5): 668–682.

Zuberi, T., and Bonilla-Silva, E. (eds) (2008), *White Logic, White Methods: Racism and Methodology*, Landham, MD: Rowman and Littlefield.

Index

9 781526 160300